WITTGENSTEIN'S METAP

Wittgenstein's Metaphilosophy

PAUL HORWICH

CLARENDON PRESS

OXFORD
UNIVERSITY PRESS

Great Clarendon Street, Oxford, OX2 6DP,
United Kingdom

Oxford University Press is a department of the University of Oxford.
It furthers the University's objective of excellence in research, scholarship,
and education by publishing worldwide. Oxford is a registered trade mark of
Oxford University Press in the UK and in certain other countries

© Paul Horwich 2012

The moral rights of the author have been asserted

First Edition published in 2012

Impression: 1

All rights reserved. No part of this publication may be reproduced, stored in
a retrieval system, or transmitted, in any form or by any means, without the
prior permission in writing of Oxford University Press, or as expressly permitted
by law, by licence or under terms agreed with the appropriate reprographics
rights organization. Enquiries concerning reproduction outside the scope of the
above should be sent to the Rights Department, Oxford University Press, at the
address above

You must not circulate this work in any other form
and you must impose this same condition on any acquirer

British Library Cataloguing in Publication Data

Data available

Library of Congress Cataloging in Publication Data

Data available

ISBN 978–0–19–958887–9 (Hbk.)
978–0–19–966112–1 (Pbk.)

Printed in Great Britain by
MPG Books Group, Bodmin and Kings's Lynn

Links to third party websites are provided by Oxford in good faith and
for information only. Oxford disclaims any responsibility for the materials
contained in any third party website referenced in this work.

Contents

Preface

> "My father was a business man and I am a business man.
> I want philosophy to be business-like, to get something
> done, to get something settled."
>
> Letter from Wittgenstein to M. O'C. Drury, 1930

Arguably, Wittgenstein's singular achievement was to have
appreciated the true nature of philosophy. And, arguably, this
insight gives his work on specific philosophical topics—language, experience, knowledge, mathematics, art, religion, and
so on—a power of illumination and demystification that cannot be found anywhere else. It is because I am myself attracted
to his particular radical perspective on the subject, and because
I think that it's so often misunderstood and undervalued, that
I have written this essay. Of course, I am uncomfortably aware
that there are already too many books on Wittgenstein—most
of them composed in the same presumptuous spirit as this one,
their authors imagining that they are peculiarly able to discern
what is vital in his work and how best to present it. What can I
say except that I hope the reader will find here an interpretation that is distinctive and compelling.

The account that I am going to suggest is guided by three
beliefs, each surprisingly controversial:

1. That Wittgenstein's ideas may be formulated clearly and
   that decent arguments may be given in support of them.
2. That the foundation of his treatments of specific issues concerning language, the mind, numbers, and so on, is his deflationary *meta*philosophical point of view—his anti-theoretical
   conception of what philosophy is—and not his claims about
   rule-following and meaning.

3. That an account of his mature philosophy can be extracted from Part I of the *Philosophical Investigations*, and that this work should be taken to override any other writings in tension with it.[1]

I am afraid that the reaction of most Wittgensteinians to this set of commitments will be that it so badly distorts the essence of his thought that there is no reason to read any further. Still I hope to convince anyone who does persevere, not only that these theses are correct, but that they dispel the elusiveness of his philosophy and help reveal its power and plausibility. Let me say a little more about each one in turn.

First, my aim is to give a clear account of Wittgenstein's ideas about how philosophy should and should not be done, to provide rational support for them, and to illustrate their application in dealing with a variety of particular philosophical problems. Such a project may not sound especially ambitious—but it will strike many professional philosophers as hopeless. For there is an uncanny convergence of opinion, amongst detractors and admirers alike, on the question of how cogent and comprehensible he is. A familiar harsh criticism is that Wittgenstein is self-indulgently cryptic and obscure, and that behind the rhetoric and fog is little of philosophical value. But it is striking that many of his supporters too would maintain that the ideas are incapable of being straightforwardly stated and justified. They think that his unconventional style, with its pithy remarks and lack of sustained reasoning, is integral to his radical anti-theoretical view of what philosophy can accomplish. So they would agree with the critics that any

---

[1] "Part I of Philosophical Investigations" is the term initially used by Wittgenstein's editors for paragraphs 1–693 of the volume. But in the most recent (4th) edition, those passages are simply called "Philosophical Investigations", and what was previously designated "Part II" is named "Philosophy of Psychology: A Fragment".

attempt to formulate his views precisely and defend them rigorously is doomed to failure. I hope to show that this point of view is wrong, and that it does a disservice to the rationally disciplined character of Wittgenstein's thought.

Second, it has long been widely held that the heart of this philosophy is a new conception of meaning. Thus Michael Dummett argues that it's the identification of the meaning of a word with its current use that leads Wittgenstein to the conservative metaphilosophical view that philosophy cannot engender a revision of ordinary practice, cannot make discoveries, and must leave everything as it is. Gordon Baker and Peter Hacker suppose that what disqualifies theoretical philosophy is its attempt to transcend 'the bounds of sense'. Saul Kripke also locates meaning at the centre. He maintains that Wittgenstein's examination of meaning results in a general, sceptical line of argument, and that his discussions of mental and mathematical phenomena are mere instantiations of that argument. Jerry Katz offers a reading according to which Wittgenstein's 'naturalism' and rejection of metaphysics are held to be consequences of his critique of systematic theories of meaning (such as Frege's) and of his falling back on the identification of meaning with use. Scott Soames agrees that this conception of meaning—peculiarly inhospitable towards the existence of surprising analytic truths—is what leads Wittgenstein to his deflationary metaphilosophy. And in a recent book by David Pears we read "That the Realist's explanation of the meanings of words in circular... is the key to understanding Wittgenstein's critical philosophy." Thus, each of these interpreters puts the discussion of meaning at the base of Wittgenstein's thought.[2] However, I believe and

[2] See Dummett's *The Interpretation of Frege's Philosophy*, Cambridge, MA: Harvard University Press, 1981, pp. 28–9, and *The Seas of Language*, Oxford: Oxford University Press, 1993, pp. 451–2; Baker and Hacker's *Wittgenstein: Meaning and Understanding*, ch. 13, "The Nature of Philosophy", Oxford: Blackwell, 1980; Kripke's *Wittgenstein on Rules and Private Language*, Cambridge, MA: Harvard

shall argue, on the contrary, that his metaphilosophy is the real foundation for his treatments of familiar philosophical issues including those that concern meaning and understanding.

More specifically, his starting point is a common-sense critique (from the perspective of uncontroversial epistemic norms) of the scientistic aspirations and methodological assumptions that govern most of what has been done, and still is done, in the name of philosophy. His conclusion is that the problems addressed within this mainstream approach are pseudo-problems and the theories proposed to resolve them are irrational. That critique has an abstract character, which takes different concrete forms depending on the topic under consideration. Thus each problem calls for its own peculiar diagnosis and treatment. And that sets the agenda for the positive therapeutic projects of Wittgenstein's philosophy.

This account of what philosophy should be does not rest on any particular view of meaning. On the contrary, his treatment of meaning is simply one application of the general therapeutic methodology that stems from that account.[3]

Quite a few admirers of Wittgenstein have held not merely that his metaphilosophy isn't central, but that it's not even *consistent* with his valuable work on various specific topics—on meaning, in particular—and should therefore be disregarded.[4] Here is Crispin Wright's rather more open-minded

University Press, 1982; Katz's *The Metaphysics of Meaning*, Cambridge, MA, MIT Press, 1991; Soames' *Philosophical Analysis in the 20th Century, vol. 2: The Age of Meaning*, Princeton: Princeton University Press, 2003, pp. 27–31; and Pears' *Paradox and Platitude in Wittgenstein's Philosophy*, Oxford: Oxford University Press, 2006, p. viii.

[3] An early and crude presentation of these ideas (directed, in particular, against Jerry Katz's divergent opinion) may be found in my "Meaning and Metaphilosophy", *Philosophical Issues* 4, 1993, 153–8.

[4] See, for example, Richard Rorty's "Wittgenstein and the Linguistic Turn", in A. Ahmed (ed.) *Wittgenstein's Philosophical Investigations: A Critical Guide*, Cambridge: Cambridge University Press, 2010, 145–61. My response—"Rorty's Wittgenstein"—appears in the same volume.

assessment, which points unerringly to the project that I undertake in this book.

> [I]t is difficult to reconcile Wittgenstein's pronounce-
> ments about the kind of thing which he thinks he ought
> to be doing with what he actually seems to do...At the
> time I write this, the complaint is justified that the great
> volume of commentary on the *Investigations* has so far
> done very little to clarify either how we should interpret
> the general remarks on philosophy so as to have our
> understanding enhanced of Wittgenstein's treatment of
> specific questions, or conversely. (What are the 'well
> known facts' arranged in the course of the Private Lan-
> guage discussion?) Wittgenstein's later views on philoso-
> phy constitute one of the least well understood aspects of
> his thought.[5]

As for my third guiding idea, the present reading of Wittgenstein is extracted almost entirely from Part I of the *Philosophical Investigation*—and for the following reasons.

In the first place, this is the only work from his so-called
later period that he carefully prepared for publication and
unquestionably wanted to be published. Who knows what he
thought of the other notes and manuscripts, found in drawers
in various parts of the world, that his executors decided to
print? These writings can no doubt be suggestive; but they
should not be accorded the authority of his *Investigations*.

In the second place, I think that the common view of Wittgenstein—that he produced two distinct philosophies—is mistaken. The trajectory of his work, including the *Tractatus
Logico-Philosophicus* and his writing in the 1930s, should be

---

[5] *Wittgenstein on the Foundations of Mathematics*, London: Duckworth,
1980, p. 162. The quoted passage is cited by Robert Fogelin in his admira-
ble *Taking Wittgenstein at his Word*, Princeton: Princeton University Press,
2009, p. 4.

seen as a series of improvements culminating in the *Investigations*. Therefore, we might well say that he produced one philosophy preceded by a variety of drafts. Or perhaps—counting "philosophies" in a more fine-grained way—that he produced *many* related philosophies including several after 1930. But to pick on the number *two* is apt to be misleading. It can foster the expectation of being able to integrate conflicting remarks from throughout the later period; and, when this proves impossible, it can encourage the conclusion that Wittgenstein's mature philosophy can't be made coherent and so isn't of any great significance.[6]

Thirdly, and most importantly, even if I am wrong to downgrade Wittgenstein's other writings, and even if I underestimate the difference between his views before and after 1930, the fact remains that a revolutionary philosophy is contained in Part I of the *Philosophical Investigations*, and this is well worth explaining, assessing, and developing, independently of what he said elsewhere.

Although I will take issue with many aspects of Kripke's celebrated account of Wittgenstein's philosophy, the spirit of his book is one that I admire and will be attempting to emulate. He presents a line of thought, not as an exact account of what Wittgenstein means, nor as what he, Kripke, would fully endorse, but rather as something that he regards as compelling and important, and that occurred to him as a result of his coming to grips with Wittgenstein's work. Similarly, my own primary concern is philosophy rather than scholarship. I do think that the ideas that will follow can be extracted, without undue strain, from Wittgenstein's text; certainly, that is how I arrived

---

[6] For similar reasons, I can't go along with Danièle Moyal-Sharrock's suggestion that Wittgenstein's writings after Part I of the *Investigations* constitute a *third* philosophy. See her collection, *The Third Wittgenstein: The Post-Investigations Works*, Aldershot: Ashgate Publishing Limited, 2004.

at them. But my main contention is that, regardless of their pedigree, they are worth taking seriously.

My hope for this project is that it might help to restore Wittgenstein's unique perspective to the mainstream of analytic philosophy. For some years now there has been a polar split between, on the one hand, the great majority of philosophers, who don't think that his ideas are relevant to their work, and, on the other hand, the Wittgensteinians themselves, who are engaged in feuds with one another that no one else cares about. It would be good if this ghettoization could be done away with.

To that end the present essay offers a clear articulation and defence of Wittgenstein's methodology, followed by applications of it to some mainstream problems in the philosophy of language and the philosophy of mind. The style throughout is analytic, there is frequent engagement with *non*-Wittgensteinian points of view, and the emphasis is on philosophical understanding rather than interpretation.[7]

This book is primarily addressed to philosophers (including advanced students)—for some prior familiarity with the subject is needed. Chapter 1, which introduces Wittgenstein's approach, is perhaps an exception. Chapter 2, the heart of the book, provides a detailed and sophisticated elaboration of that approach. Chapter 3 describes Wittgenstein's early ideas and explains where and why he came to disagree with them. (Here, the reader would be well advised to have a copy of the *Tractatus* at hand). Chapter 4 defends Wittgenstein's famous identification of the meaning of a word with its 'use', and discusses his

---

[7] One doesn't need to endorse Wittgenstein's general anti-theoretical metaphilosophy in order to appreciate that *some* problems in philosophy are spurious—based on muddled presuppositions and calling for dissolution. And so that possibility should, in every case, at least be explored (along with competing approaches), even if it is neither assumed in advance nor accepted in the end.

treatment of various paradoxes that this view must confront. Chapter 5 contrasts these ideas with those attributed to him by Kripke. And Chapter 6 projects Wittgenstein into contemporary debates about the nature of experience. These chapters are self-contained, but are best read in the order of their appearance.

As a schoolboy I happened upon the *Tractatus* in Manchester's Central Library. It was somehow impressive, and I wished I could understand it. Six years later I had my chance. I began studying philosophy in Cornell's PhD programme (having switched from physics a few months earlier). Several eminent Wittgensteinians were there—including Norman Malcolm, Max Black, and Bruce Goldberg—and I took seminars from them all. But my interests at the time were mainly in the philosophy of physics. At MIT, where I started teaching, the watchwords were clarity and rigour, Wittgenstein's philosophy was regarded with suspicion, and no one else was inclined to teach it; so it was left to me to give it a shot. In preparing my classes I came to feel that much of the unsympathetic secondary literature missed the main point, and that much of the sympathetic literature didn't take a sufficiently independent and sceptical perspective. So I began trying to work out something more satisfying. This monograph is a product of those efforts.

When I started to write it, about twenty-five years ago, the idea of prioritizing Wittgenstein's anti-theoretical metaphilosophy was much less common than it is now. Still, I believe that both this *interpretive* strategy, and the process of developing and defending the position itself, are carried further in the present work than they are elsewhere—as is the idea of insisting that Wittgenstein's ideas—for their own sake—must not be exempted from the high standards of constructive critical scrutiny to which other systems of thought are subjected within analytic philosophy.

I would like to thank my students, colleagues, and friends at the Massachusetts Institute of Technology, University College London, the Graduate Center of the City Universtiy of New York, New York University, and elsewhere—especially those most resistant to his perspective—for helping me to see what needed to be done. I shall be acknowledging a fair number of these people by name at appropriate points in the following pages. But let me not wait to mention Paul Boghossian, Josh Cohen, Hannah Ginsborg, Richard Rorty, Scott Soames, Michael Williams, and Crispin Wright, on whom I have relied for tough criticism and steady encouragement. I also owe a special thanks to Bill Child and Guy Longworth, who each read the penultimate draft and provided me (anonymously!) with detailed and insightful reactions to just about every page of it. Finally, I should say how grateful I am to the National Endowment for the Humanities, the Guggenheim Foundation, and New York University, for funding the free time needed to complete this work.

1

Wittgenstein's metaphilosophy

1.1 THE FUNDAMENTAL IDEA

Wittgenstein's most important insight is encapsulated in his remark that "Philosophy is a battle against the bewitchment of our intelligence by means of language" (PI 109). This thought may not appear to be especially momentous. But in fact it alludes to a revolutionary conception of the subject—of what it is, of how it should be done, and of what it can accomplish.[1] Moreover, since his ideas about the nature of philosophy are what shape his discussions of particular philosophical issues—concerning meaning, consciousness, numbers, necessity, beauty, and so on—his remarks about these various matters will seem disorganized and unmotivated, and will indeed be impossible to understand, unless that metaphilosophical perspective is kept clearly in mind.

Its most shocking implication is that philosophy cannot deliver the sort of knowledge that is usually regarded as its *raison d'être*. There are, he supposes, no realms of phenomena whose study is the special business of a philosopher and about which he or she should formulate profound *a priori* theories and sophisticated arguments in support of them. There are no

---

[1] Wittgenstein himself appreciated that his most significant contribution was *meta*philosophical. See G. E. Moore's "Wittgenstein's Lectures in 1930–33", in J. Klagge and A. Nordmann (eds.), *Philosophical Occasions*, Indianapolis and Cambridge, MA: Hackett Publishing Company, 1993 (see especially section H on pp. 113–14).

surprising discoveries to be made of facts, inaccessible through the methods of science, yet discoverable 'from the armchair' by means of some blend of pure thought, contemplation, and conceptual analysis. Furthermore, Wittgenstein says, the whole idea of a subject that could yield such results is based on confusion and wishful thinking.

This attitude is in dramatic opposition to the traditional view, which continues to prevail. Philosophy is widely exalted for its promise to provide fundamental insights into the human condition and the ultimate character of the universe, leading to vital conclusions about how we ought to arrange our lives. It's taken for granted that there are deep discoveries to be made about the nature of existence, how knowledge of other minds is possible, whether our actions are free or determined, what is the structure of a just society, and so on—and that philosophy's job is to provide such understanding. Isn't that why we are so fascinated by it?

If so, then we are duped and bound to be disappointed, says Wittgenstein. For these are mere pseudo-questions—the products of muddled thinking. Therefore, traditional philosophical theorizing about such matters must give way to a painstaking identification of its tempting but misguided presuppositions and an understanding of how we ever came to regard them as legitimate. But in that case,

> [w]here does [that] investigation get its importance from, since it seems only to destroy everything interesting, that is, all that is great and important? (As it were all the buildings, leaving behind only bits of stone and rubble). What we are destroying is nothing but houses of cards and we are clearing up the ground of language on which they stand. (PI 118)

Given this sort of stark pessimism about the potential of philosophy—perhaps tantamount to a denial that there is such a subject—it is hardly surprising that "Wittgenstein" is uttered with a curl of the lip in many philosophical circles. Even those who have the greatest respect for his initial work cannot contain their irritation at these later ideas. For example, Bertrand Russell's final opinion was that Wittgenstein

> ...seems to have grown tired of serious thinking and invented a doctrine which would make such an activity unnecessary.[2]

This was certainly quite a change from his earlier estimation. In 1911 the 22-year-old Wittgenstein had gone to Cambridge to study under him and had made a dazzling impression. Within a few months Russell was talking about how he could happily retire from philosophy in the knowledge that, left to Wittgenstein, it would be in safe hands![3] During the First World War Wittgenstein was a soldier and then a prisoner, and he finished writing his first book, *Tractatus Logico-Philosophicus*, which was published with Russell's help in 1921. The goal of this work was to specify the underlying structural features that must be possessed by a language if it is to be capable of representing reality. Philosophical issues were identified as the pseudo-questions that emerge when these constraints are violated.[4]

Imagining that he had thereby disposed of the major problems (and frustrated, perhaps, at the difficulty of getting his book into print), Wittgenstein gave up sustained philosophical

---

[2] *My Philosophical Development*, London: George Allen and Unwin; New York: Simon and Schuster, 1959, p. 217.

[3] See Russell's letters to Lady Ottoline Morrell, quoted in R. W. Clark's *The Life of Bertrand Russell*, New York: Knopf, 1975. For example: "He gives me such a delightful lazy feeling that I can leave a whole department of difficult thought to him, which used to depend on me alone. It makes it much easier for me to give up technical work" (p. 191).

[4] This fairly traditional view of the work is now controversial. I will attempt to justify it in Chapter 3.

activity, and for the next ten years did various odd jobs: he was a schoolmaster in three Austrian villages, a gardener in a monastery, and he helped to design and build a house in Vienna for his sister. (It is now a Bulgarian cultural centre.) In this period he did have some slight contact with philosophers (notably Frank Ramsey and certain members of the Vienna Circle) who sought him out to have the ideas of the *Tractatus* explained to them. And by the late 1920s, partially as a result of these discussions, Wittgenstein's confidence in that work had been undermined and his thirst for the subject revived.

In 1929 he returned to Cambridge to do philosophy again. Interestingly, Russell was not immediately put off by Wittgenstein's new ideas; his antipathy towards them developed only later. For in 1930, after reading Wittgenstein's latest manuscript, he wrote:

> The theories contained in this new work of Wittgenstein's are novel, very original, and indubitably important. Whether they are true, I do not know. As a logician, who likes simplicity, I should like to think that they are not, but from what I have read of them I am quite sure that he ought to have an opportunity to work them out, since when completed they may easily prove to constitute a whole new philosophy. (Report to the Council of Trinity College[5])

1.2 SCEPTICAL CONUNDRUMS

Let us now begin to examine Wittgenstein's 'new philosophy'. To a *very* first approximation, he came to think that the paradigm philosophical problems have the form:

[5] Russell's report is printed in Brian McGuinness (ed.), *Wittgenstein in Cambridge*, Oxford: Blackwell, 2008, p. 183.

How could there be such a thing as X?

—where X is some perfectly familiar, ordinarily unproblematic phenomenon, but where *a priori* considerations have been advanced whose import is that, despite appearances, X is in fact impossible. For example, one might wonder (with Descartes) how knowledge of external reality is possible, given that such knowledge would have to be derived from experience and that our experience could be just as it is even if we were merely dreaming. Or one might wonder (with Hobbes) how free and blameworthy human action could occur if everything that happens—including everything we do—is causally determined via laws of nature by events that occurred before we were born. Other commonplace phenomena whose possibility has been called into question by philosophy include motion (Zeno), time (McTaggart), space (Leibniz), causation (Hume), future facts (Aristotle), and meaning (Quine). In each case there is a focus on something whose existence is quite uncontroversial outside the context of philosophy. But we are confronted with a piece of reasoning that seems perfectly sound—its assumptions look plausible and the steps in the argument seem legitimate—arguing that, contrary to what we might naively have thought, the phenomenon is actually impossible: there can be no such things as motion, space, time, knowledge, freedom, and so on.

However, according to Wittgenstein, philosophy is incapable of establishing such dramatic results: the arguments must somehow be wrong, and their initial plausibility must derive from some language-based confusion in our thinking about them.[6] Consequently, our job is not to find out whether the

---

[6] The idea here is not that common-sense opinion is sacrosanct and can never be rationally overturned. Nor is it, more modestly, that common-sense *a priori* convictions are sacrosanct. It's rather that the methodology characteristic of philosophical scepticisms is defective. Of course, this view of Wittgenstein's is far from obviously correct, and calls for justification. See Chapter 2, Sections 2.4 and 2.5.

phenomenon in question is possible, or to try to prove that it really is or really is not, or to discern, in light of the paradoxical considerations, what its true nature must be, but rather to remove the confusion that is responsible for the misguided philosophical argument. When this has been done, we will not be left with any positive theory or new understanding. The net result will be simply that we have cured ourselves of a particular tendency to get mixed up.

1.3 ILLUSTRATIONS FROM OUTSIDE PHILOSOPHY

It is helpful to start the process of exploring this view of philosophical problems by looking at certain analogous *non*-philosophical problems. Consider the following well-known little puzzle:

> Three friends check into a cheap motel and pay $30 ($10 each) to share a room. The receptionist then realizes that it in fact costs only $25. So she hands the bellboy $5 to give back to them. He goes to their room, gives them $1 each, and keeps $2 for himself. Now, here's the question. Each of them paid $9. Three times $9 is $27. Add the $2 pinched by the bellboy. We get only $29! Where's the missing dollar? (Ponder for a minute before proceeding!)

If you are good at such brain-teasers you will quickly see that this is a pseudo-question. On the surface it appears to be a genuine question, but it really isn't. For there is no missing dollar, and it is only a certain carelessness that allows us to suppose that there is. Why should we ever have expected that the $27 ultimately paid plus the $2 stolen would equal the $30 initially handed over? Obviously (on reflection) the stolen $2 is *part* of the $27 paid. And obviously (on reflection) the proper amount to be added to that $27, if one wants to arrive at the $30 initially handed over, is the $3 given back by the bellboy. The apparent force of the question depends on being tricked into a false presupposition, and once the trick is exposed, the problem disappears. And the same goes for philosophical problems, according to Wittgenstein.

Here's another puzzle—one that that he himself liked to give in order to indicate the nature of philosophy:[7]

> Suppose that a very long piece of rope is wrapped around the equator of the Earth. Now imagine that the rope is lengthened by one yard, but that its circular form is preserved, so that the rope no longer fits snugly but occupies a circle at some slight constant distance from the Earth's surface. How great would that distance be?

Now it doesn't take much in the way of mathematical sophistication to calculate that in fact the distance would be about 6 inches—since the radius of any circle is about a sixth ($1/2\pi$) of its circumference. However, one is initially tempted to think that the uniform gap between the rope and the Earth's surface would have to be much, much less—perhaps only a few thousandths of an inch. And one may be somewhat inclined to hang on to this opinion, even in the face of the mathematical argument! Thus we have a case, similar to the more serious philosophical issues mentioned before, where something we know to be true seems impossible.

Why does it seem impossible? What is the confusion that leads us astray here? I'm not sure. But perhaps it is that we are taken in by the crude idea that if A results in B then a barely discernible modification of A could yield only a barely discernible change in B—in which case, the addition of a yard to a 25,000-mile rope cannot have a substantial effect.

---

[7] Reported by Norman Malcolm in his *Ludwig Wittgenstein: A Memoir*, Oxford: Oxford University Press, 1958, pp. 53–4.

What we can easily forget is that whether or not a change will strike us as substantial will depend on the context in which it occurs and on the perspective we happen to occupy. In abstract terms, the increase of a mere 6 inches to the initial 4000-mile radius is indeed just as insignificant as the extra yard of circumference. But from our special perspective—right on the Earth's surface—those 6 inches would be glaring.

Thus our general, heuristic principle—"Small variations have small effects"—is by no means wholly incorrect. The problem arises because we apply the principle incorrectly. And the problem disappears when we come to see that this is what we are doing. Wittgenstein's view is that philosophical problems are somewhat like this—problems engendered by confusion derived from the simplistic application of some intuitive picture of how things must be. So that what is required by way of solution is not a direct answer to a straightforward question, but rather a sort of treatment or therapy in which the operative misconception is exposed and its grip thereby loosened.

1.4 THE ROLE OF LANGUAGE

Part of Wittgenstein's view is that distinctively *philosophical* confusion arises when the misleading picture is derived from language. In the *Blue Book* he says:

> The man who is philosophically puzzled sees a law in the way a word is used, and, trying to apply this law consistently, comes up against paradoxical results. (p. 27)

And in the *Philosophical Investigations*:

> Our investigation is therefore a grammatical one. Such an investigation sheds light on our problems by clearing misunderstandings away. Misunderstandings concerning the use of words, caused, among other things, by certain

analogies between the forms of expression in different regions of language. (PI 90)

These are, of course, not empirical problems; they are solved, rather, by looking into the workings of our language, and in such a way as to make us recognize those workings; *in despite of* an urge to misunderstand them. The problems are solved, not by giving new information, but by arranging what we have already known. Philosophy is a battle against the bewitchment of our intelligence by means of language. (PI 109)

A *picture* held us captive. And we could not get outside it, for it lay in our language and language seemed to repeat it to us inexorably. (PI 115)

Let us look at a few examples of such problems, beginning with some that are relatively superficial and easy to dissolve.

If you don't know much mathematics you might be quite impressed and mystified by the contention that:

Every straight line intersects every circle—but sometimes only at imaginary points!

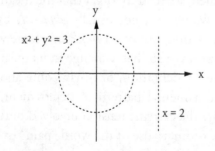

But one can be amazed only to the extent that one doesn't appreciate that the words "intersect" and "imaginary" have each been given special technical meanings—whereby, for example, the circle represented by '$x^2 + y^2 = 3$' and the line represented by '$x = 2$' are said to "intersect" at the values of x and y that simultaneously satisfy both equations, which are the so-called "imaginary points", [2, i] and [2, –i]. Unaware of these shifts in sense, one may well think that the fundamental rules governing our *ordinary* use of the words "intersect" and "imaginary" remain in force and account for their deployment in the mathematician's surprising contention—but it is impossible to see how they could possibly do so! Thus the source of philosophical bewilderment—easily removed in this case—is a natural tendency, on hearing a word, to assign it the meaning with which one is familiar.

Similarly, suppose a psychologist claims to have discovered the existence of *unconscious pain*. Now there are many fantastic things (black holes, nanochips, eleven-dimensional super-strings, and so on) whose reported discovery by science pro-vokes no particular reaction in the philosophical world. But this sort of claim is likely to hit a peculiar nerve: there will be protests to the effect that, regardless of the predictive and explanatory power of the 'unconscious pain theory', it must be rejected as incoherent—the very idea of an unconscious pain being self-contradictory.[8]

But again, the source of confusion is not difficult to identify. As just illustrated, we tend to forget that the meaning of a word is something we bestow, not usually *explicitly* by means of a deliberate stipulation, but often *implicitly*, merely by using the word in certain ways; so that a change in its meaning does not require an overt redefinition, but may come about through a shift in its fundamental pattern of deployment. As a conse-quence, despite the extreme tension involved in trying to com-bine our basic ordinary use of the word "pain" (which includes its application only to what we take the subject to be aware of) and its proposed use within the scientific theory, we resist dis-solving that tension by acknowledging a degree of ambiguity

---

[8] See Wittgenstein's *Blue Book* (pp. 22–3) for some remarks on 'the discovery of unconscious toothache'.

(which would amount to our not allowing the two uses to be combined in inference). And so we are left with a choice between either tolerating the irresoluble perplexities that this combination engenders, or refusing to accept the new theory. But this false dilemma is easily avoided. The remedy, quite clearly, is not to be mesmerized by the *word*, but to appreciate how distinct uses of it, hence somewhat distinct meanings, may evolve and proliferate.

Perhaps even more importantly, a common way for us to be misled by language, according to Wittgenstein, is that when we see a noun appearing as the subject of a true sentence, we expect there to be a *thing* to which the noun refers. This expectation comes from reflection on countless statements such as

> Neptune is a planet
>
> Boston has subways
>
> Plato taught philosophy

which suggest a universal underlying semantic structure for all sentences of that simple syntactic type: the subject, a noun phrase, picks out a particular object in the world, and the rest of the sentence denotes some property or characteristic attributed to that object.

One context in which a fixation upon this pattern can cause headaches is in the analysis of negative existential statements, such as

> Father Christmas does not exist

Over-generalizing from the previous examples, one might conclude that no such statement can be true. For in order to be true, its subject would have to succeed in designating *something*—something which the sentence goes on to say is non-existent! Therefore the statement could be true only if it were also false; and therefore could not be true. The following remark of Wittgenstein's seems quite apt:

> When we do philosophy we are like savages, primitive
> people, who hear the expressions of civilized men, put a
> false interpretation on them, and then draw the queerest
> conclusions from it. (PI 194)[9]

1.5 ODD OBJECTS: THE CASE
OF NUMBERS

But as far as Wittgenstein is concerned, the most serious dan-
ger associated with noun phrases is of a different kind. We tend
to assimilate sentences such as

> Time is one-dimensional
>
> Seven is prime
>
> My after-image is red

to the preceding cases. We suppose, in other words, that the terms
"time", "seven", and "my after-image" pick out things in the
world. Then, since the paradigmatic *thing* is a physical object—a
stone, a table, a planet, and so on—we are inclined to ask the sort
of questions about time, seven, and after-images that would normally be asked about ordinary physical objects. For example:

> Where is it located?
>
> What is it made of?
>
> How do other things interact with it?
>
> How can information about it reach us?

Our inability to give satisfactory answers to these questions can
leave the impression that the phenomena at issue—time, num-

---

[9] This is not to impugn the legitimacy and interest of questions in scientific
semantics—in particular, of the issue of what logical/semantic structure *should*
be assigned to negative existential statements. The point is merely to illustrate
the way in which paradoxes can arise from irrationally insistent overgeneralization.

bers, experiences—are either hopelessly mysterious or else could not really be as we naively take them to be:

> Where our language suggests a body, and there is none; there, we should like to say, is a spirit. (PI 36)

We quickly arrive at our characteristic questions of the form, "How is it possible for there to exist such a thing as X?", which I illustrated above. In Wittgenstein's view, however, these puzzles are merely *pseudo*-questions—the product of analogies which, perversely exaggerated, assimilate the entities named to physical objects. So we can dissolve the problems by removing the temptation to over-stretch the analogies.

For concreteness, let us focus for a moment on the case of numbers.[10] A straightforward reading of arithmetical assertions—for example, a construal of

> Seven is a prime

as analogous in semantic structure to

> Neptune is a planet

suggests a realm of mathematical reality, the numbers, whose properties it is the purpose of mathematics to discover and describe. But this can seem paradoxical and mystifying. For we can't see how locations could conceivably be ascribed to numbers. Yet how could a genuine object not exist in space or time? Nor can we see how numbers could exhibit any sort of causal influence on our beliefs about them. Yet, surely, knowledge of genuine objects would require some such interaction?

One response to these puzzles—we might call it 'mysterian platonism'—has been to acknowledge that numbers are 'objects' of an essentially bizarre kind: 'objects' that can inex-

---

[10] See Chapter 2, Section 2.6, for further details.

plicably exist 'beyond' space and time and inexplicably 'impress themselves' on our cognitive faculties.

Reacting against such mystery-mongering, another theoretical move has been to deny, given their paradoxical nature, that there could be (or, at least, that there could be *known* to be) such things as numbers—but then to remove some of the sting from this denial by maintaining that we can and should, for practical and scientific reasons, go along with the *fiction* that standard arithmetic is true. However, it is far from clear that such a have-your-cake-and-eat-it response is coherent.[11]

An alternative reaction against mysterian platonism has been to revise mathematics itself in such a way as to remove its unpalatable commitments. In particular, the intuitionist-constructivists hold that the world of mathematical objects must be a human invention or construction; this suggests to them that there can be nothing more to mathematical truth than 'provability from the (conventionally) accepted axioms of mathematics'; and this in turn leads them to abandon the classical law of excluded middle: that every statement of the form "p or not p" is true. (For let "A" be the statement "Every even number is the sum of two primes", and suppose that neither "A" nor "not A" can be proved. If truth were provability, then neither "A" nor "not A" would be true, and so "A or not A" could not be maintained.)

Then there are attempts to avoid the weirdness of ethereal platonic objects via some sort of reductionist account. But to the extent that a given proposal promises to demystify numbers by reducing them to unproblematic physical entities (such as numerals), it will seem highly implausible; and to the extent

[11] The basis for this concern is the difficulty of seeing any difference between the assertive practice (paralleled in thought) that a fictionalist recommends and a practice that would constitute genuine belief. See "A World without Isms", Chapter 12 of my *Truth-Meaning-Reality*, Oxford: Oxford University Press, 2010, esp. pp. 260–4.

that it seeks to avoid this implausibility by proposing to reduce them to other abstracta (such as logical or set-theoretic entities), then no significant demystification will be achieved.

Finally, it might be hoped that the needed clarity and understanding are best promoted by means of a *superficial* systematization of our arithmetical beliefs: for example, a Peano-style axiomatization. But such a thing is not easy to come by (as Gödel proved). Moreover, it is hard to see how a mere 'compression' of our convictions could touch any of the ontological or epistemological puzzlement that they initially provoked.

Despite their opposition to one another, the fictionalists, constructivists, logicists, axiologists, and mysterian platonists share a fundamental assumption: namely, that to take our mathematical discourse at face value requires the adoption of a metaphysical picture with many attendant difficulties. In other words, all these theorists feel the force of a certain dilemma: either accept arithmetic understood naively and be confronted with extreme philosophical perplexities, or avoid those perplexities but pay the price with a peculiar mathematics, or a contrived construal of mathematical practice, or both.

Wittgenstein's view was that we must expose and exorcise the single misconception that is responsible for this false dilemma. We should learn to see that neither arithmetical discourse nor the natural interpretation of it as referring to an abstract, mind-independent reality need necessarily carry with them the propriety of puzzlement about the nature, location, and accessibility of that reality.

The basic mistake, in his view, is the expectation that philosophy can and should deliver *a priori* theories that—like good scientific theories—are simple, unifying, and explanatory. It's this background presupposition that inclines us to exaggerate the analogies between talking about planets (for example) and talking about numbers; to therefore raise the same questions about numbers that we normally ask about planets; and to be perplexed when we can't answer them. Wittgenstein's therapy—his reminding us of the highly idiosyncratic character and function of arithmetical discourse—relieves the grip of these temping over-simplifications without requiring any modification either of standard mathematics, or of the naïve idea that numbers are abstract objects, or our naïve aspiration to discover what is true about them.[12]

1.6 QUESTIONS AND OBJECTIONS

Having briefly described and illustrated Wittgenstein's conception of philosophy, I would like to end the chapter by mentioning some of the many sceptical questions that this introduction should provoke—issues that I will address in the next chapter.

First, could there be a *precise* articulation of Wittgenstein's metaphilosophical view, including clear ways of characterizing 'over-stretched analogies', 'pseudo-problems', and 'philosophical perplexities', and an account of the processes by which aspects of language induce these phenomena?

Second—turning from the content of his doctrine to the justification for accepting it—what general reason is there to agree with his claim that nothing of any depth is to be learned by doing philosophy in the traditional theoretical way? This is certainly not self-evident; yet he does not appear to provide any argument, over and above a series of examples, for adopting such a pessimistic point of view.

---

[12] Perhaps this naïve view still qualifies as a form of "platonism".—In which case, what I am suggesting is that platonism *per se* is not necessarily objectionable. What *is* objectionable is the position for which I introduced the label "mysterian platonism"—the philosophical theory that goes beyond our naïve view in supposing that numbers are intrinsically mysterious, calling for involving inexplicable conceptions of 'object' and 'intuitive access'. See Chapter 2, Sections 2.3 and 2.5.

Third, there would appear to be solid reason to *dis*agree. Surely there are philosophical problems in, for example, ethics, mathematical logic, naturalistic epistemology, and the foundations of physics—problems addressed by people who rightly take themselves to be philosophers—that do not have the character Wittgenstein describes, and from whose solution we think important knowledge might well be gained.

Fourth—and a further objection—he says that the goal of philosophy is not to formulate and establish theories, but rather to clear away confusions produced by language. But is not this claim about the nature of philosophy itself a theory? So isn't Wittgenstein's metaphilosophy self-contradictory?

Fifth—and bearing on both the nature of, and basis for, that view—is it clear that his scepticism about the prospect of radical discoveries within philosophy precedes and helps explain his other doctrines—in particular, his account of *meaning* as *use*? For it is widely held, on the contrary (for example, by Baker, Dummett, Hacker, Katz, Kripke, Pears, and Soames—see my Preface), that Wittgenstein's metaphilosophical conservatism—the sacrosanct status of 'ordinary language'—itself issues from his conception of meaning.

Insofar as we aspire not merely to understand Wittgenstein's thought but to reach some truth of the matter about the nature of philosophy, it is essential to try to answer these questions. It must be conceded, however, that there are initial grounds for doubting that satisfactory responses can be found. The fact that Wittgenstein himself did not answer them should give us pause. But in addition he might seem to suggest that any attempt to organize his ideas within a systematic, rational structure will inevitably distort them. For he says, in the Preface to the *Philosophical Investigations*:

> The best that I could write would never be more than philosophical remarks; my thoughts were soon crippled if I tried to force them on in any single direction against

their natural inclination. —And this was, of course, connected with the very nature of the investigation. For this
compels us to travel over a wide field of thought criss-
cross in every direction.

However, it is important to distinguish two strands of thought
here. One of them is the observation that philosophy is holistic: that its central problems are so intertwined that we cannot
treat any of them thoroughly without addressing the others.
But of course, philosophy is far from unique in having this
character. Nor does 'holism' preclude a respect for clarity and
rigour.

One might also see in this passage an expression of Wittgenstein's distaste for explicitly setting down arguments, for abid-
ing by the standard norms of academic presentation, and for
spoon-feeding his reader. But I believe these attitudes to be
more a product of his moral and aesthetic sensibility than an
inevitable reflection of the substance of his thought. Accordingly, I shall be working on the assumption that it *is* possible to
explain Wittgenstein's philosophy in a more conventional,
rational, orderly way than he does himself—clearly articulating
its basic principles, reconstructing persuasive arguments in
favour of them, and spelling out their consequences. It seems
to me that this assumption is vindicated in what follows. Wittgenstein's importance for us must surely depend on its being
correct.

2

A critique of theoretical philosophy

Traditional philosophical questions about the nature of numbers, time, knowledge, truth, justice, beauty, free will, and so
on, derive their fascination, according to Wittgenstein, from
conceptual tensions (paradoxes) that stem in turn from a
perverse exaggeration of linguistic analogies. So in his view
the aim of a reasonable philosophical methodology should be
to dissolve such puzzles—to expose the irrational overgeneralizations from which they emerge.

In contrast, attempts at *theory* construction are *not* the
proper response. Such projects he argues, just compound those
original mistakes. For both our initial over-stretchings and the
various theorization strategies that are designed to deal with
the paradoxes they cause are encouraged by the same misguided
assumption: namely, that the phenomena at issue are susceptible to non-empirical projects of theorization oriented, just as
science is, towards the discovery of simple regularities, deep
explanations, and pre-theoretical errors. Therefore, a decent
approach must aim to undermine the appeal and seeming legitimacy of such projects, proposals, and puzzles, by exposing and
criticizing the scientistic conception of philosophy that engenders them.

Thus, for Wittgenstein, the important revelations that are
typically promised within our subject are impossible. In so far
as *theses* are propounded in philosophy, they should be barely
more than observations about the use of words—reminders

offered to help loosen the grip of over-stretched analogies. The most we can hope for is the *elimination* of our traditional concerns.[1]

This, in a nutshell, is his revolutionary metaphilosophical perspective. Chapter 1 offered a preliminary account of it, but several important questions and objections were left in abeyance. The present chapter will address those challenges to the view, thereby clarifying it and giving it a measure of support.

We will begin by looking (in sections 2.1–2.3) at the traditional way of philosophizing that Wittgenstein opposes, making explicit its methodological assumptions and describing the various kinds of theoretical construct it engenders. After that (in sections 2.4 and 2.5) I'll develop his interlocking reasons for condemning both this practice itself, and its specific products, as irrational. The forgoing picture of 'problem creation, inflationary theorization, and therapeutic deflation' will then (in section 2.6 and 2.7) be articulated as an eight-stage sequence of ideas, and illustrated with case studies from the philosophies of arithmetic, time, truth, and value. We turn (in section 2.8) to a rebuttal of the accusation that Wittgenstein's account is incoherent in that it violates its own anti-theoretical requirements. And we'll examine (in section 2.9) the explanatory and epistemological relations between his meta-philosophy and his "use conception" of meaning.

---

[1] As Wittgenstein puts it in the *Blue Book* (p. 18): "Our craving for generality has [as one] source . . . our preoccupation with the method of science. I mean the method of reducing the explanation of natural phenomena to the smallest possible number of primitive natural laws; and, in mathematics, of unifying the treatment of different topics by using a generalization. Philosophers constantly see the method of science before their eyes, and are irresistibly tempted to ask and answer in the way science does. This tendency is the real source of metaphysics, and leads the philosopher into complete darkness. I want to say here that it can never be our job to reduce anything to anything, or to explain anything. Philosophy really is 'purely descriptive'."

2.1 T-PHILOSOPHY

The above remarks about "traditional philosophy" do not purport to cover *all* of the loosely related forms of intellectual pursuit to which the label "philosophy" has ever been applied, but only to the one against which Wittgenstein was reacting—the one he rightly regarded as dominant at the time (and which remains dominant).

On that conception—which I will call "T-philosophy", to suggest both "traditional" and "theoretical"—the aim is construction and defence of important philosophical theories. But what is to qualify as "an important philosophical theory"? To a first approximation it's a non-obvious body of *a priori* principles—one that offers a complete, systematic, precise, and basic account of some pervasive yet puzzling phenomena. Thus we have Kripke's theory of truth, Lewis' theory of possibility, the *Tractatus* theory of language and metaphysics, Kant's theory of ethics, Frege's theory of arithmetic, Grice's theory of meaning, and so on.

In order to qualify as a *theory* (according to T-philosophy) the constituting principles must have a certain generality and depth. They must organize, unify, and explain common-sense commitments—and have the potential to correct them. And they must be initially controversial—deriving credibility, not from sheer self-evidence, but from their possession of theoretical virtues such as internal coherence, compatibility with what is known, and explanatory power.

In order to qualify as *philosophical* (according to T-philosophy) such principles must be, in some sense of the term, "*a priori*". They cannot be supported, as scientific theories are, by the perceptual observations of colours, shapes, spatio-temporal coincidences (such as measurement values), and the like. This is the basic respect in which investigations within T-philosophy differ from those within physics, biology, psychology, and the other empirical sciences.[2]

And as for what is of *importance* to T-philosophers, they are not especially concerned with electrons, or fish, or football, or ammonia, or unemployment, or tectonic plates—but rather with meaning, beauty, necessity, and so on. The focus is on concepts and phenomena that strike them as peculiarly pervasive, fundamental, rich, and idiosyncratic—and therefore as providing theorization projects that are peculiarly challenging.[3]

One might object that a great deal of theorizing by philosophers is clearly *not a priori*: for example, their work in empirical semantics, in the foundations of quantum electrodynamics,

---

[2] Timothy Williamson (in *The Philosophy of Philosophy*, Oxford: Blackwell, 2007) supposes, quite plausibly, that philosophical knowledge (as traditionally conceived) has been confined to "knowledge in which experience plays no strictly evidential role" (p. 169). He himself prefers to call this "armchair knowledge" rather than "*a priori* knowledge", on the grounds that the latter term has often been understood more narrowly within philosophy, to exclude knowledge produced by cognitive capacities that have been molded in part by experience. My own terminological preference, however—reflected in my definition of "T-philosophy"—would be to retain "a priori", acknowledging that its sense should be explicated in something like the broader way he suggests. After all, "armchair knowledge" is surely at least as ambiguous. It's unclear, for example, whether it requires merely that the knower is in an armchair at the time he makes the judgement—or also that he has spent his entire life there.

[3] It might be thought, since *arithmetic* also purports to arrive *a priori* at non-obvious results, that it too will qualify as T-philosophy, as just defined. And that would imply, it might be thought, first, that those defining criteria could not adequately capture a form of traditional *philosophizing*, and second—given the undisputed rationality of mathematics—that projects satisfying those criteria could not, simply on that account, be defective.

But these concerns are easily assuaged. For notice that arithmetic proper (as opposed to the *philosophy* of arithmetic, which includes axiomatization projects) does not in fact satisfy the above criteria, since it arrives at its number-theoretic conclusions by demonstrative proof rather than by the forms of conjectural inference relied upon in T-philosophy. And it is precisely the expectation that those forms of inference might deliver radical or otherwise interesting results that, as we will see, is the focus of Wittgenstein's critique.

in cognitive neuroscience, in evolutionary biology, and in the history of ideas. But this complaint would be inappropriate, since there has been no suggestion here that the term "philosophy" can't be properly applied to empirical projects. The claim was merely that there is a traditional and still prevalent conception of the subject (T-philosophy) which requires a priority, and this is the conception that was Wittgenstein's target. Anyway, it is obvious that philosophy, however broadly construed, won't include *everything* that members of philosophy departments get up to in the office. Einstein was not doing physics when he campaigned against nuclear weapons, and Kant was not doing philosophy when he conjectured that planets derive from nebulae.

A potentially devastating objection to theorizing within the norms of T-philosophy stems from scepticism about the very existence of *a priori* knowledge. If there is indeed no such thing—if, as Quine argued, a person's beliefs form an holistic system *all* of whose elements are more or less directly responsive to her experience—then we must acknowledge that philosophical theories, including those listed above, are somehow *a posteriori*, appearances notwithstanding.

However, it's worth observing that few philosophers consider themselves, qua philosophers, to be engaged in science—not even in a relatively speculative, vague, and embryonic form of it. It does seem clearly wrong to think of Russell's logical atomism, Leibniz's monadology, McTaggart's account of time, or Rawls' theory of justice in that way. So even if Quine's hyperempiricism is *in fact* correct, it remains perfectly possible that philosophy is and has been dominated by a conception of the subject as oriented towards *a priori* theorization.

But *is* Quine's view correct? His web-of-belief model, in so far as it purports to cover commitments of *every* kind, is not especially plausible. It works nicely as an account of how *scientific* opinions evolve. But many of our beliefs—such as those about logic, right and wrong, numbers, and our own feelings and sensations—are not constrained by observation in the way that the model would imply. And why should they be? Linguo-conceptual activities and their associated norms serve a variety of purposes—discovery of the laws of nature being only one of them. So there is no good reason to expect epistemology in general to coincide with the epistemology of science.[4]

Although T-philosophical theories are not scientific, they are 'scientistic': that is to say, the goals and methods that lie behind them are inspired by, and modelled upon, those of the empirical sciences. The objective, as in science, is deep truth, profound understanding—fundamental principles that will explain relatively superficial facts and will have the authority to modify our naïve pre-theoretical convictions.

Amongst theoretical constructions of this kind, some are at the *same level* as the facts which they aim to cover, and others purport to characterize the *underlying nature* of the facts at that level. Thus we find *superficial systematizations*—for

---

[4] There are many competing theories of the basis of *a priori* justification. Amongst the most popular are that it is rationalized or explained by (i) knowledge of meanings, (ii) intuitions, (iii) reliability of belief-producing mechanisms, (iv) considerations of coherence or (v) what is *taken* to be *a priori* justified. —And there is also the Wittgensteinian view that *a priori* justification has *no* theoretical basis. I myself favour this last idea: namely, that what are in practice treated as basic facts of *a priori* justification—that one ought to believe, for example, that if dogs bark then dogs bark, that 3 has a successor, that lying is wrong, that a given red-looking thing probably *is* red, and that if all observed emeralds have been green then the next one will be too—are epistemologically and explanatorily *fundamental*. This is not to deny, of course, that there may be a battery of evolutionary, cultural, and cognitive mechanisms that produce such normative convictions. But these causal factors will neither justify those convictions nor help to explain their truth. See my "Ungrounded Reason", *Journal of Philosophy*, CV:9, 2008 (reprinted with revisions in *Truth-Meaning-Reality*)—which begins with the following remark of Wittgenstein's: "It is so difficult to find the *beginning*. Or better: it is difficult to begin at the beginning. And not try to go further back" (*On Certainty*, 471).

example, Peano's axiomatization of arithmetic, the rules of truth-functional propositional logic, Mill's utilitarianism, and the minimal theory of truth. And these contrast with *foundational theories* such as Frege's logicist reduction of arithmetic, semantic explanations of epistemic justification, moral constructivism, the verificationist theory of truth, and logical atomism.

2.2 INTUITION → GENERALIZATION → PARADOX

In both cases the goal, as in science, is a body of simple and precise generalizations that can accommodate the relevant data. Of course, the data here are not scientific. Instead of sensory perceptions, one relies upon basic *a priori* convictions (so-called "*a priori* intuitions"): for example, that the numeral "3", as we understand it, is a singular term; that "good", like "red", has the logical power of a predicate; that if dogs bark then it is *true* that dogs bark; that humans are *essentially* human, that a belief in life on Mars could be *reasonable* only on the basis of empirical evidence, and so on. But although such convictions are not strictly *observational*, they are supposed to play the same theory-constraining and theory-justifying roles as do observations in science.

Starting from such data, and with the optimistic expectation that simple and illuminating laws await our discovery, we are led toward the theories that are T-philosophy's ultimate objective. We tend to arrive in the first place at generalizations like these:

- Numbers are objects.
- Goodness is a substantive property.
- Every instance of '<p> is true ↔ p' is true.

- A justified belief must have argumentative backing.
- A decision can be free only if it is not causally determined.
- No belief is intrinsically motivating.
- Knowledge of a given fact requires some causal relation between the subject's state of belief and the fact known.

Such principles—intuitively supported and appealingly simple—can seem irresistible. But, on the other hand, they often conflict either with other strong convictions or with one another:

- Surely, numbers don't occupy positions in space and time and have no material constitution. But how, in that case, could they be genuine objects?
- Surely, some beliefs are justified. But if justification is a matter of good argument, the premises of any such argument would themselves have to be justified, requiring further arguments...and so on, *ad infinitum*; so justified belief would be impossible!
- Surely, my decision to write these words was free. But for all we know our laws of nature are deterministic—in which case *no* decision is free.

Thus we obtain the paradoxes with which our subject is notoriously pervaded. Over and over again we are torn between conflicting inclinations about what to think, and can rarely agree on satisfying ways of settling the issue. Some other well-known examples were mentioned in Chapter 1: the conflicts between, on the one hand, our naïve belief in future facts, meanings, time, space, and the external world, and on the other hand, theoretical arguments to the effect that such beliefs are mistaken.

But not all philosophical paradoxes take the form of a clash between theory and pre-theoretical intuition. In some cases, the clash is between our various *theoretical* convictions. For example:

- We might feel compelled to accept that if someone claims *that p* (no matter what sentence is put in place of "p") then what he says is *true* if and only if p. (For example, the claim that dogs bark is true if and only if dogs bark.) But this general thesis turns out to be in contradiction with principles of logic that are no less compelling. (The liar paradox.)[5]

- We might be unshakeably convinced both that 10,000 grains of sand are enough to make a heap, and that any heap of sand will still qualify as such if only a single grain is removed from it. But we can then deploy principles of classical logic to infer that 9,999 grains is enough to make a heap; and, having established this, that 9,998 is enough ... and so on, step by step, until we reach the absurd conclusion that just 1 grain is enough to make a heap. And parallel problems afflict just about every property—being a rich man, being a red surface, being a large number, and so on. (The sorites paradox.)

---

[5] Consider "This very statement is untrue". If that is true then things are as it says they are, so it is untrue. But, according to classical logic, from the fact that a proposition <p> entails its own negation we can infer <not-p>. So we can conclude that the initial statement is untrue. However, if it *is* untrue, well that is exactly what it says about itself, so it is not untrue. But then the same principle of classical logic allows us to conclude that it is *not* untrue. So we have proved a contradiction ("It is both untrue and not untrue")—which, again according to classical logic, we must not accept.

More precisely, this kind of paradox arises (in its simplest form) with respect to the claim that whatever statement satisfies a certain definite description, "D", is not true—where it turns out that that very claim is the unique satisfier of the description. For example, let "D is not true" abbreviate "The proposition expressed by the third quoted sentence in footnote 5 of Chapter 2 of *Wittgenstein's Metaphilosophy* is not true". In that case:

<D is not true> = D

Therefore, given Leibniz's Law, we have

<D is not true> is true ↔ D is true

But, given the equivalence schema for truth

<D is not true> is true ↔ D is not true

And so we arrive, by transitivity, at the contradiction

D is true ↔ D is not true

- It may seem very plausible that, from a purely self-interested point of view, we should always act so as to maximize our expected personal gain. Yet that principle is incompatible with another natural idea: namely, that we should never be in the slightest motivated by the desire for events whose occurrence we know we cannot help to bring about. (Newcomb's paradox.)[6]
- We may be inclined to think both that a thing's identity is preserved as its ageing components are gradually replaced *and* that if all those old parts were recombined the resultant object would be the same as the original one. But, given the transitivity of identity—i.e. "(x=y and y=z) → x=z"—those thoughts are inconsistent. For the two later objects (one fully refurbished and the other recombined) are obviously not identical to one another; so they can't both be identical to the earlier thing. (The ship-of-Theseus paradox.)

Puzzles of these types no doubt arise in other fields too, from time to time. But they are especially common in philosophy. And although there may be *some* temptation to think that this peculiarity issues from the self-contradictory nature of so many of the phenomena that we study, a more plausible diagnosis is that it reflects certain distinctive elements of our methodological goals and assumptions. And one might well

---

[6] Suppose you see that a certain transparent box, B, contains a thousand dollars and you know that a certain opaque box, A, contains either a million dollars or nothing. Suppose further that you must choose between being given either the contents of both boxes or the contents of A alone. And suppose that you know that your decision has been accurately predicted, and that the million dollars was placed in A if and only if it was predicted that you will choose it alone. Evidently, your expected gain is maximized by choosing box A alone. But, on the other hand, it's now too late for you to causally influence how much was placed there—so it might well seem obviously best for you to chose both boxes, since you'll get that amount, whatever it was, plus the visible extra thousand! For further discussion, see chapter 11 of my *Asymmetries in Time*, Cambridge, MA: MIT Press, 1987.

suspect that a careful scrutiny of these elements will reveal them to be, intrinsically defective. This suspicion will be confirmed in section 2.4.

2.3 THEORETICAL REACTIONS

The epistemic tensions that arise at the initial stages of T-philosophical investigation are not typically perceived by its practitioners as deterrents to that activity or as casting doubt on its legitimacy. On the contrary, they tend to serve as a stimulus to yet more elaborate projects of the same kind. They provoke alternative strategies of theoretical resolution, typically falling into one or other of the following categories:

(A) Sceptical theories

As we have seen, there's a kind of thesis, characteristic of philosophy, that impugns the reality of some phenomenon whose existence is ordinarily regarded as obvious: for example, free choice, motion through space, causal relations between events, and the experiences of other people. And, in some cases, one might be persuaded to resolve such a conflict with common sense by supposing that common sense has indeed been refuted.

In their more ambitious (metaphysical) form—also known as "error theories"—such sceptical proposals go as far as to assert that the phenomena do not exist (for example, Zeno's denial of motion, McTaggart's of time, Hilbert's of numbers, and Mackie's of moral facts). In their weaker (epistemological) form, the claim is merely that we are *not justified* in believing that these things exist (for example, van Fraassen *vis-à-vis* electrons and the like, Field *vis-à-vis* numbers, and Rosen *vis-à-vis* possible worlds).

Either way, a sceptical theory would seem to imply that our assertoric practice with respect to the phenomena at issue ought to be abandoned. For if there are no such phenomena, or if it is unreasonable for us to believe that there are, then the practice is either false or irrational or both. However, the advocates of sceptical theories commonly attempt to make their view less inconveniently radical by advocating a 'fictionalist' stance: we are advised to continue to engage in the old assertoric practice, but without believing what we are lierally saying.

(B) Revisionist theories

These resemble error-theoretic forms of scepticism in renouncing certain pre-theoretical intuitions—but they are less extreme. They do not deny the very existence (or knowability) of the phenomena in question, but do relinquish certain normally held views about them. They reject, for example, the mind-independence of numbers, or the difference between meaning and reference, or the tensed nature of certain facts, or the possibility of unverifiable truth, or the coherence of *de re* necessity, or the intrinsically motivating character of ethical belief.[7] Thus, whilst allowing that there *are* such things as numbers, or meanings, or temporal facts, or truths, or necessities, or ethical beliefs, it is held that our opinions about them must be substantially revised.

---

[7] I don't mean to suggest that non-philosophers would articulate these 'normal' commitments in the compressed and jargon-laden way that I have just expressed them. Still, it will be generally accepted that even if life had never happened to evolve, the number of planets would still have been eight; that saying, at 3 pm, "It is now raining" does not express exactly the same thought as saying "It is raining at 3 pm"; and so on.

(C) Mysterian theories

Here I have in mind a type of theory, peculiar to philosophy, in which certain phenomena are regarded as *truly* paradoxical and *essentially* bizarre.[8]

To take one of Wittgenstein's examples: the relation between our understanding of a word and our specific uses of it can seem puzzling in that, on the one hand, answers to the countless questions about whether or not to apply it to this or that object (or possible object) must somehow derive from our grasp, at a given time, of what we mean by the word; but on the other hand, it's hard to see how anyone's faculty of understanding could have 'leapt ahead' and considered what to say in every such case. And a somewhat tempting response to this problem, emphasized (but criticized) by Wittgenstein, is simply to accept that this bizarre and inexplicable 'leaping ahead' is exactly what happens. In a strange way (on this view) the state of meaning a given thing by a word really does encompass infinitely many decisions about how it will and would be applied.[9]

Consider, as a second example, the above-mentioned puzzle over whether numbers are *objects*. Instead of responding to the conflicting considerations by arguing that since objects must be material, numbers cannot be objects—or by arguing on the other hand that since the referent of any singular term is an object, numbers trivially qualify—the mysterian theorist is inclined to say that numbers are *somehow* objects, but of an

[8] I borrow the term "mysterian" from Owen Flanagan (see his *The Science of the Mind*, Cambridge, MA: MIT Press, 1991, p. 313) and Colin McGinn (see his "Can We Solve the Mind–Body Problem?", *Mind* 98, 1989, 349–66) who apply it to those who believe that *consciousness* is essentially incomprehensible.
[9] See PI 187–97. A reading of these passages is offered at the end of Chapter 4. Did he perhaps have in mind Brentano's "noetic rays"?

ineradicably paradoxical kind, since the paradigm objects are material.[10]

Similarly, the mysterian theorist of 'the passage of time' will *embrace* the conceptual tension between the apparent existence of some such objective phenomenon and the apparent impossibility of making sense of it. He will maintain that there is indeed such a thing whilst granting that it is hopelessly baffling.[11]

(D) Conservative systematizations

These emerge from an acknowledgement that the intuitions that paradoxically conflict with our temptingly simple generalizations are in fact *falsifying* information, and from a commitment to devise accounts that will fully accommodate *all* the data. Such projects include:

- Ongoing attempts to give an accurate conceptual analysis of "S knows that p", in light of counter-examples to the received definition of it as "S's belief *that p* is both true and justified". ('Gettierology')
- Efforts to produce an ethical theory that accommodates our intuitions to the effect that the rightness of an act depends not only on its results but also on which of them are 'means' and which 'ends'. ('Trolleyology')
- Attempts to construct the correct paradox-free theory of truth—one that will optimally incorporate restrictions either of classical logic, or of the principle that every statement articulates its own condition for being true, or of both. ('Cretanology')

---

[10] Arguably, Gödel exemplifies this tendency. He maintains that numbers are abstract objects, so we cannot interact causally with them. But he postulates a mysterious quasi-perceptual mechanism—an extraordinary faculty of intuition—by which we are able to appreciate their presence and properties.

[11] See, for example, the work of Henri Bergson, Storrs McCall, and John Lucas.

As illustrated in these cases, the intuitive data involving a given philosophically interesting concept are typically so messy that the prospect of a simple systematization of them all will be extremely remote. Still, it may be that these data can be divided into disjoint subsets that individually look more amenable to such accounts. So a fairly common theoretical move is to suggest that simplicity will be promoted by supposing that the phenomenon breaks into several forms or kinds (corresponding to the several subsets). For example, philosophers have distinguished within the great variety of facts, those that are 'metaphysically real'; within the many types of object, those that are 'robust'; and within the free choices, those that are 'genuinely' free.[12]

2.4 THE IRRATIONALITY OF SCIENTISM

So far I have merely been trying to *describe* the science-like goals, methods, forms, and products that define T-philosophy. With Wittgenstein, I take this to have been, and still to be, a mainstream approach to our subject. I have not yet ventured any normative judgements about it, one way or the other. But now I want to present and develop Wittgenstein's reasons for regarding it as misconceived.

---

[12] *A priori* reductive analyses—the philosopher's stock in trade—can fall within any of the four categories of theory that have been distinguished in this section. Some (such as logical behaviourism) have a sceptical import, some (such as the identification of numbers with numerals) are revisionary, some (such as certain correspondence definitions of truth) invoke mysterian notions, and some (such as Frege's reduction of arithmetic to logic, and Reichenbach's reduction of temporal order to causal order) are intended to be conservative. It's important to achnowledge also the difference between substantive theories like these, and trivial definitions (such as "brother" means "male sibling"), which do not qualify as *theories* properly so-called, as I characterized them in Section 2.1 and as Wittgenstein uses the term. See Section 2.8 for further discussion of that conception of 'theory'.

What's supposed to be so wrong with a scientistic approach to *a priori* domains? Why isn't it, on the contrary, an excellent idea to take methodological principles that have proved spectacularly successful within the empirical sciences and apply them to philosophy? Why shouldn't we expect these methods to deliver just the sorts of immensely valuable understanding here as they did there?

At this point one might well observe that whatever its initial promise, this strategy has not in fact panned out! Our subject is notorious for its perennial controversies and lack of decisive progress—for its embarrassing failure, after over two thousand years, to settle any of its central questions.

Now it may be said, in response, that these disappointing results might be attributed not to any faults in the defining features of T-philosophy, but to the peculiar depth and difficulty of those questions—or instead, perhaps, to its improper execution, to the laziness and lax standards prevalent amongst philosophers.[13] So we cannot simply infer the incoherence of philosophical scientism from its disappointing upshot to date. That conclusion could be justified only in light of a scrutiny of its essential nature and the exposure of patently defective ingredients.

But such ingredients are not hard to identify One is the illusion that significant theoretical progress can be made by disambiguating what are normally regarded as unified concepts. Another is an irrational distortion that tends to occur when the demand for simplicity is carried over from empirical science to *a priori* philosophy. Another is the absence of legitimate epistemic constraints that are strong enough to deliver theoretical knowledge within T-philosophy. And a fourth is the question-

---

[13] See Timothy Williamson's "Must Do Better"—an Afterword to his *The Philosophy of Philosophy*.

able value of believing philosophical theories that are *true*. Let me say a little more about each of these problematic features.

Relevant to all of them is the fact that our linguo-conceptual practices, and the basic *a priori* commitments associated with them, are extremely *messy*. For the most part these practices evolved not for the sake of helping us to *understand* the world, but to serve a variety of much more humdrum practical purposes and to serve them in a way that conduces to the complex contingencies of our nature, our culture, and our environment. So we should not be surprised to find, as we indeed do find, that it is no easy matter to provide examples of ordinary notions governed by *simple* commitments. It is by now well known that *explicitly definable* meanings/concepts are few and far between. But meanings/concepts whose deployments issue from other forms of simple commitment (such as inferential roles) are also uncommon. Most are too vague, or open-textured, or family-resemblance-like, or paradox-prone for any such neat formula.

It is sometimes supposed (as at the end of Section 2.3) that order can be achieved by appreciating that what might superficially seem to be a unified phenomenon in fact divides into more than one kind (for example, that 'robust' objects are different from other objects, that 'metaphysically real' facts are different from other facts, and so on). But it is hard to see how any genuine gain in overall simplicity can be accomplished by drawing such distinctions. When the 'special' kind is defined by means of explicit criteria, we can easily see that the simplicity of our theory of it is purely stipulative and has been bought at the expense of sweeping all the original messiness over to the other side. Moreover, such explicit criteria are rarely agreed upon. More commonly, the question of exactly how the presumed distinction is to be drawn is taken to be a deep and intractable problem. But what this judgement really reflects is that there is no reason to prefer one criterion to another, because none of them can yield an *overall* gain in simplicity and thereby constitute a genuine discovery.

Thus *individual* concepts tend to be ineradicably messy. But we find further complexity in the considerable differences *amongst* concepts. Even within the category of monadic predicative concepts there are endless variations in the shapes of the principles governing their deployment. Consider: RED, GAME, GOOD, BEAUTIFUL, PRIME, MAGNETIC, TRUE, ... [14]—Simplicity can be expected neither in the descriptions of particular meaning-constituting practices nor in the description of some common form that all such practices might be thought to display.

Moreover, any complexity in our basic usage of a given term (i.e. our accepting "p(t)", "q(t)", "r(t)", etc.) will induce a parallel complexity in the various *facts* to which that usage commits us (i.e. the fact that p(t), the fact that q(t), the fact that r(t), etc.). So if the usage isn't nicely systematizable, the claimed reality won't be either.

Of course, there is no less messiness in the *sensorily perceived* phenomena that provide the data for *scientific* theorization projects—projects which, nonetheless, are often extremely successful. So why think that *philosophy* must be hobbled by its messy data? The answer is that a scientist looks for, and often finds, simplicity at some deeper level (such as the individualistic or microscopic). The superficial facts are then explained as the causal products of simple underlying laws in combination with a messily varied spatio-temporal array of particular circumstances.

---

[14] I am using words in small capital letters as names of the meanings of those words. For example, "RED" names the meaning of (i.e. the concept expressed by) the word "red".

For discussion of the variety of ways in which different meanings/concepts are constituted, see section 4 of Chapter 5.

But no such strategy can be successfully employed in T-philosophy. For its application requires phenomena that (a) are arranged in space and time, (b) stand in causal relations to one another, and (c) are accessed via inference to the best explanation. But *a priori* reality (that is, what can be known *a priori*) does not exhibit these features. Therefore, there is no prospect of accounting for the messy data of T-philosophy via simple theories at some more fundamental level. So it is not surprising that this is never attempted.

Instead, after the discovery of a satisfyingly simple and *almost* adequate regularity, a standard move is to declare victory and go home. The recalcitrant intuitions are blithely deemed incorrect. For example, it's true of just about every potential belief, that it could be rational only if it has argumentative support. And so a philosopher might well become convinced on this basis that there is a general *a priori* law here—that *all* rational beliefs must meet that condition—notwithstanding the implication of such a law (via well-known regress considerations) that there could be no such thing as rational belief. Admittedly, not many philosophers will be prepared to go quite so far. But hardly less dubious is the more common view that although certain of our unsupported convictions are treated in practice as legitimate, the absence of justification makes their real legitimacy puzzling and questionable.

Now this policy—allowing simplicity to override data—cannot be defended as merely a sensible matter of extending the norm of 'respect for simple theories' from the empirical sciences to *a priori* domains. For, as just noted, the scientist does not insist on a non-existent simplicity in the observed facts. He does not conclude that any troublesome data must be illusory. Instead he postulates an underlying unobservable realm in which a simple regularity really does hold.—And, by combining this segularity with an ineliminably messy array of extraneous factors he aims to explain *all* the observed phenomena.

Thus the norm of simplicity characteristic of theoretical philosophy is not merely an extension of what has been well vindicated in science.[15] —It is an unprincipled and irrational distortion of the scientific norm.[16]

A fall-back position—less ambitious but more intellectually responsible—is to acknowledge that *all* the intuitive data must be accommodated, even though no satisfying simple account of them will usually be obtainable; and then to set oneself to devise general principles that are as simple as possible.

But a difficulty now—the third objection to T-philosophy— is that any achievable level of simplicity will be insufficiently constraining. It is an old point from the philosophy of science that our body of data—no matter how substantial it is—can always be accommodated by infinitely many competing general hypotheses. Simplicity must be brought in to help us decide between them. But the lower the degree of simplicity demanded, the greater the number of competing hypotheses that will exemplify it. The upshot, for the present context, is

[15] Granted, science is prepared to discount observational beliefs when there is reason to think that they resulted from unreliable perceptual processes. And granted, certain basic *a priori* convictions might also be discredited in some such way. In either case, this may well be the verdict on judgements that are widely disputed, or that are made in circumstances notorious for interfering with good cognitive functioning—such as when the subject is tired, or drunk, or distracted, and so on. However, the *a priori* intuitions at issue here tend to be fairly uncontroversial (outside philosophy at least); nor are they recognizably unfavourable cognitive conditions.

[16] Another objection to the T-philosopher's distorted norm of simplicity is that, in so far as it does not specify any extent of data dismissal that is too great a price to pay for a simple theory, it provides virtually no limit on what can be maintained. As Wittgenstein says: "We have got onto slippery ice where there is no friction and so in a certain sense the conditions are ideal, but also, just because of that, we are unable to walk. We want to walk: so we need *friction*. Back to the rough ground!" (PI 107). And Kant had made similar remarks about the attractions and dangers of theoretical metaphysics. Its practitioners are compared to "The light dove, cleaving the air in her free flight, and feeling its resistance, [who] might imagine that its flight would be still easier in empty space" (*Critique of Pure Reason*, B8).

that our norms of theory choice will not usually be strong enough to issue in determinate results. So the truth of a philosophical theory will typically be impossible to know.

Look at the character of the "progress" in our attempts to discover the correct accounts of right and wrong, of truth (in the face of the liar paradox), of knowledge... What we tend to find are increasingly elaborate refinements of alternative approaches, with no prospect of rational convergence.

This sets the stage for the fourth questionable feature of scientistic T-philosophy: its presupposition that *true* philosophical theories are *worth* knowing. The grounds for scepticism on this point are that none of the explanations of the objective value of true belief available elsewhere appears to carry over to philosophy.

One such explanation is that true scientific theories tend to foster pragmatic success. Empirical beliefs play a distinctive role in decision-making; for any deliberation involves assumptions about the probable causal consequences of the various actions we might perform. And we should expect the truth of such assumptions (and of the theories from which they are derived) to increase the probability that the decisions they help engender will promote our goals. But T-philosophical theories do not enter into deliberation in that way; so their value cannot be explained pragmatically.

A more promising alternative—no doubt available in science—derives from the value of sheer *understanding*, of knowing the basic explanatory principles. Isn't that also the point of *philosophical* theorizing? Certainly, it is supposed to be. But note the above-mentioned fact that in the *a priori* domain we cannot reasonably deploy the picture of increasingly profound layers of reality—the lower-level facts explaining the higher-level ones. Thus we do not have genuine explanatory depth in philosophy. So it is hard to see what sort of "understanding" its theories could conceivably provide.

Arguably, any dramatically simple systematization will be revelatory and worth discovering 'for its own sake', even if it does not qualify as deeply explanatory. But, as we have seen, the messiness of our conceptual practices suggests that such accounts can be expected only in rare and uninteresting cases (such as bachelor).[17]

A final possible rationale for systematic theorization may be thought to reside in its essential role in obtaining the solutions to paradoxes. It may be thought that it is not enough to respond to a paradox merely by admitting that *some* mistake in *some* tempting assumption must have been made. For, surely, we will not have succeeded in getting to the bottom of the problem unless we have *identified* the mistake, understood why we were inclined to make it, and figured out what we should be saying instead. But how can all that be done without having what we take to be a better systematic account of the phenomenon—a better *theory*—than we had before?

I would like to look with particular care at this way of trying to explain the value of true philosophical theories.

Consider again the liar paradox. Certain simple rules governing, on the one hand, TRUTH, and on the other hand, our *logical* concepts (NOT, IF, EVERY, and so on), have become entrenched in our thinking. And perplexity can result from the fact that in certain cases—such as consideration of "This statement is not true"—these rules are seen to conflict with each other. Anyone whose response is to feel, nonetheless, that none of them could conceivably be incorrect, will experience the tension characteristic of paradox.—"This *must* be right, but *cannot* be right." But someone might, in contrast, appreciate (i) that what strikes us as "overwhelmingly natural" does so in virtue of our human psychology and needs,

---

[17] Truth in *mathematics* is worth pursuing for the sake of the role of mathematical discoveries in the empirical sciences—and also for its own sake, but only when what is proved is 'interesting', that is, satisfyingly simple.

and (ii) that distinct conceptual practices, which evolved for entirely different purposes, can well serve those purposes yet clash in certain unanticipated and unimportant contexts. This person's initial attachment to the conflicting natural rules will be reduced accordingly, so he is not ensnared by the paradox. He isn't stymied and bewildered—even if he has not yet settled the further theoretical question as to which particular adjustment to the old combination of rules will be simplest and best.

Of course, with some paradoxes it may become evident, on reflection, what went wrong and what needs to be corrected. There was a mistake that could and should have been recognized as such, independently of the paradox it helped to engender. But in other cases (like the liar paradox) the only symptom of something having gone wrong is the dawning of the contradiction; none of the ingredients, taken individually, could have been antecedently identified as mistaken. Here the issues of what should be done are issues of what on balance to believe—issues hinging on considerations of consistency and simplicity, akin to problems in science. They are problems within T-philosophy, and Wittgenstein has no time for them:

> Philosophy may in no way interfere with the actual use of language; it can in the end only describe it.
>
> For it cannot give it any foundation either.
>
> It leaves everything as it is.
>
> It also leaves mathematics as it is, and no mathematical discovery can advance it. A "leading problem of mathematical logic" is for us a problem of mathematics like any other. (PI 124)
>
> It is the business of philosophy, not to resolve a contradiction by means of a mathematical or logico-mathematical discovery, but to make it possible for us to get a clear view of the state of mathematics that troubles us: the state of affairs *before* the contradiction is resolved. (And this does not mean that one is sidestepping a difficulty.)

> The fundamental fact here is that we lay down rules, a technique, for a game, and that then when we follow the rules, things do not turn out as we had assumed. That we are therefore as it were entangled in our own rules.
>
> This entanglement in our rules is what we want to understand (i.e. get a clear view of). (PI 125)

Thus a Wittgensteinian treatment of a philosophical paradox need not include everything that one may be inclined to demand of a "full resolution". For him, what is crucial is to dissolve the sense of bafflement; and that is achieved once we have understood and eliminated its sources—once (a) we have seen exactly how it is that if we combine certain assumptions and inferential proclivities (that are not normally combined) we are taken somewhere surprising, somewhere we do not want to go, and (b) we have fully accepted and absorbed the implication that this combination of commitments must be adjusted. The next step—compulsory, one might have thought—would be to try to restore consistency in the optimal way, to work out which of them ought to be rejected. What specific modification will enable us to retain as much as we can whilst making it no longer possible to derive a contradiction? But for Wittgenstein this project is not compulsory, and attempts to execute it are extraneous to the form of critical philosophy that he recommends.

If the cases or contexts in which certain of our assumptions turn out to engender paradox are merely hypothetical or very rare, or if the 'right' modification of them would have no practical significance, then, from a purely *pragmatic* point of view, we can remain contented with those assumptions. As for the *theoretical* point of view—that of a pure concern for 'explanatory understanding'—Wittgenstein would say (as I have been emphasizing) that this perspective is one we must beware against. For there is no particular reason to expect a simple resolution, hence no rational prospect of their being such a thing as "the best way out".

In the case of the truth paradoxes, what we encounter in the literature is an expanding profusion of proposals, proofs, and formal pyrotechnics. But has anything really worth discovering been discovered? Have the paradoxes actually been solved? Have they almost been solved? Are we at least considerably closer to their solution? There is no basis for a positive answer to any of these questions. On the contrary, it is not unreasonable to suppose that the explosion of alternative approaches—each one elaborated in increasingly sophisticated detail—provides evidence for the sceptical view, mentioned above, that the available norms of theory choice are too weak to ever yield something we might regard as "the solution". Granted, competing theoretical approaches must to some extent be 'worked out', before one can expect convergence on the best one. But in this instance all we ever see is 'working out'. Eventual rational convergence is an item of faith.[18]

---

[18] Stephen Schiffer argues (in *The Things We Mean*, Oxford: Oxford University Press, 2003, pp. 68, 69, 198) that classical philosophical paradoxes result from defective meanings (concepts)—meanings whose constituting tendencies of deployment clash with one another. And he claims that one can thereby explain why no classical a paradox has ever been truly solved—that is, why intelligent and dedicated philosophers have never been able to settle on which of the conflicting doxastic procliuities is wrong. (It is because every one of them is dictated by the problem's ingredient concepts.) This, he thinks, is why progress in philosophy is so slow and slight in comparison with the sciences. But we might question, both the explanatory value and the plausibility of Schiffer's idea. For notice: (a) that the mistakes that provoke certain paradoxes need *not* be especially hard to identify. (In each of the *sceptical* paradoxes, for example, there's always a premise that generalizes irrationally from our actual practice—see section 2.5); (b) that, in many cases, proposed solutions do *not* call for conceptual revision; (c) that, anyway, conceptual change is commonplace, and so a pattern of word-use would *not*, on account of being meaning-constituting, be particularly resistant to revision; and (d) that if Schiffer's motivating assumption were granted (namely, that the inability of highly intelligent philosophers to reach consensus on the solutions to the classical paradoxes shows that there *aren't* any solutions to them), then we might equally well infer from the fact that his own theory is still not generally recognized as correct, that it is *not* correct! (For more detail, see "The Nature of Paradox", Chapter 11 of my *Truth–Meaning–Reality*.)

Let me stress that this is not to deny that some philosophical theories are true and the others are false. Nor need it be denied that some at least *tiny* value attaches to *any* true belief. But, even so, most truths are not sufficiently important to be worth bothering with. And it remains to be seen why the true philosophical theories should not be consigned to that category.

A final point worth noting is that just as some people enjoy tiddlywinks, others golf, and others bungee jumping—and why not?—so some will be simply fascinated by this or that branch of philosophical theory. And it is surely a good thing, other things being equal, that all these desires be satisfied. But the objection to such theorizing that I have been exploring—its fourth defect—is that in contrast to science there appears to be no objective reason to desire *true* theoretical belief in *a priori* philosophy. For what is discoverable will contribute neither to successful deliberation nor to significant understanding. As long as there is no illusion on this point—as long as someone derives pleasure merely from an exploration of alternative arcane positions in logical space—let him by all means carry on.[19]

2.5 KINDS OF THEORY AND THEIR PECULIAR DISCONTENTS

These general criticisms of traditional philosophy—of *a priori* theorization projects—take different particular forms depending on the particular type of theory (of those outlined in Section 2.3) that is attempted.

---

[19] Some of the material in this section was drawn from my "Williamson's Philosophy of Philosophy". However, my thinking about the confusions of scientistic philosophy benefited greatly from Williamson's published response to this paper and from our subsequent correspondence. The paper appears, together with his "Reply to Paul Horwich", in *Philosophy and Phenomenological Research* 82, 2011.

Against reformist accounts

The central objection to such proposals—including error theories, epistemological scepticisms, and less radical revisionist theses—is that they fly in face of our data.

For example, the theory, "Knowledge of *any* fact requires that one's belief be causally related to that fact", does not square with the datum, "We know that there are prime numbers". Granted, the recalcitrant data here are *intuitive*, rather than *empirical*; it immediately *seems* to us correct to think certain things. But notice that the data that might be marshalled in favour of the theory are of exactly that kind. It *seems* to us that if someone's *belief* in the conspiracy against him is not somehow brought about by the *existence* of that conspiracy (or by its causes), then he cannot be said to *know* about it. And if such data are weighty enough to lend initial *support* to a generalization, then they are surely weighty enough to *refute* it! It would have been perverse to continue to insist that all swans are white, after a bunch of black ones had been observed. And it is no less perverse to insist on the above generalization about knowledge once confronted with the conflicting intuitions.

Or consider David Lewis's radical suggestion that merely possible events (such as Gore's having won the 2000 US Presidential election) are no less *real* than actual events (such as Bush's having won). He is drawn to that conclusion by a striking analogy between possible worlds and times. Just as some things are true at certain times and not at others, so some are true in certain possible worlds and not in others. But an event qualifies as *real*, even if it is not happening right now, as long as it happens at some time or other. So should not we suppose, similarly, that an event is real, even though it does not occur in the actual world, as long as it occurs in some possible world? No, we should not! For as elegant as that proposal may be, it is obviously false. Our fundamental practice with the concept REALITY is to restrict its application to what *actually* has been the case, is the case, or will be the case. Thus the genuine analogy between times and possible worlds, like all analogies, is limited—and Lewis has overstretched it. He is allowing simplicity to trump data—but with no attempt to explain how those data could be mistaken.

Of course, the advocates of such a theory see matters the other way around: they think its beautiful simplicity makes it so highly plausible that the conflicting initial indications should be recognized as false. But there is no established epistemic norm to sanction that position. In the empirical sciences (as we have seen) experience is king; simple laws at that level are not expected; but their operation at a more profound level can be made plausible in so far as they cohere with *all* the data. Yes, there is the possibility of discrediting observation reports by showing that the abnormal contexts in which they occurred interfered with the reliability of our perceptual/cognitive mechanisms. But the intuitive judgements at issue here are entirely normal with respect to both their contents and the conditions in which they are made. Thus, lying behind reformist theories in philosophy is an invalid distortion of scientific methodology.[20]

---

[20] As Daniel Hutto (in his *Wittgenstein and the End of Philosophy: Neither Theory nor Therapy*, Basingstoke: Palgrave, 2003 second edition, 2006, p. 213) puts Wittgenstein's view:

> Once we forgo the dream of a unified science and come to realize that our more homely needs are what should drive conceptual development wherever it occurs, it becomes clear that in many cases, *contra* the expectations of revisionists, there is no genuine need to develop or revise our existing concepts.

And he backs up this interpretation with the following passages from Wittgenstein's *Last Writings on the Philosophy of Psychology*:

> Why don't we form a simpler concept?—Because it wouldn't interest us.—But what does that mean? Is it the correct answer?
> Should I say: Our concepts are determined by our interest, and therefore by our way of living?
> Sometimes it happens that we later introduce a new concept that is more practical for us.—But that will only be in very definite and

Against mystery-mongering

Let us now turn to what I have been calling "mysterian theories". Rather than coming down on one side or the other of a paradox, such theories take it to reveal the ineradicable strangeness of the phenomenon at issue. But the uncomfortable truth is that paradoxes are blameworthy confusions in *us*, not bizarre features of the world; and so, instead of marvelling at them and catering to them, we ought to be trying to understand where we have gone astray.

Here is how Wittgenstein expresses this point in response to the mysterian view of how the meaning of an expression ("Add 2") determines its use (the series of answers, "2", "4", "6", ...):

> ...your idea was that that act of meaning the order had in its own way already traversed all those steps: that when you meant it your mind as it were flew ahead and took all the steps before you physically arrived at this or that one.
>
> Thus you were inclined to use such expressions as "The steps are *really* already taken, even before I take them in writing or orally or in thought." And it seemed as if this were in some *unique* way predetermined, anticipated—as only the act of meaning can anticipate reality. (PI 188)
>
> ..."in a *queer* way the use itself is in some sense present."—But of course it is, 'in *some* sense'! Really the only thing wrong with what you say is the expression "in a queer way". The rest is all right; and the sentence only seems queer when one imagines a different language-

small areas, and it presupposes that most concepts remain unaltered. Could a legislator abolish the concept of pain? The basic concepts are interwoven so closely with what is most fundamental in our way of living that they are therefore unassailable. (*Last Writings on the Philosophy of Psychology*, Volume 2, §§43–4e).

> game for it from the one in which we actually use it. (PI
> 195)[21]

Similarly, the mysterian view of numbers—that they are
indeed objects but of an incomprehensible kind (see pp. 31–2)
—involves the same sort of confused assimilation of distinct
linguo-conceptual practices—in this case, the one for material
things and the one for numbers. And this leads to the idea that
there would be something magical about an object with no
spatio-temporal properties or substantial composition. Thus
the mysterian and the sceptic are deeply similar. They agree that
numbers are essentially paradoxical. One goes on to infer that
such things could not possibly exist, whereas the other views
their extreme weirdness with equanimity, as not at all disquali-
fying. But they begin with the same mistake.

Our final example came from the literature on 'the passage
of time'. It is sometimes maintained that "in a queer sense"
pastness advances. On the one hand, we are supposed to imagine a material feature of the universe that inexorably spreads
through reality, like an infectious disease, or a conquering
empire extending its reach. But, on the other hand, it is
acknowledged that these images are not literally correct, that
no such quasi-material feature could exist. And things are left
at that. The 'motion of the Now' just *is* bizarre![22] However, as
Wittgenstein suggests, this sort of reification of our confusion
is always a step in the wrong direction:

> In our failure to understand our use of a word we take it
> as the expression of a queer *process*. (As we think of time
> as a queer medium, of the mind as a queer kind of being.)
> (PI 196)

---

[21] For a closer reading of these passages, see Chapter 4, Section 4.3.
[22] Further discussion of what lies behind the "mystery of temporal passage"
can be found in Chapter 6, Section 6.1.

Against systematization

It remains to examine what is the matter with the final theoretical strategy that was distinguished in Section 2.3: namely, *conservative systematization projects*, whose response to paradox is to acknowledge that something must be rectified in the oversimple philosophical theory (or combination of theories) that engenders it.

This is perhaps the least bad form of philosophical theorization. It does not blithely discount intuitive data with the help of a distorted norm of simplicity. Nor can it be convicted of shameless exoticism and flirting with contradictions. The data are respected; simple accounts of them are sought but not demanded; such accounts are gratefully accepted when they happen to work out; and they are modified (to the detriment of their simplicity) whenever necessary.

This is all admirably responsible. But why bother? In Section 2.4 I argued at length that we should not—that nothing of any objective value can be expected to result—and there is no point in spelling out those considerations again. But let me repeat the main conclusions.

The trouble with such systematization projects is that in all but a few cases the complexity of our data makes it unreasonable to expect interesting results. More specifically:

• The apparently messy data concerning a given concept cannot be cleaned up by postulating *ambiguity*—that is, by supposing there to be more than one concept at issue.
• It will rarely be possible to capture *all* the data in a simple systematization. But the tendency to dismiss intuitive convictions solely on the grounds that they stand in the way of such a theory is obviously illegitimate.
• Moreover, there are no explanatory layers in *a priori* reality; so there is no prospect (as there is in science) of a revelatory *underlying* simplicity either.

- If a *complex* systematization is all that can be achieved then there are bound to be equally good alternatives; in which case we won't have legitimate epistemic norms that will enable us decide between them. So knowledge will be impossible.
- Anyway, possession of the *truth* in those cases will have no instrumental or intellectual value; so there is no objective reason to pursue it.[23]

2.6 THE GENERAL FORM OF A PHILOSOPHICAL ISSUE

Implicit in the Wittgensteinian position that I've been presenting is the idea that philosophical problem areas tend to share a certain abstract structure. Let me now make that structure explicit. I'll begin by illustrating it with the case of *numbers* (already discussed in Chapter 1), and then move on to some further examples.

Case I: NUMBER

In the genesis and resolution of the philosophical problems regarding entities of type X, (e.g. the numbers) one can discern eight elements or stages:

(1) *Scientistic expectations.* The assumption that simple, deep, radical, *a priori* principles could very well await our discovery.

  e.g. A theory of what numbers are, and of how their existence and characteristics can be known

---

[23] Although Wittgenstein believed that his greatest contribution was his critique of traditional theoretical philosophy, he was nonetheless far from dismissive of it, or of its practitioners. As he reportedly said to his friend, Drury: "Don't think that I despise metaphysics. I regard some of the great philosophical systems of the past as among the noblest productions of the human mind...Count yourself lucky to have so much time to study such a great man as Leibniz." From M. O'C. Drury, "Conversations with Wittgenstein", in R. Rhees (ed.), *Recollections of Wittgenstein*, Oxford: Oxford University Press, 1984 (see p. 105).

(2) *Linguistic analogies.* The terms for Xs exhibit forms of use that bear a striking resemblance to the uses of a certain more prominent class of words.

> e.g. *The numerals, "1", "2",..., are singular terms, functioning like the names of people, planets, and so on.*

(3) *Generalization.* As a consequence, we philosophers may become inclined to suppose that Xs are entities of the same kind as the referents of those analogous words.

> e.g. *So numbers are just like material objects.*

(4) *Linguistic idiosyncrasy.* However "X"-terms also exhibit certain linguistic peculiarities. In various respects their use is quite different from that of the otherwise analogous words. These differences incline us to deny that Xs have certain of the features characteristic of the referents of those more prominent words.

> e.g. *Unlike the situation with most ordinary names, there are no circumstances in which it is appropriate to accept sentences of the form, "The number n is made of material M", or "n occupies place p", or "n's existence causes e". So numbers—unlike ordinary objects—are taken to have no substance, no location, and no causal powers.*

(5) *Paradoxical tension.* There is a clash between the things that the various disanalogies and analogies dispose us to prioritize: on the one hand, the special features of Xs, but on the other hand, their strong resemblance to the referents of the analogous terms.[24]

> e.g. *It is hard to see how numbers could be genuine objects and yet have no material constitution, not exist in space or time, and not be capable of causal interaction. It is also hard to see, since they cannot be causally responsible for our arithmetical beliefs, how any such beliefs can qualify as knowledge.*

---

[24] Wittgenstein is prone to assert that philosophical puzzlement results from "misunderstandings of language"—and, more specifically, that these often take the form of our exaggerating analogies in use between words in different regions

(6) *Philosophical bewilderment.* These paradoxical tensions can easily induce a peculiar form of puzzlement, an amazement at how there could possibly be such things as Xs, a sense that the phenomena in question are deeply mysterious, almost magical.

> *e.g. How bizarre numbers are! How could such paradoxical things exist? What would they have to be like?*

(7) *Philosophical theorization.* Typical alternative responses to this sort of puzzlement are:

- *Sceptical: denying the very existence or knowability of Xs— but typically recommending, in view of the pragmatic advantages of our discourse about them, that this discourse be retained.*

  > *e.g. Fieldian fictionalism: whereby numbers simply do not exist (as far as we know), although it is useful to pretend they do.*

- *Revisionist:* advocating some less extreme alteration in our ordinary view of Xs.

  > *e.g. Dummettian intuitionism: whereby arithmetical reality is constructed by us—therefore not all the classical rules of proof (such as reductio ad absurdum) can be relied on.*

of language. (For example, we may regard numerals as more like names of planets than they really are.) However, one might well wonder what reason there is to think that it is fundamentally *language* that we are confused about. Why not suppose, rather, that there are certain analogies between, for example, numbers and planets—the phenomena themselves!—and that *these* are what we irrationally overstretch? The answer is that those apparent alternatives are not substantially different. In accepting a sentence we are believing its propositional content—we are committing ourselves to something about the world. Therefore, an overreaction to analogies between the "3"-sentences we accept and the "Mars"-sentences we accept is the same thing as an overreaction to analogies between what we take to be true of 3 and what we take to be true of Mars. Wittgenstein's essential point is that philosophical problems derive from a certain form of irrational reasoning—which can be described as moving from beliefs to beliefs or, equivalently, from accepted sentences to accepted sentences. For further discussion, see Section 2.9. See also my "Naturalism, Deflationism, and the Relative Priority of Language and Metaphysics", in H. Price (ed.), *Expressivism, Pragmatism and Representationalism*, Cambridge: Cambridge University Press, 2013.

- *Mysterian:* embracing the essentially puzzling nature of Xs.

  e.g. Godelian platonism, whereby the bizarreness of numbers is accepted: the strange combination of their being, on the one hand, immaterial, non-spatio-temporal, and non-causal, but on the other hand, no less robustly object-like as are physical things, and capable of exhibiting a peculiar non-sensory influence on our beliefs.

- *Conservatively systematic:* continued searching for principles concerning Xs that will accommodate, explain, and streamline our a priori beliefs about them.

  e.g. Peanian axiomatization, whereby all our arithmetical beliefs are claimed to be deducible from a handful of basic arithmetical postulates.

(8) *Therapeutic dissolution.* We must come to appreciate that any such theoretical response is wrong-headed. The strategy of (self-)persuasion should combine a general critique of scientism (along the lines of Section 2.4) with objections (along the lines sketched in Section 2.5) to the various specific forms of theory to which scientism can give rise.[25]

  e.g. The ground for scepticism about numbers (whether or not this scepticism is tempered by fictionalism) is the conviction that in order to exist, or to be known, they would have to have (but in fact fail to have) the metaphysical and epistemological nature of material things. For otherwise they would be "too weird"! But this conviction stems from an irrational exaggeration of the analogies in use between numerals and other names. We can perfectly well acknowledge that numbers are objects (in the ordinary sense) without expecting them to have all the characteristics of material things and without being puzzled that

---

[25] Daniel Hutto (in his *Wittgenstein and the End of Philosophy: Neither Theory nor Therapy*, pp. 216–20) suggests that Wittgenstein's ultimate aim is not confined to the therapeutic rooting out of confusion and dissolution of puzzle-

*they do not. Intuitionistic revisionism is in broad sympa-
thy (for the same bad reasons) with this sceptical concern,
but hopes to avoid scepticism by supposing that arithmetic
claims express mental constructions rather than facts about
numbers (as intuitively conceived). However this analysis
proves to be contrived and implausible. Gödel's mysteri-
anism is also based on the same basic mistake—the impression that numbers conceived of as 'objects unlike material
things' would be extraordinarily bizarre. But instead of
concluding that they cannot exist, it allows that the world
can perfectly well contain entities that are truly paradoxical. And as for systematization, the general worry (that we
have no right to expect the phenomena to be amenable to
such theorization) is vindicated in the case of Peano's axiomatization by Gödel's incompleteness theorem.*[26]

ment, but that he engages in these activities merely as a means to his main goal: namely, *clarification*—an improved understanding of important concepts, such as meaning, sensation, and justice (facilitating their proper deployment).

Now a resistance to tempting misconceptions and misapplications can in itself qualify as a form of clarity and good understanding. As Wittgenstein says: "...the clarity we are aiming at is indeed complete clarity. But this simply means that the philosophical problems should completely disappear" (PI 133). But Hutto evidently thinks that Wittgenstein has something more in mind. For this kind of 'implicit' clarity would not take us beyond the sort of therapeutic result which he regards as a mere means to Wittgenstein's real objective. However, it is hard to see what the further kind of 'conceptual clarity' could be. Is it, perhaps, possession of an *explicit* account of how the concept is, and is not, to be deployed? But one might well wonder whether such a thing would have any significant value. What could be the point of an assortment of explicit warnings about mistakes to avoid, given that, post therapy, those mistakes are anyway avoided? And if 'full clarification' of a concept requires a complete and simple account of its deployment, the goal would be a systematic theory—quite *un*-Wittgensteinian, as we have seen.

[26] My apologies to those who will be justifiably irritated by the brevity and assertiveness of these remarks. They are intended as a mere indication of the lines along which a Wittgensteinian therapeutic treatment of perplexities about NUMBER could go. Please keep in mind that the aim was is to help clarify his general method, rather than to engage in serious philosophy of mathematics.

In order to give more substance to this eight-stage schema, let me sketch its application to some other problematic concepts: first, *time*, which Wittgenstein treats briefly in the *Blue Book*;[27] and then *truth* and *goodness*, which are barely mentioned in his later work. The point of these exercises is to further explain the proposal and add to its plausibility, both as a piece of Wittgenstein interpretation and as a fruitful metaphilosophical perspective. But even better tests will come in subsequent chapters when we use this framework to deal with two of the topics that he addresses in detail in the *Philosophical Investigations*: namely, *meaning* and *experience*.

Case II: Time

(1) *Scientism*. Our concepts are not as fundamentally different from one another as they might appear to be; so we should strive for theoretical unification.

(2) *Analogy*. There is a similarity between the use of duration predicates (such as "five minutes apart") and distance predicates (such as "five metres apart").

(3) *Generalization*. We are inclined, as a consequence, to think of a temporal interval as like a line in space.

(4) *Idiosyncrasy*. We deploy past, present, and future tenses of verbs: depending on whether something occurs before, during, or after the time of utterance, we say "It existed", "It exists", or "It will exist". We suppose, therefore, that at any moment of time no more than that moment actually exists.

(5) *Paradox*. Putting these ideas together, we imagine the measurement of a time interval as analogous to

> ... the process of measuring a *length*—say, the distance between two marks on a travelling band which passes us,

---

[27] See the *Blue Book*, pp. 26–7, and PI 89–90.

and of which we can only see a tiny bit (the present) in front of us. (*Blue Book*, p. 26)

This picture combines the idea that a time interval is just like a line segment, with the idea that we can be aware, at any time, of only one point of the interval. But in that case, as

> Saint Augustine…argued: How is it possible that one should measure time? For the past cannot be measured, as it is gone by; and the future cannot be measured because it has not yet come. And the present cannot be measured for it has no extension. (*Blue Book*, p. 26)

(6) *Bewilderment*: So time is deeply weird:

> Augustine says in the *Confessions* "quid est ergo tempus? si nemo ex me querat scio; si querenti explicare velim, nescio." (PI 89)

That is, when asked what it is we are at a loss—although, given our unhesitating everyday use of temporal concepts, we seem to know perfectly well.

(7) *Theories*: In reaction to this perplexity there has been a tendency to reach one of the following kinds of conclusion:
   • *Sceptical*: Time does not exist (McTaggart)
   • *Revisionary*: Tensed facts are analysable in terms of untensed facts. (Russell)
   • *Mysterian*: Time, in a bizarre way, *passes*, 'present-ness' *moves* inexorably into the future. (Bergson, Lucas, McCall)
   • *Conservatively systematic*: Tense logic. (Prior)

(8) *Therapy*: The correct response to the puzzle, however, is to recognize that it arises needlessly from a tendency to over-draw the analogy between our terms for duration and length. To combat this tendency we should

> (c)ompare what we mean by "measurement" (the grammar of the word "measurement") when applied to a distance on a travelling band with the grammar of the word applied to time. (*Blue Book*, p. 26)

> We will see, contrary to Augustine's rhetorical suggestion, that our practice in the ascription of predicates like "five minutes apart" does not require that all the parts of that to which it applies be simultaneously present. Rather, just as lengths are typically measured by comparison with certain *standard* lengths (such as marks on a ruler), so intervals of time are measured by reference to standard durations (such as pendulum swings).

Of course, it would be absurd to suggest that this snappy treatment disposes of the many perplexities surrounding time—or even of the single one crystallized in Augustine's remarks. My aim again is simply to instantiate, with a second case, the abstract stages into which I think Wittgenstein divides the rise and fall of philosophical problems. The same goes for the following examples of *truth* and *goodness*, which I shall set out just as cryptically.

Case III: Truth

(1) *Scientistism.* The nature of truth may be captured in simple *a priori* principles.

(2) *Analogy.* "Is true" has the syntactic and logical character of predicates such as "is red" or "is magnetic". For example, we suppose that "true"—just like those other predicates—may be used to articulate instances of Leibniz' Law. For example: from "What he said is true" and "He said that there is life on Mars" we may conclude "That there is life on Mars is true".

(3) *Generalization.* Exaggerating this analogy:—since these other predicates stand for substantive properties; (i.e., properties with characterizable underlying natures) we tend to assume that "true" too is used to attribute a *substantive* property. So we can reasonably ask how truth is constituted at an underlying level.

(4) *Idiosyncrasy.* In contrast with other predicates we do not apply "true" on the basis of its manifesting certain telltale symptoms—marks of truth that would be more or less the same whichever proposition were in question. Rather, we are prepared to assert the *truth* of precisely those things that we are prepared to assert. Putting it schematically, we suppose that truth is a property that the proposition <p> possesses just in case p.

(5) *Paradox.* We concluded initially that all true propositions owe their possession of the property of truth to the same *underlying* characteristic. But we find ourselves quite unable to discover what that characteristic is. We are unable to answer the question, "What is truth?" We cannot find a single truth-constituting property, f-ness, that the proposition <dogs bark> will possess if and only if dogs bark, that the proposition <altruism is good> will possesses if and only if altruism is good, and so on. All attempts at an analysis of our concept of truth prove to be either circular or refuted by obvious counter-examples.

(6) *Bewilderment.* Truth is an enigma—too profound for theoretical elucidation.

(7) *Theories.* The forms of alternative response to this perplexity have been:

- *Sceptical*: Absolute truth does not exist. (Foucault, Ahrendt, Derrida, MacFarlane)
- *Revisionary*: Various sorts of statement, normally taken to be true, cannot really have a truth value—for example, ethical pronouncements, definitions, and sentences of arithmetic. (early Wittgenstein, Ayer)
- *Mysterian*: Truth is a *correspondence* (in some queer sense) with *facts* (in some queer sense). (early Wittgenstein)
- *Conservatively systematic*: For example, that the basic theory of truth (enabling us to systematize all the facts about it) consists in compositional principles explaining

the truth of sentences in terms of the referents of their parts, plus grounding constraints. (Tarski, Kripke)

(8) *Therapy*. The so-called 'deflationary' perspective calls attention to the special utility of the truth predicate as a mundane logical device enabling the articulation of certain otherwise inexpressible generalizations, such as "All instances of <p or not-p> are true". This function meshes perfectly with our acceptance of the above-mentioned triviality: that each proposition specifies the circumstances in which it is true. No theory of the form, "x is true if and only if x has the underlying property f-ness," is called for, and none should be expected.

Case IV: Good

(1) *Scientism*. A presupposition of there being some simple *a priori* account of the nature of normative properties.

(2) *Analogy*. "Good" is a predicate, operating in inference in the same way as "destructive", "impetuous", "pleasurable" etc., which stand for properties.

(3) *Generalization*. The belief that one's prospective action would possess a property like 'destructiveness' could never, by itself, suffice to provide *motivation* for performing or avoiding it; one would in addition need to *desire* that one's action will (or won't) have the property. Therefore (by analogy), "good" too stands for a property whose recognition cannot be *intrinsically* motivating.

(4) *Idiosyncrasy*. But a person's conviction that his doing a given thing would be good does in fact suffice, all by itself, to somewhat incline him to do it.

(5) *Paradox*. (3) and (4) are glaringly inconsistent.

(6) *Bewilderment*. Goodness (and other normative attributes) are extremely odd! Can we really countenance the existence of such properties?

(7) *Theories*. These include examples of the

- *Sceptical*: Nothing is good (or bad). (Mackie)
- *Revisionary*: Granted, various things, such as generosity, are good. But such pronouncements do not express genuine beliefs and can be neither true nor false. (Ayer)
- *Mysterian*: Goodness is an extraordinary property, whose presence can, in some inexplicable way, be intuited, and whose detection is, in some inexplicable way intrinsically motivating. (Moore)
- *Conservatively systematic*: All our ethical convictions are deducible from the basic moral principle that it is good for there to be as much happiness in the world as possible. (Mill)

(8) *Therapy*. It must be appreciated that although "good" (and other normative terms) function *logically* like other predicates (in obeying the predicate calculus)—so that we can properly speak of the *property* of being good, and of *statements* and *beliefs* about which things possess that property—in other respects their use is unique. The special linguistic function of affirming "X is good" is to express, and to induce in others, an inclination to perform and encourage certain actions that are dictated by X. This makes it intelligible how certain beliefs about what is good are motivating, and it demystifies how we are able to arrive at them.

It bears repeating emphatically that these quick case studies are not offered as anything like complete solutions (neither Wittgenstein's nor my own) to the problems of number, time, truth, and goodness—though I do believe that they may well be along the right lines. They are offered as illustrations of what I take to be his conception of how the most characteristic problems in philosophy emerge, and of how they should, and should not, be handled.

The immediate grounds for attributing these opinions to him lie in his explicit metaphilosophical remarks. (See especially, paragraphs 89–133 of *Philosophical Investigations*.) But substantial further justification for the above analysis—evidence both for its being Wittgenstein's view and for its rough correctness—will come in subsequent chapters when we examine his relatively detailed treatments of *understanding* (Case V) and *experience* (Case VI).

In the meanwhile I would like to address a variety of important sceptical questions concerning Wittgenstein's metaphilosophy and the possibility of finding arguments in favour of it.[28]

2.7 EXCEPTIONS

Wittgenstein thinks that each distinctively philosophical problematic exemplifies something like the structure articulated above. However, it is not his view, nor is it plausible, that every one of them fit precisely into that mold. We do indeed in every case find irrational overgeneralization, conceptual tension, a special kind of bewilderment, various misguided forms of philosophical theorizing, and the need for therapeutic dissolution. However, not all such problems are rooted, as above, in the overstretching of analogies between, on the one hand, the terms and concepts of philosophical interest, and on the other hand, the terms within some more prominent domain of conceptual/linguistic activity. In addition, we must recognize a somewhat different source of irrational overgeneralization.

---

[28] Simon Blackburn argues (in *Truth: A Guide*, Oxford: Oxford University Press, 2005, pp. 129–36) that it is a "bizarre misreading" of the later Wittgenstein to construe him as opposed to deep philosophical theorizing. On the contrary he sees Wittgenstein as the inspiration for his own theoretical programmes in which certain assertoric practices (notably, ethics) are recognized as having an entirely *non*-descriptive function, as capable of no more than *quasi*-truth, and as calling for an ingenious and painstaking explanation of how, given the *non*-cognitive states that are really expressed by its sentences, the discourse nonetheless displays the superficial form of a genuinely descriptive domain. [*footnote continues*]

Consider, for example, the concept of JUSTIFICATION. As mentioned earlier, we might come to think that a belief—any belief—may qualify as justified only if it is based on a good argument. Certainly, many beliefs are like that. But the notorious Agrippan regress considerations show that if the *universal* requirement were correct, then *nothing* could be justified! For any such 'good argument' would have to be based on premisses that are themselves justified—requiring further arguments with justified premisses...and so on, *ad infinitum*. Thus we have a paradox; we encounter the usual array of unsatisfactory 'theoretical' responses to it; and we have Wittgenstein's characteristic alternative way out—that is, recognition of our initial hypothesis as the irrational exaggeration that it is.[29]

To support his "anti-quietist" view of Wittgenstein's metaphilosophy Blackburn offers two kinds of textual evidence. First, he cites remarks about ethical precepts, mathematical theories, basic empirical assumptions, and declarations of intention, in which Wittgenstein complains about the ordinary practice of categorizing them as true or false. And second he notes Wittgenstein's emphasis on the importance of not being mislead by the superficial similarities between different domains of discourse and of the need to recognize their distinctive functions and distinctive ways of executing them. However, I would say that neither of these forms of evidence is compelling. Regarding the first, Blackburn himself acknowledges that "Wittgenstein certainly held a minimalist or deflationist theory of truth"—a view implying that *every* declarative sentence expresses a truth-apt proposition. And so Wittgenstein's cited remarks to the contrary must be seen as mistakes, backslidings into his earlier *Tractatus perspective,* and inconsistent with his new fundamental commitments. And regarding the second alleged evidence, all it reveals is Wittgenstein's conviction that philosophical puzzlement results from our tendency to overstretch analogies between different domains of discourse, and of the need to dissolve that puzzlement by reminding ourselves of the crucial differences between them. It reveals no interest in Blackburn-style 'expressivistic' theoretical projects. Unsurprisingly, Wittgenstein neither engages in them nor recommends them.

[29] For illuminating discussions of Wittgenstein's treatment (in his *On Certainty*) of epistemological issues, see Danièle Moyal-Sharrock's *Understanding Wittgenstein's On Certainty,* Basingstoke, Palgrave Macmillan, 2004; William Child's *Wittgenstein,* London: Routledge, 2011, pp. 191–213; Michael Williams' "Wittgenstein's London, Refutation of Idealism", Denis McManus (ed.), *Wittgenstein and Scepticism,* London Routledge, 2003, and his "Wittgenstein on Truth and Certainty", in B. Weiss and M. Kölbel (eds.), *Wittgenstein's Lasting Significance,* London: Routledge, 2004.

In general, if a word's deployment in a broad and prominent range of contexts exhibits a neat pattern, one naturally expects that pattern to extend to *every* context. But this conclusion may turn out to clash with what we actually are inclined to say—engendering an epistemic tension. We might respond to such a tension in a variety of ways (as illustrated above)—perhaps by embracing the weird features of the concept expressed, by renouncing it altogether, by concluding that the recalcitrant applications must be given up, or by feeling that our quandary can be settled only in light of some soothing conceptual analysis or axiomatic systematization. But, as we have seen, none of these responses will be reasonable or appropriate, according to Wittgenstein. For our basic error, and what needs to be rectified, was the assumption—itself an overgeneralization from the singular traits of *scientific* theorizing—that the fundamental facts concerning any property are very likely to be simple...*so* likely, that *prima facie* indications to the contrary might reasonably be discounted as erroneous.

In cases of this sort the "linguistic analogy" is not between the use of certain special-purpose terms (such as "true") and the use of a more prominent class of terms (such as empirical predicates). It is, rather, between a term's use in some relatively rare context, and its usual pattern of deployment. But that difference does not make much difference—neither to the kind of puzzlement that ensues, nor to the forms of misguided theorizing that tend to be provoked by it, nor to the more appropriate (therapeutic) way of dealing with it.

2.8 AN ANTI-THEORETICAL THEORY?

Wittgenstein's distinction between 'theories' in philosophy and mere 'descriptions' is best explained by reference to the differences between, on the one hand, those presuppositions and products of T-philosophy that he criticizes and, on the other hand, his own remarks about language use and philosophical practice that are made either in the course of that general critique of T-philosophy or in his dissolution of the topic-specific problems that arise within that approach to the subject. Understanding his distinction in this way, then an accusation of incoherence against Wittgenstein will be vindicated if, and only if, his critique (including the therapeutic observations that issue from it) involves claims of the very kind that he is condemning.

Applying this interpretative proposal, we can say (roughly speaking) that, by a *theory*, Wittgenstein has in mind a hypothesis about some non-evident reality—an attempt to unearth facts that are not out in the open, that cannot be discerned merely by looking in the right direction, with an unprejudiced eye and a clear head, but that can be known only via some form of conjectural inference.

This is not at all to identify the *non-theoretical* with the *indisputable*. For even phenomena that are perfectly open to view may, for a variety of reasons, not be noticed and may therefore be disputed. Rather, the mark of a non-theoretical fact is that, given appropriate reminders, thought-experiments, and other forms of assistance, one can be brought to recognize it as obvious:

> The aspects of things that are most important for us are hidden because of their simplicity and familiarity. (One is unable to notice something—because it is always before one's eyes.) The real foundations of his enquiry do not strike a man at all. Unless *that* fact has at some time struck him.—And this means: we fail to be struck by what, once seen, is most striking and most powerful. (PI 129)

And these ideas are reinforced in the contrast he draws between the 'descriptive' approach of his *Philosophical Investigations* and the 'theoretical' approach that he took in the *Tractatus*:

> ...if we too in these investigations are trying to under-
> stand the essence of language—its function, its structure,—
> yet *this* is not what those [*Tractatus*] questions have in
> view. For they see in the essence, not something that lies
> open to view and that becomes surveyable by rearrange-
> ment, but something that lies *beneath* the surface. Some-
> thing that lies within, which we see when we look *into* the
> thing, and which an analysis digs out. (PI 92)

Such theorizing is now to be shunned. There must be no
attempt to *explain* our linguistic/conceptual activity (PI 126)
as in Frege's reduction of arithmetic to logic; no attempt to
give it *epistemological foundations* (PI 124) as in meaning-based
accounts of *a priori* knowledge; no attempt to characterize
idealized forms of it (PI 130) as in tense logics; no attempt to
reform it (PI 124, 132) as in Mackie's error theory or Dummett's
intuitionism; no attempt to *streamline* it (PI 133) as in Quine's
account of existence; no attempt to make it more *consistent* (PI
132) as in Tarski's response to the liar paradoxes; and no
attempt to make it more *complete* (PI 133) as in the settling of
questions of personal identity for bizarre, hypothetical,
'teleportation' scenarios.

But none of these prohibitions precludes metaphilosophical
investigations and conclusions of the sort that Wittgenstein
himself endorses. One can certainly find meanings of the word
"theory" relative to which he would have to be construed as
contradicting himself—urging a *theory* according to which *theorizing* is illegitimate. But if the term "theory" is used in the
sense suggested—as picking out the irrational products of
T-philosophy, theses concerning phenomena that are hidden,
not open to view—then Wittgenstein does not propound one.

Granted his account is controversial, not widely regarded
as even remotely correct, let alone obviously correct. But, as
we have seen, this feature of a doctrine is entirely consistent
with its being *potentially* obvious. And that is the case here.

The considerations we have mentioned that support Wittgenstein's critique of the goals and practices of T-philosophy are potentially obvious facts and are intended to make it obvious that T-philosophy is indeed irrational.

Granted also his view is a generalization. But Wittgenstein's objection is not to generalizations *per se*, but to the T-philosophical tendency to distort the epistemic norm of simplicity to the point that certain generalizations are *insisted* upon, even in the face of counter-examples.

And granted, finally, his view is evaluative. But again it was never part of his objection to T-philosophy that some of its contentions concern what should or should not be believed. After all, our basic normative convictions can be as obvious as anything can. And so Wittgenstein is often happy to combine (though not, of course, *inferentially*) the empirical observation that we all (including himself) find a certain normative fact obvious (for example, that such-and-such way of thinking is irrational) with an outright assertion of that fact.

In sum: given a modicum of interpretive charity, it is hard to see any basis for the charge that Wittgenstein's metaphilosophy requires him to engage in some of the very intellectual activities that it denounces.[30] And so there is simply no need for any of the radical escape tactics that have been urged on his behalf.

---

[30] See Meredith Williams' *Blind Obedience* (London: Routledge, 2010, esp. chapter 1) for a sensitive reading of the principal metaphilosophical segment (§89–133) of the *Philosophical Investigations*. Unlike myself, however, she sees a conflict between the purely therapeutic goals that are recommended there and various (alleged) features of Wittgenstein's actual philosophical method. Specifically:

(a) His aiming for "complete clarity", which Williams regards as an illusion akin to the *Tractatus'* theoretical goal of 'final analysis'.
(b) The need for an explanation of "why and how philosophical theorizing goes wrong"—of what ensures that philosophical theories are inevitably mistaken and can never amount to valuable discoveries.

For example, Karl Popper[31] suggested that Wittgenstein's 'anti-theoretical metaphilosophical theory' might be rescued from incoherence by construing it as not itself *philosophical*, and therefore as not applicable to itself. Rather, he recommends that it be seen as an *empirical* theory—an inductive generalization of data to the effect that whatever has so far been proposed by philosophers has turned out to have a certain sort of confused origin and a certain dismal fate. And it is certainly true that Wittgenstein constantly reminds us of how our words are actu-

---

(c) And the (supposed) fact that such an explanation will turn out to require a revolutionary account of 'normative similarity'.

Thus, she says, "[t]he philosophical problematic is not eliminated, it is changed. Without the theoretical diagnosis of philosophical error, which involves an alternative understanding of the normativity of language, the arguments cannot fully persuade the philosopher to give up his project" (p. 18).

My reactions in a nutshell are that:

(a*) Wittgenstein's talk of "complete clarity" alludes to whatever context-dependent, person-relative level of understanding is needed to ward off philosophical confusion. This is not an incoherent ideal (on a par with the *Tractaus'* theoretical conception of "ultimate analysis"), and is perfectly achievable. (See my footnote 25 for further discussion.)

(b*) Although we are indeed owed an account of what exactly is wrong with philosophical theorization, the right account (or so I have argued) goes no further than a characterization of the therapeutically treatable confusions of scientistic T-philosophy.

(c*) And the conceptions of intrinsically-normative meaning and rule-following that Williams sees as essential to Wittgenstein's perspective (and which might indeed stand in tension with the therapeutic metaphilosophy) are *not* in fact his conceptions. In Chapters 4 and 5 I both support this interpretation—namely that Wittgenstein took those phenomena to be constitutionally *non*-normative—and defend the idea itself. I argue against the view (which is endorsed by Williams and many others) that "a purely causal account [of rule-following] cannot make space for the distinction between correct and incorrect action" (p. 192).

[31] Karl Popper, "The Nature of Philosophical Problems and their Roots in Science", *British Journal for the Philosophy of Science*, Vol. 3 No. 10, August 1952, 124–56. I myself advocated something like Popper's view in "Meaning and Metaphilosophy", *Philosophical Issues* 4, 1993, 153–8.

ally used—that is, of certain empirical facts. However, the point of such observations is *not* to provide inductive evidence for an empirical theory, but to unsettle our penchant for scientisitic oversimplification. And that motivating idea, which is evidently normative, is not one that Popper's strategy of argument is capable of arriving at. Furthermore, although examples of unsuccessful theorizing are telling, their role is illustrative and heuristic. The *justification* for his doctrine rests (as we saw in Section 2.4) on wholly abstract considerations.—One can reason *a priori* from the methodological nature of traditional theoretical philosophy that it is doomed to engender the conceptual tensions characteristic of distinctively philosophical puzzlement—tensions deriving from irrational over-generalization.

Moreover, it is worth noting that Wittgenstein himself explicitly considers and rejects the idea that philosophy and metaphilosophy might be quite different from one another:

> One might think: if philosophy speaks of the use of the word "philosophy" there must be a second-order philosophy. But it is not so: it is, rather, like the case of orthography, which deals with the word "orthography" among others without then being second-order. (PI 121)

Another defence against alleged self-contradiction that is sometimes offered on Wittgenstein's behalf is that his metaphilosophy be regarded as an *activity* rather than a *thesis*. But although one aspect of his position is indeed a certain distinctive way of *doing* philosophy (including the avoidance of other ways of doing it), this activity is surely the product of his *beliefs* about the peculiar nature of the subject—beliefs that he explicitly articulated.

A conceivable manoeuvre at this point would be to argue that he would distance himself from any such *explicit statements*; that he would maintain, in the spirit of the *Tractatus*, that they are merely heuristic aids—ladders to be eventually thrown away—and that what they attempt to put into words must really be *shown* in practice and cannot meaningfully be *said*. In Chapter 3 I will address and criticize Wittgenstein's earlier reliance on this notoriously murky distinction. But for now, suffice it to say that a merit of the *Philosophical Investigations* is to have done away with it!

2.9 DOES WITTGENSTEIN'S METAPHILOSOPHY REST ON HIS VIEW OF MEANING?

He takes it to be evident (once surrounding confusions have been eliminated) that the meaning of a word consists in its use.[32] This idea implies, one might think, that our practice with respect to a word *cannot* be unfaithful to its meaning.—Which suggests, in turn, that no correct philosophical analysis of the meaning of a term could possibly provide reason either to alter, or to maintain, existing practice with respect to its use. Thus a respectable philosophy will have the power neither to revise nor justify our common sense conceptions: it cannot but leave everything as it is. Notwithstanding this fact, traditional philosophical theorizing involves *departing* from the ordinary usage of words:

> ...philosophical problems arise when language *goes on holiday*. (PI 38)

It might seem, therefore, that from the 'use' account of meaning, one can infer that philosophical theories are meaningless—and hence that philosophical theorizing is inevitably misguided.

This way of deriving his metaphilosophy from his account of meaning is commonly attributed to Wittgenstein;[33] but I do

---

[32] For a thorough discussion of this doctrine, see Chapter 4.

[33] See, for example, Baker and Hacker, *Wittgenstein, Meaning, and Understanding*, Chapter 13, "The Nature of Philosophy":—

not think that it can really capture his intentions. Cerainly there are no particular passages in which he attempt to justify his claim about the ineffectuality of theoretical philosophy on the basis of his identification of the meaning of a word with its use. And that's unsurprising For in the first place he has no *need* to justify it that way, since it emerges from the considerations developed earlier in this chapter. And in the second place he *could* not do so, for the above-sketched derivation is badly flawed; there is in fact no legitimate route from the 'use' theory of meaning to the idea that philosophy cannot revise or sustain our linguo-conceptual practices.

To see this, let me set out, more carefully, what that route is supposed to be:

(i) Meaning = use.
(ii) Therefore any deployment of a word outside its ordinary usage would be meaningless.
(iii) But philosophical theorizing does involve departures from ordinary usage.
(iv) Therefore philosophical theories are meaningless.
(v) Therefore we must confine ourselves to removing the temptation to engage in philosophical theorizing.

But this reasoning is glaringly invalid—specifically the step from (i) to (ii). If that move were allowed then the consequences

---

... philosophy is extraordinary in that it adjudicates the bounds of sense. It clarifies which questions are intelligible and which investigations are in principle relevant or irrelevant for answering them. This view Wittgenstein held and argued for throughout his career. (p. 259) Oxford

See also David Pears, *The False Prison*, vol. 2, Oxford: Oxford University Press, 1987; and Jerrold Katz, *The Metaphysics of Meaning*, Cambridge, MA., MIT Press, 1991.

The following critique of this way of understanding Wittgenstein is extracted from "Wittgenstein's Metaphilosophical Development", Chapter 8 of my *From a Deflationary Point of View*, Oxford: Oxford University Press, 2004.

would be far more radical than could have been intended by Wittgenstein or than can be accepted by us.

In the first place, a vital constraint on how the term "use" must be understood in the context of Wittgenstein's account of meaning is that there be the possibility of appreciating that we have been saying (and thinking) false things—that is, applying words incorrectly. It must be possible to discover that certain common uses of words are in fact mistaken.[34] (For example, we have now learned that we were wrong to think, "The sun revolves around the Earth".) But in that case, the notion of 'use' that Wittgenstein needs cannot dictate that a theory would have to be meaningless if it involved departures from what is ordinarily said. And that goes for *philosophical* theories too. In other words, the use conception of meaning is not by itself capable of explaining why philosophy shouldn't be amongst those disciplines that enable us to discover errors in accepted usage.

In the second place, although an everyday word might be deployed in a *radically* novel way (in violation of its ordinary meaning) within the context of a philosophical theory, it does nonetheless have *some* use within that theory. Therefore the use conception—far from certifying the word as meaningless—will entail that it *does* have a meaning. This sort of commandeering of terms is common in science: familiar words (such as "energy", "fish", and "language") are pressed into unfamiliar, explanatory service and thereby given new and technical meanings.[35] So why should it not happen within philosophy too? And in that case, why would metaphysical theories be any less intelligible than scientific ones?

Thus an identification of meaning with use cannot get us to the conclusion that philosophical theorizing is misconceived.

[34] See Chapter 4, Section 2(G), for elaboration of this point.
[35] Remember the examples of "imaginary" and "pain" from Chapter 1, Section 1.4. The bewilderment that can be provoked by the technical uses of these words comes not from their inability to yield *genuine* meanings but from a failure to recognize that they yield *different* meanings.

Moreover, it is evidently not the case that the products of T-Philosophy are invariably meaningless, and nor does Wittgenstein need to claim that they are. Given his purposes it suffices to show that the problems that such theories are attempting to solve do not exist, and that the theories are uncalled for and unjustified. Some of them may indeed be meaningless. But others are merely irrational; and some could even turn out to be true—although this would emerge on the basis of non-philosophical considerations (such as science) and not from their offering solutions to philosophical pseudo-problems.[36]

2.10 TWO PHILOSOPHIES?

Wittgenstein is often credited with having invented two distinct philosophies—one appearing as the *Tractatus Logico-Philosophicus* when he was thirty years old, and the other devised after he returned to Cambridge a decade later, and published posthumously as the *Philosophical Investigations*.

---

[36] Huw Price's appraisal of metaphysics (see his "Naturalism Without Representationalism", in D. Macarthur and M. de Caro (eds.), *Naturalism in Question*, Cambridge, MA: Harvard University Press, 2004, 71–88) has much in common with Wittgenstein's—but there are some deep differences. The starting point for both lines of thought is naturalistic observation of human linguoconceptual activity, and both reach the conclusion that metaphysics is illegitimate. But the routes they take are not at all the same. In the case of Wittgenstein, his initial observations are intended to provoke the recognition that our metaphysical proclivities are based on overstretched analogies and other forms of irrational overgeneralization. But Price's line of argument relies on a couple of interlocking assumptions that Wittgenstein does not make: (i) that any legitimate metaphysical conclusion would have to be deduced from linguistic premises; and (ii) that no respectable inferential route of that sort exists. And although the second of these ideas is certainly plausible (—for why on earth should we expect to be able to deduce non-linguistic facts from linguistic data?—), the first one would be rejected by most fans of metaphysics, and it is not at all clear that they would be mistaken in doing so. For further discussion, see my "Naturalism, Deflationism, and the Relative Priority of Language and Metaphysics".

Indeed many philosophers hold the first work in much higher regard than the second, and think it a shame that Wittgenstein did not continue to develop his earlier ideas.

This characterization of Wittgenstein's career is seriously mistaken.[37] For his philosophy evolves towards the mature position of the *Investigations* (which is further elaborated in subsequent work), and the *Tractatus* should be seen as a first approximation to that position. After all, the most distinctive and important of his ideas is already present in the *Tractatus*: namely, his view of traditional philosophical perplexities as pseudo-problems based on confusions stemming from features of language. Thus it is somewhat perverse to maintain that Wittgenstein, and philosophy, would have been better served if he had developed the *Tractatus* point of view—since that is exactly what he did do, and his *Investigations* are the result. In the next chapter I will present a reading of the *Tractatus* that makes clear exactly what Wittgenstein retained from that position and exactly how he revised and improved it.[38]

[37] And not because the actual number of his philosophies is perhaps three, or four! See the Preface for a little further discussion of this issue.

[38] My thanks to Yu Guo for his valuable comments on a draft of this chapter.

3

Tractatus Logico-Philosophicus

3.1 OUTLINE

Few philosophical works have been as ambitious yet short, and as influential yet obscure, as Wittgenstein's *Tractatus*. It purports to lay the whole subject to rest in fewer than eighty pages of cryptic text, sufficiently tough going to provoke complaints even from the likes of Frege and Russell who were ideally placed to understand it. Yet it transformed subsequent philosophy, most notably by inspiring the logical empiricism of the Vienna Circle and by providing the basis of Wittgenstein's further revolutionary ideas.

My intention here is certainly not to offer a full interpretation of this remarkable book, but merely to sketch its main lines of thought: to identify the principal theses and the relations of justification between them. The goal is to illuminate Wittgenstein's mature philosophy of the *Philosophical Investigations* by looking back to how he arrived at it.[1]

A special difficulty in settling on a satisfactory reading of the *Tractatus* is that many—perhaps all—of what at first appear to

---

[1] A couple of warnings. First: things move along fairly quickly in this chapter—perhaps too quickly for those with no previous exposure to the *Tractatus*. Second: substantial arguments will be given in support of each element of the overall interpretation to be proposed here. However, there was insufficient space for the detailed critique of alternative readings that would be needed to fully justify it.

be its central doctrines are, by the end of the book, supposed to
be exposed as "senseless":

> 6.45   My propositions are elucidatory in this way: he
>   who understands me finally recognizes them as
>   senseless, when he has climbed out through them,
>   on them, over them. (He must so to speak throw
>   away the ladder, after he has climbed up on it).
>   He must surmount these propositions; then he
>   sees the world rightly.

So just because we start by reading

> 1   The world is all that is the case.

we cannot infer without further ado that Wittgenstein *endorses*
this idea, that the *Tractatus* is intended to advocate it; and similarly for the pronouncements that follow. Rather we must
confront the problem of distinguishing those he makes *wholeheartedly* from those he does not finally stand by.

And there are some further intimately related issues of interpretation. What is Wittgenstein's ultimate view of the latter
class, the propositions that are eventually to be "recognize[d] ... as
senseless"? Does he nevertheless retain a sort of quasi-commit-
ment to the quasi-ideas that one might improperly attempt to
communicate with them? If so, how? But if not—on the
grounds that these propositions are truly nonsensical—then
how is it possible for their enunciation to reveal anything, or to
be of any philosophical value at all?

My plan is to postpone these questions for a while (until
Section 3.6)—focusing to begin with on the positive theory
that Wittgenstein seems at first sight to be propounding.

A wide range of philosophical topics is covered in the *Tractatus*; but most of the issues are located in one of four overlap-
ping areas:—metaphysics, meaning, the logical sub-structure
of language, and metaphilosophy. The relationship between
Wittgenstein's views in these domains is *prima facie* as follows.

At the start of the book he makes a series of metaphysical claims, presented as obvious, including (a) that there is a stock of basic entities ('objects'), the ultimate constituents both of our world and of all merely possible worlds; (b) that certain combinations of these entities actually exist, forming *atomic facts*; and (c) that all the other facts that make up the real world are constructed, with the help of logic, on the basis of the atomic ones.

Second, he specifies what it takes to *represent* a state of affairs.—Representing is a matter of picturing or modelling, and a possible arrangement of worldly things is modelled by certain arrangement of elements when they stand for the things and when they are arranged in the same way as the things are arranged.

Third, by combining the picture theory of meaning with his metaphysical doctrines he can deduce what character any language will need to have if it is to be capable of representing reality. It must contain (a*) unanalysable terms ('names') that refer to the basic objects, (b*) elementary propositions, each consisting of some of these terms combined in a certain way (i.e. embedded within a certain logical structure), and true if and only if the referents of those terms are actually combined in exactly that way,[2] and (c*) various other propositions, but only in so far as their truth values are logically determined by those of the elementary propositions.[3]

---

[2] In this chapter I follow Wittgenstein's (or his translators') usage of the term "proposition"—that is, to refer to a *sentence with its meaning*, and not, as is more common these days, to refer merely to the *meaning* itself that a sentence might have.

[3] It might be thought, contrary to the direction of thought sketched in these last paragraphs, that Wittgenstein infers the metaphysical character of reality from assumptions about linguistic form—and, moreover, that he subscribes to the 'idealist' explanatory view that structure is imposed on the world by language. But this reading has various counts against it. First, Wittgenstein gives

And fourth, he is then in a position to elaborate and defend his distinctive conception of *philosophy*—as a subject whose characteristic problems derive from violating the above requirements. He argues that the metaphysical nature of reality cannot be explicitly *described*, because any such attempt will break the rules for constructing meaningful propositions. That nature can merely be *shown*—it is *implicitly* revealed in the character of our propositions. For example, he supposes that a properly constructed language can contain no *predicate* meaning "is an object"; so "There are objects" has no sense; rather, some sort of commitment to the existence of objects is implicit in our use of names and of the object-variable, "x". Therefore, coherent questions about the meaning of "exists" and the nature of existence cannot arise. They are pseudo-questions. Indeed, *all* traditional philosophical puzzles, questions, and claims are held to derive from such mistakes. They are fostered by the fact that the actual content (or lack of content) of a proposition, as revealed by a full conceptual analysis, is often heavily disguised by its superficial form. Thus, legitimate philosophical activity must be confined to conceptual clarification and the dissolution of pseudo-problems.

---

no explicit indication that he intends the epistemological or explanatory relations between his doctrines to diverge so radically from the order in which they appear in the book. Second, although it is indeed plausible to suppose that *our intuitions* about metaphysical structure are merely the expression of our linguistic proclivities, it appears to be only later, in his *Philosophical Investigations*, that Wittgenstein comes to appreciate and acknowledge this point. For example:

> We predicate of the thing what lies in the method of representing it. Impressed by the possibility of a comparison, we think we are perceiving a state of the highest generality. (PI 104)

And third, even if linguistic structure is indeed *epistemologically* prior to metaphysical structure, that would not imply any parallel *explanatory* priority. So there would be no basis for moving to the thesis—implausibly anti-realist—that the *actual* structure of the world (as opposed to our *beliefs* about that structure) is somehow the product of our language.

These four clusters of ideas are the central components of the *Tractatus*. Let us now examine them a little more thoroughly.

3.2 METAPHYSICS

The metaphysical pronouncements with which Wittgenstein begins his book offer the following account of how reality is composed. First, there is a fixed supply of indivisible, necessarily-existent, so-called 'objects'. Each such object may be combined with a variety of other basic objects to make a variety of *atomic* facts—where the possibility of a given combination depends on the intrinsic natures of the objects involved, and where (in virtue of the objects' mutual independence) the actual existence of a given combination entails neither the existence nor the non-existence of any other possible combination. Finally, the bifurcation of possible atomic facts into those that are actual and those that aren't logically determines a *totality* of actual facts (including, for example, conjunctive and disjunctive facts)—and that is *the world*.

One might be inclined to interpret

> 2.01   An atomic fact is a combination of objects (entities, things)

as saying that any such fact consists in one or another *substantive* relation between two or more things—for example, 'x is *between* y and z', or 'x is *brighter* than y'—and that some such non-logical relation is to be identified with the *structure* (configuration, or way the objects are combined) of the atomic fact. However, this interpretation assumes that Wittgenstein is distinguishing such substantive properties (and relations) from what he calls "objects". And that assumption does not square with his examples of 'objects', which include universals such as redness and blueness:

2.251   Space, time, and colour (colouredness) are forms
of objects.

Nor is it easy to see how a proposition—an arrangement of
referring elements—could (in accord with 2.15) have *exactly
the same* structure as the fact it represents if that structure
were a *substantive* relation between objects. The word "Venus"
is surely not brighter than the word "Mars"! Thus a better
interpretation is to suppose that Wittgenstein lumps together
what we ordinarily distinguish as objects and properties
(including relations) into the general category, *entity*—which
he thinks of as containing 'objects' of various types. An
atomic fact is then a purely *logical* combination of such
entities.[4]

Another distinctive feature of the *Tractatus* metaphysics is
the special status accorded to logic:

4.312   My fundamental thought is that the "logical
constants" do not represent.

So there are no *logical objects*—no elements of reality corresponding to terms such as "not" and "or". Rather (as we shall
see more clearly in the next section) the logical terms are supposed to be nothing but expressive devices: their function is
merely to provide us with propositions that are relatively non-
committal—enabling us to convey not simply that there exist
such and such atomic facts but, more cautiously, that whatever

---

[4] Here are a couple of further virtues of this reading. It would explain why
all possible elementary facts are given solely by the objects:

2.124   If all objects are given, then thereby are all *possible* facts also
given.

And it would also explain why the intrinsic nature of an object is determined by
which other objects it may be combined with:

2.141   The possibility of its occurrence in atomic facts is the form
of the object.

the totality of atomic facts may be they fall within (or outside) a certain specified range of alternative totalities.

3.3 MEANING

The second major component of Wittgenstein's system is an account of meaning—a theory articulating the nature of *representation*.

This theory is composed of three main theses: first, a specification of how a *picture* (or model) is able to represent what it does; second, the idea that basic ('elementary') *propositions* represent in exactly this way—that they are literally pictures of possible facts; and third, an explanation of how logical terms may be introduced, enabling the construction of meaningful sentences that go beyond the elementary, pictorial ones.

Consider, to begin with, a possible situation consisting of various things standing in a certain relation to one another. Wittgenstein's view is that in order for a picture to depict that state of affairs it must also consist in various things—pictorial elements—standing in a relation to one another. Moreover, these elements must refer to the things in the represented state; and the relation holding between the elements must be *the same* as the relation between those things.

> 2.15   That the elements…are combined with one
>   another in a definite way, represents that the things
>   are so combined with one another.

Think, for example, of a simple map, which has letters referring to cities, and lines referring to railway links:

One of the representing facts here is

> that there is a line between "O" and "L"

and it depicts the possible fact

> that there is a railway link between Oxford and London

In this example the representing elements are the letters "O" and "L", and the property of *being a line*; the referents of these elements are, respectively, Oxford, London, and the property of *being a railway link*; and the arrangement in which the elements stand may be indicated as follows:

> that there is an exemplification of... between... and...

Thus, in order to arrive at what is represented by this arrangement of elements we simply put the referents of those elements into the very same arrangement.

Turning now to the second component of Wittgenstein's theory of meaning, his idea is to illuminate *linguistic* representation by showing how it can be assimilated, via the above account, to the much less mysterious case of *pictorial* representation.

The railway example is an instance of *spatial* representation in virtue of the fact that the arrangement of both representing elements and represented things is spatial: it involves the relation of *between-ness*. But some systems of representation—*linguistic* ones—are purely *logical*: their representations share only a logical structure with the fact represented. Consider, for example, the proposition "John loves Mary" (and let us pretend, for the sake of illustration, that it is an *elementary* proposition). In this case the representing state of affairs is

> that the word "John" precedes the word "loves" which precedes the word "Mary"

and the represented possible fact is

> that John loves Mary

Now one might be initially tempted to assume that the elements of the representing picture are the words "John", "loves", and "Mary". But this cannot be right. For under that supposition—given that what is represented must be that the *referents* of the pictorial elements exemplify the very same relation as do the elements themselves—we would have to say that the represented state of affairs is

> that John precedes love which precedes Mary

—an absurdity.

In fact, the only way of accounting for the representational power of the sentence, via Wittgenstein's picture theory, is to suppose:

- that the representing elements are "John", "Mary", and the relation, *x precedes the word "loves" which precedes y*
- that these elements are arranged in the logical structure, 'that x#y'
- that the elements refer, respectively, to John, Mary, and the relation, *x loves y.*

These suppositions give us just what is needed. By embedding the represented objects in the structure of the representing fact, we arrive at precisely the possible fact that is intuitively represented.[5]

Thus we can understand what Wittgenstein has in mind in cautioning that

> 3.1432   We must not say, "The complex sign 'aRb' says 'a
>   stands in relation R to b'"; but we must say,

---

[5] For a similar account of Wittgenstein's picture theory see the excellent commentary by Erik Stenius, *Wittgenstein's Tractatus: A Critical Exposition*, Oxford: Blackwell, and Ithaca: Cornell University Press, 1960; 2nd edition, 1964.

> " *That* 'a' stands in a certain relation to 'b' says
> *that* aRb".

The "certain relation" between 'a' and 'b' is that the first of them is written immediately before 'R' and the second immediately after it.

Although one might be tempted to read Wittgenstein as maintaining that *all* propositions are pictures—for we do encounter formulations that are not explicitly restricted (for example, "4.01: The proposition is a picture of reality")—I doubt that this interpretation can be sustained. For, as we have seen, he is insistent that reality is exhausted by the *atomic* facts; and hence that the logical constants ("and", "or",...) do not represent. Therefore, if logically complex propositions were pictures, we would have to suppose that the logical terms enter into the pictorial *relation* between representing elements. And that would imply that they also enter into the relation between *represented* elements, which they obviously do not: the fact represented by "I am cold and wet" obviously does not contain the *word* "and". Thus it does not appear to be possible to apply the picture theory to logically complex propositions (at least, if it is agreed that the logical constants do not represent).[6]

Moreover, Wittgenstein has no need to apply his theory so broadly, since he gives the following alternative account of how

It is worth noting that Wittgenstein's proposal is close to one of Frege's fundamental ideas: namely, that a sentence is the result of applying (in a certain order) certain function-expressions to certain argument-expressions, and that—at the level of reality—the *meaning* of the sentence is the result of applying (in the *same* order) the meanings of those function-expressions to the meanings of the argument-expressions. Wittgentein diverges from Frege by (1) focusing exclusively on meaning qua *reference*; (2) supposing that both the representing and represented entities are *facts* rather than objects; and (3) confining this account of representation to *elementary* propositions (as we will see immediately below).

[6] As we will now see, Wittgenstein certainly does not deny that the logical terms have distinctive 'meanings' in *some* sense. So the possible state of affairs corresponding to a logically complex sentence is a compositional function of how those terms (amongst others) are distributed within it. However, that

non-atomic propositions can be meaningful. Consider a proposition containing only 'names' and standard logical terms of the predicate calculus. Its truth value will be logically determined by the truth values of elementary propositions. Conversely, any such proposition logically determines that the assignment of truth values to the elementary propositions must be one of a specific range of alternative assignments. Thus the possibility represented by a fully analysed, predicate-calculus proposition is the possibility that the totality of existing atomic facts is one of a specific range of alternative totalities. Therefore, as long as a proposition is definitionally equivalent to a fully analysed, propositional calculus proposition,[7] its meaning may be identified with such a possibility.

3.4 THE STRUCTURE AND LIMITS OF LANGUAGE

From the accounts he has just given of the nature of reality, and of what would be required to represent that reality,

---

compositionality is *not* a result of these terms designating logical elements within reality (for example, objects called "not", "or", etc.), and thereby helping to constitute a picture of the world. Thus:

> 4.0311 One name stands for one thing, and another for another thing, and they are connected together. And so the whole, like a living picture, presents the **atomic** fact [my emphasis].
>
> 4.0312 The possibility of propositions is based on the principle of the representation of objects by signs.
> **My fundamental thought** is that the "logical constants" do not represent. That the *logic* of the facts cannot be represented [my emphasis].

[7] At this point one should add "and as long as this analysing proposition is neither a tautology nor a contradiction". For, since propositions of these two kinds are not contingent, Wittgenstein regarded them as not conveying 'genuine' possibilities and therefore as lacking sense ("sinnlos").

Wittgenstein is able to draw conclusions about the character and scope of any representationally adequate language. These results concern

(i) The existence of elementary propositions.
(ii) The general form of a proposition.
(iii) The theory of entailment and the mutual independence of elementary propositions.
(iv) The rules of logical syntax.

I will take them up in turn.

In the first place, if it is to be capable of picturing the atomic facts, a language must contain primitive terms ('names') that refer to the simple objects.—Additional words must be explicitly definable in terms of these primitives (together with logical terms). For each such primitive there will have to be certain others with which it can coherently be combined to form elementary propositions, and yet others with which it cannot be so combined. These possibilities define the logical type to which the term belongs; they must match the combination-possibilities of the objects to which they refer. Moreover—and again matching the corresponding objects—the way in which terms combine to form these propositions must be (as Frege emphasized) that some are *functional* in logical type (for example, "_ flies", i.e. *x precedes "flies"*) and are exemplified by others, so forming a proposition.

Secondly, an adequate language must be capable of representing *all* the facts, no matter what they might happen to be or how complex they are: it must contain a proposition for each such possible fact. But any possible fact is the possibility that the atomic facts are such as to determine it—which is a possibility of the following form: either the totality of existing atomic facts contains just *these* ones, or it contains just *those*, or... Therefore, in order to represent each possible fact, it suffices for a language to have, in addition to the elementary

propositions, certain further propositions—one for each collection of assignments of truth values to the elementary propositions. And—as we saw at the end of Section 3.3—this will be
so if the language contains the standard logical terms, "or",
"and", "not", "every", and so on. With these resources it can
articulate every possible disjunction of conjunctions of positive
and negative atomic facts.

If the language is not to go too far—if it is not to allow
senseless assertions (i.e. assertions to which no 'genuinely' possible facts correspond)—then each of its propositions must
amount to a disjunction of conjunctions of positive and negative elementary propositions. But every predicate-logic proposition, provided that it is composed merely of the primitive
vocabulary and standard logical terms, is logically equivalent to
one of these disjunctions. Therefore, an adequate language may
not contain a proposition unless its full conceptual analysis
reduces it to a predicate-logic proposition, all of whose non-
logical terms are meaningful primitives.

Wittgenstein speaks of 'the general form of a proposition' as
being a *variable*, ranging over all the propositions that can be
constructed in accordance with these rules. As he puts it:

6　　　The general form of truth-function is: $[p, \xi, N(\xi)]$.
　　　　This is the general form of a proposition.

6.01　This says nothing else than that every proposition
　　　　is the result of successive applications of the oper-
　　　　ator, $N(\xi)$, to the elementary propositions.

—where $N(\xi)$ is defined as the conjunction of the denials of all
the propositions whose form is ξ.[8]

---

[8]　5.502　$N(\xi)$ is the negation of all the values of the propositional
　　　　　　variable ξ.

　　5.51　If ξ has only one value then $N(\xi) = -p$ (not p), if it has two
　　　　　　values then $N(\xi) = -p.-q$ (neither p nor q).

This claim is the product of two separable ideas: first, that each legitimate proposition is the result of successive applications of the usual logical operators to elementary propositions; and second, that all such operators are definable in terms of "$N(\xi)$". Of these ideas, the second is much less important. For although it permits a certain aesthetically pleasing simplification of the view, Wittgenstein does not need it in order to specify how any legitimate proposition must be constructed.[9] Thus he is able to do what, in his Preface to the book, he said he was aiming to do: namely, "to set a limit to thought, or rather—not to thought, but to the expression of thoughts...".

Thirdly, a *truth ground* of a proposition is defined as any assignment of truth values to elementary propositions that determines that the proposition is true. Moreover, it is obvious that a proposition A entails proposition B just in case there could not be a fact corresponding to A unless there were also a fact corresponding to B. So Wittgenstein is in a position to infer that A entails B if and only if every truth ground of A is a truth ground of B. Notice, however, that this account works only in so far as the *elementary* propositions are *independent* of one another. It must be supposed that, given any two such propositions p and q, then none of the following is the case: p entails q, p entails –q, q entails p, q entails –p. And this condition will indeed be satisfied if, as Wittgenstein assumed, the possible atomic facts are mutually independent. But it follows that "point k is red" and "point k is green" cannot be elemen-

[9] Robert Fogelin (*Wittgenstein*, London: Routledge and Kegan Paul, 1976) argues persuasively that we should give up the second thesis. He shows that "$N(\xi)$" lacks the expressive power of the combination of standard logical operators. See also Scott Soames, "Generality, Truth Functions, and Expressive Capacity in the *Tractatus*", *The Philosophical Review* XCII, No. 4, 1983, 573–89.

tary propositions (describing possible atomic fact); for they are not mutually independent.[10]

Fourthly, Wittgenstein adopts Frege's logic, and follows his strict observance of the distinction between logical categories—viz. names, 1st-level function-expressions, 2nd-level function-expressions, and so on—reserving separate types of variable for each one. Given a good logical syntax of this sort, it will be the case, he argues, that no function can be its own argument (because, if the function-expression is "f(x)", then the argument-expression must be a name; and if the function-expression is "F(#(x))", the argument-expression must be a 1st-level function-expression, and so on). The point of these rules of logical syntax is to avoid paradox. And, as we will see, the same motive lies behind other strictures: for example, the above-mentioned claim that there can be no predicates meaning "is an object" or "is a concept", and that these notions will instead have to be expressed by distinctive types of variable, "x" and "#_".

3.5 METAPHILOSOPHY

Wittgenstein's account of how philosophy should, and should not, be conducted would appear to flow naturally from these theses concerning metaphysics, meaning, and linguistic structure.

---

[10] It is worth noting that the existence of such groups of incompatible, *apparently* simple properties does not immediately refute Wittgenstein's 'independence' claim. For one may be able to locate further properties in terms of which the incompatible ones may be defined, and which themselves *do* satisfy that condition. Consider, for example, green, red, blue, and colourless. Let the property H be *green or red* and let J be *green or blue*. Then clearly H and J are logically independent of one another. And the colour properties may be defined in terms of them, as follows: green = H&J, red = H&–J, blue = J&–H, and colorless = –H&–J. This technique may be extended to cases involving an arbitrary number of mutually incompatible predicates.

It has been shown that each significant claim must have a unique, complete conceptual analysis into a particular sentence of predicate logic. He emphasizes, however, that the right analysis may be extremely hard to discern. For there are often great differences between the superficial grammatical forms of sentences and their underlying logical forms. This is nicely illustrated by Russell's theory of descriptions, according to which "The F is G" reduces to "$(\exists x)(Fx \ \& \ (y)(Fy \rightarrow y = x) \ \& \ Gx)$". Therefore mistakes in analysis can easily occur. Moreover, sentences may be constructed that *look* significant, but which really are not—as a good conceptual analysis of them would reveal. Traditional philosophical questions and statements fall into this category, according to Wittgenstein. They are disguised nonsense:

> 4.003　They belong to the same class as the question whether the good is more or less identical than the beautiful.

And a complete conceptual analysis will show that their apparent depth and interest, indeed their very coherence, is an illusion.

An important case in point, he thinks, is the temptation to *say* explicitly (or raise questions about) what can only be *shown* implicitly by the structure of propositions: for example, that the world contains basic objects. For Wittgenstein's rules of logical syntax do not allow a predicate meaning 'is an object'. Therefore, "Are there objects?" will not yield, under analysis, a genuine question, though on the surface it seems perfectly significant.

The rationale for such restrictions comes from the need to avoid paradox. Consider, for example, Frege's notorious difficulty with the concept HORSE: that since it is designated by "the concept HORSE"—which being a singular term, must refer to an *object*, not a concept—the concept HORSE is not a concept! In supposing that the metaphysical category of the entity to which an expression refers cannot be explicitly specified, but only shown by the sort of expression it is, such paradoxes are pre-empted.[11]

Thus Wittgenstein would wholeheartedly endorse—indeed, he carries further—what Frege had said about the value of 'ideography', i.e. logical syntax:

> If it is one of the tasks of philosophy to break the domination of the word over the human spirit by laying bare the misconceptions that through the use of language often almost unavoidably arise concerning the relations between concepts and by freeing thought from that with which only the means of expression of ordinary language, constituted as they are, saddle it, then my ideography, further developed for these purposes, can become a useful tool for the philosopher.[12]

3.6 THROWING AWAY THE LADDER

One might well think that Wittgenstein's project in the *Tractatus* is to present and propound the above-sketched theory of reality, meaning, the logical structure of language, and the nature of philosophy—a theory enabling him, as he promised at the outset, to "draw a limit to thinking" and to give an undermining diagnosis of traditional philosophy. However, there are substantial grounds for questioning whether this was in fact his intention. For, not only do just about all of the work's own

---

[11] See Gottlob Frege, "Concept and Object", *Translations from the Philosophical Writings of Gottlob Frege*, ed. P. Geach and M. Black, Oxford: Blackwell, 1952. The influence on Wittgenstein of this aspect of Frege's work is emphasized by Peter Geach in "Saying and Showing in Frege and Wittgenstein", *Acta Philosophica Fennica* Vol. 28, Nos. 1–3, 1976, 54–70.

[12] G. Frege, *Begriffsschrift*, Preface.

theses and arguments fall on the wrong side of the specified limits, but this is obviously no mere oversight on Wittgenstein's part, since he himself eventually draws attention to it—emphasizing at the end of his book that what has come earlier is by its own lights devoid of sense, and attempting to reassure us that there is no genuine tension between the meaninglessness of those pronouncements and their philosophical utility. To repeat:

> 6.54 My propositions are elucidatory in this way: he who understands me finally recognizes them as senseless, when he has climbed out through them, on them, over them. (He must so to speak throw away the ladder, after he has climbed up on it).
>
> He must surmount these propositions; then he sees the world rightly.

And then, the book's bottom line:

> 7 Whereof one cannot speak, thereof one must be silent.

So, are we to conclude that Wittgenstein's aim was the very opposite of what one might easily have taken it to be initially: not to advocate the theory enunciated, but rather to demolish it—or at least a good part of it!

Perhaps. However, such a conclusion would itself be by no means unproblematic. For it is not easy to see how the pronouncements of the *Tractatus* could shed light on anything—how they could help us to see anything "rightly" (even their own meaninglessness)—if they were total nonsense. Wittgenstein's resort to the image of 'using a ladder and then throwing it away' will need to be translated into a clear explanation of how the book could conceivably be enlightening.

To that end, it might help to suppose on his behalf that his "senseless propositions" should not be equated with "gibberish", but should be taken to involve some less extreme defect—one that does not preclude their somehow being "elucidatory". In particular, the defect might be that these propositions are elements of a theory that is at once (i) definitive of our notions of 'object', 'fact', 'refers', and so on, yet (ii) internally inconsistent.—In which case, Wittgenstein's overall line of argument may be seen as a form of *reductio ad absurdum* whose moral is that the central notions of metaphysics and semantics must be abandoned—i.e., that a decent logical syntax will not contain predicates purporting to express them.[13]

But although this response seems plausible as far as it goes, and might explain how the *Tractatus* propositions could have a certain narrow negative import, one might doubt whether that could be *all* Wittgenstein has in mind in saying that our engagement with them puts us in a position to "see the world rightly".

For that enlightened state is supposed to be one in which we who occupy it entirely refrain from *any* philosophical assertions, and react to those of another person by subjecting them to conceptual analysis and thereby exposing their nonsensicality. Moreover, these reactions are supposed to be governed by strict constraints. We are to 'assume' (or at least to behave as though we are assuming) that a more or less Fregean specification of the possible logical forms is correct, that certain terms are the objectively primitive ones, that each meaningful sentence has a determinate conceptual analysis articulated in terms of the primitives and the proper logic, and that such analyses can be almost impossible to discern, so that we easily fail to appreciate what a sentence means (or fail to see that it in fact has *no* meaning). But how could these positive insights—

---

[13] As already mentioned, it is not unlikely that he had in mind, amongst other things, the paradox concerning the concept HORSE, which seems inevitably to arise within the Fregean view of *reference*—a view Wittgenstein may well have regarded as definitive of the notion.

explicit or implicit—result merely from the above-sketched *reductio*?

It would seem rather that, although there are not supposed to be any fully cogent formulations of those ideas, still Wittgenstein's formulations do somehow manage to steer us in the right direction. If they were not able to do that, it is hard to see how we could possibly reach the correct destination—which is presumably why Wittgenstein enunciated them! It would seem, therefore, that Wittgenstein is 'committed' (in *some* sense) to his metaphilosophical propositions. And since these emerge from his propositions about metaphysics, meaning, logic, and language, he must be 'committed' to those as well.

Thus, the 'reductio' reading leaves us with an overall view that is of questionable coherence. And in addition it seems impossible (without considerable strain) to reconcile it with either Wittgenstein's own prior statements of intention or his subsequent statements about what his intentions were. Why would he announce in the Preface that he plans to "draw limits to thinking" (precisely what the subsequent theory proceeds to explicitly do), and that "the truth of the thoughts communicated here seems to me unassailable and definitive"? And why would he refer in the *Philosophical Investigations* to the mistaken opinions espoused in his earlier work, and go on to give a systematic critique of them—his old doctrines concerning language, logic, meaning, and ontology? Could he really have forgotten that he never intended to espouse them?![14]

In the face of these difficulties, I think we should not so quickly dismiss the more straightforward, old-fashioned reading of the *Tractatus*, whereby he is really expressing some sort

[14] Peter Sullivan struggles illuminatingly with these issues in his "What is the *Tractatus* About?", in B. Weiss and M. Kölbel (eds.), *Wittgenstein's Lasting Significance*, London: Routledge, 2004.

of attachment to the propositions he appears to be endorsing. Perhaps Wittgenstein felt that even though his metaphysical, logical, semantic, and metaphilosophical proclivities cannot accurately be expressed through *statements* in the way that he initially tries to, there is nonetheless something right about them—something profound that is manifested in our grammatical structures and linguistic activities. Perhaps he took "his propositions" to more or less roughly convey quite a few important things, despite the fact that such things cannot really be articulated in either language or thought!

Lacking a third option, we must confront the unwelcome choice between those on the table. One interpretation has it that most of the theory articulated by Wittgenstein is reduced to absurdity and wholly rejected. But this fails to explain how we manage to arrive at the rich battery of attitudes and practices that he associates with "seeing the world rightly". And it fails to square with what, in a *variety* of writings, he clearly indicates to be the import of the book.[15] Whereas the alternative interpretation takes him to retain a mysterious sort of allegiance to that theory, despite its falling on the wrong side of the limits of language and thought—implying an inclination on Wittgenstein's part to allow that what cannot be adequately *said*, and can only be adequately *shown*, might nonetheless be *badly and roughly said*.[16]

---

[15] See, for example, Wittgenstein's *Notes Dictated to G. E Moore*, reprinted in *Notebooks* 1914–1916. The relevance of this material is emphasized by David Pears in his *Paradox and Platitude in Wittgenstein's Philosophy*, Oxford: Oxford University Press, 2006, p. 5.

[16] These alternatives illustrate the two principal strategies of *Tractatus* interpretation to be found in the literature. The second one offers a traditional reading—a so-called Standard Interpretation—according to which Wittgenstein *endorses* his metaphysical remarks while recognizing that what they are attempting to communicate cannot really be *said* but merely *shown*. The first exemplifies the more recently popular so-called Resolute (or Austere) Interpretation, according to which he rejects his metaphysical pronouncements as plain unsalvageable nonsense. For good examples of the Standard Interpretation see Frank

It seems to me that the less unappealing, more charitable of these two readings is the second one. Granted, the *Tractatus* would have been a better work without its murky quasi-endorsement of propositions that it designates as unsayable (and unthinkable). And granted, an important norm of interpretation is to avoid the imputation of serious errors. But on the other hand we must beware the infamous fallacy of 'the infallible Wittgenstein'. And we should not forget that the *Tractatus* doctrine of the 'unsayable' would not be its only significant defect, as he himself, later on, was perfectly ready to admit.[17]

Ramsey (*Critical Notice of L. Wittgenstein's Tractatus Logico-Philosophicus*, *Mind* N.S. Vol. 32, No. 128, October 1923, 465–78), Elisabeth Anscombe (*An Introduction to Wittgenstein's Tractatus*, Hutchinson, 1959), Max Black (*A Companion to Wittgenstein's Tractatus*, Cambridge: Cambridge University Press, 1964), Norman Malcolm (*Ludwig Wittgenstein: A Memoir*, 2nd edn., Oxford: Oxford University Press, 1974), Peter Geach ("Saying and Showing in Frege and Wittgenstein"), David Pears (*The False Prison*, vol. 1, Oxford: Oxford University Press, 1987; and *Paradox and Platitude in Wittgenstein's Philosophy*, Oxford: Oxford University Press, 2006), Marie McGinn ("Between Metaphysics and Nonsense: Elucidation in Wittgenstein's *Tractatus*", *Philosophical Quarterly* 49, 1999 491–513), Peter Hacker ("Was He Trying to Whistle It?", in Alice Crary and Rupert Read, (eds.), *The New Wittgenstein*, London: Routledge, 2000), and Ian Proops ("The New Wittgenstein: A Critique", *European Journal of Philosophy* 9:3 2001, 375–404). For the Resolute Interpretation see Cora Diamond ("Throwing Away the Ladder: How to Read the *Tractatus*", *Philosophy* 56, 1981; reprinted in her *The Realistic Spirit*, Cambridge, MA: MIT Press, 1991), James Conant ("Must We Show What We Cannot Say", in R. Fleming and M. Paine, (eds.), *The Senses of Stanley Cavell*, Lewisburg, PA: Bucknell University Press, 1989), Thomas Ricketts ("Pictures, logic, and the limits of sense in Wittgenstein's *Tractatus*", in H. Sluga and D. Dunn, (eds.), *The Cambridge Companion to Wittgenstein*, Cambridge: Cambridge University Press, 1996, Warren Goldfarb ("Metaphysics and Nonsense: On Cora Diamond's *The Realistic Spirit*", *Journal of Philosophical Research* 22, 1997, 57–74), and Michael Kremer ("The Purpose of Tractarian Nonsense", *Nous* 35, 2001, 39–73).

[17] For a couple of especially thorough and compelling presentations of the case in favour of a standard reading see Peter Hacker, "Was He Trying to Whistle It?", and Ian Proops, "The New Wittgenstein: A Critique". For helpful resistance to my particular line on 'Wittgenstein's ladder', I am grateful for conversations with Thomas Ricketts and Meredith Williams.

3.7 SELF-CRITICISM

In the Preface to the *Philosophical Investigations* Wittgenstein says that he has come to recognize "grave mistakes" in his first book. What are these mistakes?

It is useful to divide his complaints about the *Tractatus* into three groups: first, those directed against presuppositions of the approach; second, objections to the integrated theory of reality, meaning, and language that he presented as satisfying those presuppositions; and third, the critique, arising from these objections, of his original metaphilosophical point of view.

As we have seen, the primary aim of the *Tractatus* was to specify systematically everything that could meaningfully be said, and this was done by characterizing a logico-semantic structure that any adequate language would allegedly have to have. Thus his project presupposed that

(T1)   Language has an essential nature.

However, it is argued in the *Investigations* (PI 18–21 and PI 65–116) that virtually any use of words, no matter how messy or impoverished, can be a language: the concept LANGUAGE, like the concept GAME, applies to a fuzzily circumscribed variety of activities that share no particular set of defining characteristics but merely bear certain *family resemblances* to one another.[18]

---

[18] ...someone might object to me: "You take the easy way out! You talk about all sorts of language-games, but have nowhere said what the essence of a language game, and hence of language, is: what is in common to all these activities, and what makes them into language or parts of language. So you let yourself off the very part of the investigation that once gave you yourself most headache, the part about the general form of propositions and of language."

And this is true.—Instead of producing something in common to all that we call language, I am saying that these phenomena have no one thing in common that makes us use the same word for all,—but that they are *related* to one

The specific form taken by Wittgenstein's early essentialism about language was governed by the idea that

(T2)   The central function of language is the description of reality.

Thus, according to the *Tractatus*, a simple sentence is descriptive by virtue of picturing a possible state of affairs and saying that this state of affairs is actual. But he points out in the *Investigations* (PI 23–27) that there are countless meaningful uses of language other than descriptions of facts: for example, ordering, speculating, story-telling, joking, thanking, and praying.— And there are no limits to the further uses of language that might evolve. So the *Tractatus* conception of language is dangerously over-simplified.

Turning now from the presuppositions of his approach to the substantive theories to which they led him: Wittgenstein maintained, as we have seen, that there is an absolute distinction between, on the one hand, the basic elements of reality ('objects') and on the other hand, complexes which are constructed in a definite way out of those elements. Given the required isomorphism between reality and any representationally adequate language, this bifurcation implies a corresponding absolute distinction amongst words between, on the one hand, primitive, indefinable terms ('names'), whose meanings consist simply in their reference to basic features of the world, and on the other hand, all other significant (non-logical) expressions, whose meanings are given by rules that specify, for each sentence containing them, a determinate synonymous sentence formulated in terms of the primitive and logical

another in many different ways. And it is because of this relationship, or these relationships, that we call them all "language". (PI 65)

For a clear and insightful discussion, see Michael Forster's "Wittgenstein on Family Resemblance Concepts" in A. Ahmed (ed.), *Wittgenstein's Philosophical Investigations: A Critical Guide*, Cambridge: Cambridge University Press, 2010.

vocabulary. However, in the *Investigations* Wittgenstein offers several interrelated criticisms of this theory.

In the first place he questions the assumption that the meaning of a word—what we know when we understand the word—is the entity for which it stands (PI 1–15). He turns his back on the idea that

> (T3)   The meaning of a word is its reference

remarking that such a view is natural only for a limited range of terms (e.g. names of people). Instead, he urges the idea that the meaning of a word is its *use*. A mastery of its use is what we must display in order to be said to understand a word, and it is what a definition (an explanation of its meaning) is attempting to impart.

In support of this transition, he reminds us that given a conception of meaning as naming, we will have to say that if some constituent of a sentence does not refer then the sentence does not correspond to any possible state of affairs and so does not say anything. That is,

> (T4)   An empty name is meaningless.

However, in the *Investigations* (PI 39–45) it is acknowledged that empty names may nonetheless have a function. Hence,

> When Mr. N.N. dies one says that the bearer of the name dies, not that the meaning dies. And it would be nonsensical to say that, for if the name ceased to have meaning it would make no sense to say "Mr. N.N. is dead." (PI 40)

More accurately, Wittgenstein's position on this issue is not that the *Tractatus* conception of meaning as reference is *false*, but rather that such models of language—models in which reference is emphasized—flatten out the diversity in word-use to the point that features of philosophical importance are disguised. (Just as "Big Ben" refers to Big Ben, so "five" refers to five.) Thus we can indeed say that someone who understands a language knows what its words stand for. However, such knowledge consists in a mastery of the use of words, and it is the similarities and differences in such patterns of usage that we must appreciate in order to deal with philosophical problems.[19]

Given this shift in perspective, another component of his earlier theory that Wittgenstein comes to abandon is the idea that

> (T5) Understanding a language involves operating a calculus according to definite rules.

In the *Tractatus* such rules are definitions, which determine the proper analysis of each sentence and thereby provide a precise specification of its truth conditions and inferential properties (without which the sentence would be meaningless). But in the *Investigations* (PI 65–88) he reminds us that language is full of indeterminacy: nearly all words are vague, their proper application often irremediably uncertain. Moreover, this is no defect (as the *Tractatus* strictures implied); for it does not detract from the use and usefulness of words, and so does not in the slightest interfere with the existence of *perfect* understanding. In fact, pervasive indeterminacy is only to be expected

[19] It is far from obvious that Wittgenstein came to fully *reject* his earlier view of what meaning is. On the contrary, he explicitly acknowledges that the word "meaning" is ambiguous: *Investigations* paragraph 43 defines meaning as use, but only

"For a large class of cases—though not all—in which we employ the word 'meaning'..." Clearly he is not saying—as is often wrongly supposed—that it is only the meanings of *some* words that may be identified with their uses. Rather, he is allowing that there are various cases in which, in speaking of a word's "meaning", we have in mind something else: for example, its referent, or its pragmatic force, or some concurrent intention. And this observation squares perfectly well with the *Tractatus* emphasis on meaning qua referent. Thus Wittgenstein's use conception of meaning does not contradict his *Tractatus* position. His change of view concerns not what meaning is, but which brand of meaning is philosophically important. For further discussion see Chapter 4 Section 2(E).

iven that languages evolve to help us engage with the phenomena we *actually* encounter, not all possible phenomena.

A related revision concerns the Tractarian view that

> (T6)   There is a set of basic entities from which all facts
>   are composed, and, correspondingly, a set of basic
>   words in terms of which all meaningful expres-
>   sions are defined.

Wittgenstein argues against the idea that the words of a language
(and the corresponding features of reality) divide objectively into
two distinct classes: the relatively few *primitive* elements, and the
majority that are *defined* in terms of (or *composed* from) those
primitives (PI 46–64). For, in the first place, he now sees that the
meaning-constituting use of a term will very rarely take the special form of a strict explicit definition. Thus nearly all words turn
out to be primitive; so the *Tractatus* theory can have almost no
explanatory bite. And in the second place, even when the uses of
terms *are* related in such a way that one can specify some in
terms of others, there may well be alternative ways of doing so,
and no objective fact of the matter as to which is correct. It may
well be possible to characterize the meaning of word "A" in terms
of the meanings "B", "C", and "D"; but this would not preclude
the possibility and occasional utility of explaining "B" in terms
of "A", "C", and "D". For in his view the construction of an
'appropriate' hierarchy of meanings/concepts will be substantially context-dependent: considerations of psychology (that is,
feeling of naturalness) and purpose will help to determine which
definition is most reasonable. Conclusion: there are no metaphysically fundamental ingredients of reality. And there is no absolute
and objective set of basic meanings.[20]

---

[20] Remember Nelson Goodman's observation that although *we* would
explain "grue" in terms of "green" and "blue" with a definition of the form "x is
grue = x is green and observed before time T or blue and not observed before
T", one could equally devise a definition of "green" in terms of "grue" and

In addition, Wittgenstein comes to think that he had mis-understood the nature of logic. In the *Tractatus* he held that

(T7)   Logic provides an *a priori*, metaphysically neces-sary structure for thought and for the world.

He characterized all the logical forms that may be generated from a certain stock of basic logical operations, and he main-tained that every significant sentence (and every fact) must reduce to something with one of those forms. As he later expressed that view:

> "Thought is surrounded by a halo. Its essence, logic, presents an order, in fact the *a priori* order of the world: that is the order of possibilities, which must be common to both world and thought. But this order, it seems, must be utterly simple. It is prior to all experience, must run through all experience; no empirical cloudiness or uncer-tainty can be allowed to affect it. It must rather be of the purest crystal. But this crystal does not appear as an abstraction; but as something concrete, indeed, as the most concrete, as it were the hardest thing there is. (*Trac-tatus Logico-Philosophicus*, No. 5.5563)" (PI 97)

His objection to this way of thinking is not so much that it's false, but that it's rhetorically overblown to the point of incom-prehensibility. For our certainty that all decent propositions must fall within the specified space of alternative forms arises from *stipulation*, rather than from the recognition of a deep feature of reality. Commenting on that attempt to draw the limits of language by a specification of all possible logical forms, he now says:

"bleen". And there could be creatures, very unlike us, who would find that alternative order of explanation perfectly natural. See Goodman's *Fact, Fiction, and Forecast*, 1955 (4th edition, Cambridge, MA: Harvard University Press, 1983, esp. pp. 74–81).

"(*Tractatus Logico-Philosophicaus*, 4.5): "The general form of propositions is: This is how things are." That is the kind of proposition that one repeats to oneself countless times. One thinks that one is tracing the outline of a thing's nature over and over again, and one is merely tracing round the frame through which we look at it". (PI 114)

And it is far from compulsory that this "frame" be *logical*. The feeling that there is something uniquely profound about logic is undermined by his across-the-board conception of meaning as use. For just as some convictions stem from our use of "and", "or", and "every", others stem from our use of other terms. Thus there is no characterization of what makes something a 'logical constant' that could justify attributing to these terms (or to the sentence structures that they define) a peculiarly sublime metaphysical status.

Finally, and correlated with the renunciation of his parallel accounts of language and reality, there is a small but momentous change in Wittgenstein's *meta*philosophical view. The *Tractatus* asserts that philosophical questions are provoked by confusion (rather than by ignorance, which is the source of *scientific* questions); that they therefore articulate pseudo-problems which can at best be eliminated, not solved; that, consequently, no philosophical explanations, theories, or discoveries are possible; and that the operative confusions originate in misunderstandings about language. Moreover, when he comes to specify the precise nature of these misunderstandings, he adds that

(T8)   Philosophical confusions arise because of the considerable distances between the superficial forms of certain propositions and their ultimate conceptual analyses in terms of fundamental primitives. This distance can be so great that we can easily fail to appreciate a statement's real meaning. And in the case of certain statements, we fail to appreciate their complete lack of meaning.

But there is an inconsistency between, on the one hand, his anti-theoretical view that philosophy can do no more than expose pseudo-questions for what they are, and on the other hand, the idea—embodied in the semantic and logical doctrines that, according to (T8), are needed for the diagnosis and treatment of such pseudo-questions—that one *can* legitimately produce philosophical theories of considerable intellectual value. Thus Wittgenstein prohibits philosophical theorizing on the basis of a philosophical theory!

What he has to do to resolve this incoherence, and what he *does* eventually do in the *Philosophical Investigations*, is to modify his earlier account of how philosophical confusion arises—retaining most of it, but abandoning the component that is responsible for the internal conflict: namely, thesis (T8). Thus Wittgenstein continues to hold that our puzzlement derives from illusions engendered by language; and so he continues to hold that philosophy cannot yield theoretical knowledge. But he comes to see that the precise source of our language-based misunderstanding is not the gap between superficial grammatical form and 'underlying logical form'—a notion he abandons—but is rather something with *no* theoretical presuppositions: namely, our tendency to insistently over-generalize. More specifically, he replaces (T8) with the idea that philosophical confusion resides in the tendency to stretch analogies in the uses of words, to be unnecessarily perplexed by the conceptual tensions that result, and to wrongly feel that an *a priori* theory of the phenomenon in question is needed to demystify it.

As we saw in Chapter 2, section 6, his later diagnosis is that the words in a certain small class are seen to function in many respects like the words in another more prominent class. However, there are crucial differences which we tend to overlook, and as a consequence we are inclined to raise improper (hence unanswerable) questions about the phenomena characterized by terms in the smaller class. We thereby fall into conceptual bewilderment; we are stymied by the paradoxical 'queerness' of these phenomena; and the cure appears to be one or another form of *a priori* account of them. But according to Wittgenstein, the peculiar puzzlement we feel is one from which no *theory*, properly so-called, can adequately deliver us. What is needed, rather, is a rooting out of its irrational sources. And this is the methodology he employs in the remainder of the *Investigations* as he proceeds to treat problems surrounding the concepts of meaning and experience.

3.8 CONCLUSION

To summarize: Wittgenstein maintained in the *Tractatus* that what is essential to language is its capacity to represent facts—a capacity deriving from rules that specify the truth conditions of each sentence as truth functions of elementary sentences whose constituents refer to absolutely basic ingredients of reality. However, he comes to think that this account is misconceived and vacuous. *Language* (like *game*) has no defining character, and it is misleading to focus on representation (i.e. description) to the neglect of other linguistic activities. Words indeed purport to refer to bits of reality; but it is in a mastery of their *use* that our understanding of them consists. And this form of meaning has no particular concern with indefinable primitives or simple 'objects', gives no special status to logic and its proprietary terms, and is happy with substantial realms of indeterminancy both in how we are *disposed* to apply our words and when it would be *correct* to apply them. As before, philosophical problems are said to derive from linguistic illusions—but these stem from mistaken analogies rather than missing analyses. Thus there is no longer any call for a theory articulating 'the essential structure of language and reality'— indeed, no room for *any* sort of philosophical theory.

4

Meaning

4.1 WITTGENSTEIN'S OBJECTIVES

Wittgenstein's treatment of meaning—one of the main topics of his *Investigations*—is important both in its own right and as a rich illustration of his singular approach to issues in philosophy. My primary goal so far has been to explain and defend that approach. I have shown how, in his view, philosophical problems originate in scientistic over-simplification—one is prone to insist upon exaggerated linguo-conceptual similarities and, as a consequence, falls into paradox and into a sense of the phenomena in question as peculiarly perplexing. And I have elaborated his idea that the only appropriate response to this sort of puzzlement is to expose the mistakes that provoked it—so that the upshot will be an absence of confusion rather than the establishment of theoretical knowledge. The purpose of the present chapter is to provide a reading, from this metaphilosophical perspective, of Wittgenstein's discussion of meaning and understanding.

Within that domain, the idea for which he is most famous is that the *meaning* of a word may be defined as its *use* in the language. It would be quite wrong, however, to think that the point of his discussion is to expound and support that opinion. For he would of course reject any suggestion that this identification qualifies as a genuine *theory*—hence, in need of *support*—rather than a mere definition, as trivial and obvious as the synonymy of "bachelor" and "unmarrried man". So it is hardly surprising that, although he reminds us of the usage of the word "meaning" that reveals our commitment to this definition, he offers no arguments in favour of it. —He takes it for granted from the very outset of his book and relies on it throughout.

The actual aims of Wittgenstein's treatment of meaning and understanding are twofold. In the first place he wants us to appreciate various defects in the theory of these phenomena that he himself had advanced in the *Tractatus*. These self-critical remarks—mostly located in paragraphs 1–100—continually invoke, as obvious, the intimate association between understanding a word and mastery of its use. And in the second place—mainly in paragraphs 138–242—he attempts to defuse a cluster of philosophical problems that emerge from reflections on meaning. These puzzles consist in the difficulty of reconciling the seductive idea of meaning as some sort of conscious mental phenomenon with its intimate relation to use. Thus, both components of his discussion of meaning *presuppose* the correctness of his famous definition of it.

Since Wittgenstein's earlier work and his subsequent objections to it were dealt with in the last chapter, I will not spend much time on that material here, but will focus rather on the second part of his discussion. I would like to show how well his elaboration and resolution of the problems that he addresses fit into the eight-stage metaphilosophical framework that was articulated in Chapter 2 (section 2.6). However because, as I have just mentioned, the conceptual tensions with which he is concerned only arise on the assumption that 'meaning = use', it is vital to appreciate from the start exactly what he has in mind by this equation. The point of the next section will be to make that relatively clear. We will then be able, in Section 4.3 (and guided by our eight-stage schema), to interpret the passages from 138 to 242 in which Wittgenstein addresses what he takes to be the central perplexities about meaning.

In the next chapter I will turn to an influential alternative construal of these passages: Kripke's 'skeptical interpretation'— according to which Wittgenstein's aim was to develop an argument to the effect that there are no 'genuine facts' as to what words mean. I will question the validity of this argument, and contrast it with Wittgenstein's own line of thought.

4.2 WITTGENSTEIN'S DEFINITION OF "MEANING" AS "USE"

The very first thing Wittgenstein does in his *Investigations* is to cast doubt on a tempting Augustinian view of meaning (which somewhat resembles his own earlier perspective in the *Tractatus*)[1]. This view is that almost all words are conventionally associated with observed aspects of reality, and that we learn a language by attending to the behaviour of its speakers and noticing which such associations have been established. But in fact, as he now recognizes, it is only a small subset of terms that are learned in roughly this way; and only within that narrow domain does the functioning of language depend on a perception-mediated, causal correlation between words and things (or properties). In most cases the deployment and utility of an expression may be fully explained without any mention of substantive word-world relations of that sort. But in *all* cases there is such a thing as 'knowing how and when to *use* a term'. *That* is what lies behind the term's deployment and provides the criterion for someone's understanding it.

Wittgenstein does not deny that words stand for (refer to, or signify) aspects of reality—even in discourse about numbers, values, possibilities, experiences, and so on. His central point, rather, is that this "signification" is determined by usage—even

---

[1] See Saint Augustine's *Confessions*, I viii 13.

when there is no conventional association between utterances of the word and observations of its referent. Thus our inscription "5" stands for the number 5 in virtue of how we operate with it in counting and calculation. There is no word-world causal correlation here—but there is disquotational reference nonetheless. Similarly, "pain" designates pain partly in virtue of our tendency to apply it to ourselves as an expressive alternative to grimacing, crying, jerking away, and so on, and not because we have *observed* a pain (see Chapter 6). Every word's purporting to refer to what it does consists in its being used in a distinctive way; but only for a few of them does that usage involve one or other form of causal association between the word and some object or type of object. As he puts it:

> Now what do the words of this language *signify*? What is supposed to show what they signify, if not the kind of use they have? (PI 10)

> For a large class of cases—though not for all—in which we employ the word 'meaning' it can be defined thus: the meaning of a word is its use in the language. (PI 43)

But exactly what does Wittgenstein have in mind here? Why the qualification: "For a large class of cases—though not for all..."? Precisely what does he mean by the "use" of a word? Is that supposed to be its *function*, or is it some *practice* with the word? Is he thinking of *norms* or *rules* of use, or mere *regularities* or *dispositions*? Might a word's use be described by specifying which *beliefs we intend to express* with its help? Moreover, no matter how these various matters are decided, his proposal surely is not going to be *generally accepted*; but in propounding a controversial hypothesis, is he not guilty of contravening his anti-theoretical metaphilosophy? In the remainder of this section I will offer brief answers to these questions and hope thereby to take us in the direction of a clear and plausible formulation of his use-conception of meaning.

(A) Constitution of meaning versus rearticulation of meaning

Often, the question "What is the meaning of such-and-such?" is a request for an explicit definition—for something along the lines of: the meaning of "bachelor" is UNMARRIED MAN. We answer by *rearticulating* the meaning, relying on a synonymous expression whose constituents are supposedly more fundamental than the word to be defined. So if that word is already basic—for example, "red"—we are at a loss for a decent response.

But paragraph 43 is not concerned with that sense of the question. It is concerned rather with the facts in virtue of which *any* given word (whether defined or indefinable) has the meaning it does—with the underlying characteristics that are responsible for its possessing that particular meaning. Thus Wittgenstein is addressing a problem about the constitution of a certain range of properties: namely, the various 'meaning-properties' that words can have. Just as one might ask what it is for something to be red, or to be magnetic, or to be true, and so on, in a similar spirit one can ask what it is for a word to mean RED, or for it to mean AND, or for it to mean ELECTRON. These are the questions that his remark is intended to answer—or at least to put us in a position to be able to answer. He is suggesting that each word's meaning what it does consists in certain facts about its use.

(B) Behavioristic versus semantic or intentional aspects of use

But what is supposed to qualify, in the present context, as the *use* of a given word? In particular, does Wittgenstein have in mind a tendency to *do* certain things with it, where this is characterized in behavioural terms perhaps (e.g. our disposition, in certain circumstances, to utter certain sentences containing it)? Or might the relevant use of a word be something that we need *semantic* concepts or *intentional* concepts in order to articulate (e.g. that the word is used to *refer* to dogs; or—*à la* Grice—that it is used with the *intention* of helping to communicate our *beliefs* about dogs)?

I want to advocate the first of these answers. This is the one that we would expect given that he is aiming to *fully* demystify the concept of meaning, and thereby to demystify what he takes to be the derivative and equally puzzling concepts of *reference*, *intention*, and *belief*. As he says in the *Blue Book* (pp. 4–6), he wants to explain how 'life' is given to signs that are otherwise 'dead'. And the 'life' of a sign surely includes its remarkable capacity both to reach into reality and to help express the contents of thoughts.

As already indicated, he adopts a *deflationary* view of the truth-theoretic notions. Note the trivial equivalence schema

$$\textbf{p} \text{ is true} = p \qquad \text{(where '}\textbf{p}\text{' stands for the proposition that } p)$$

which he endorses in PI 136—and which naturally extends, for predicative and nominal concepts, to

$$\textbf{f} \text{ is true of } x = f(x)$$

and

$$\textbf{n} \text{ refers to } x = n \text{ is } x$$

Thus the notion of truth—TRUTH—is explained in terms of that of PROPOSITION (i.e. sentence meaning), which will on pain of circularity have to be explained *independently* of TRUTH. Therefore, he cannot be supposing that the notion of proposition be analysed in terms of the notion of *truth* condition. Similarly, the concepts, IS TRUE OF (i.e. IS SATISFIED BY) and REFERS, are explained in terms of the concepts we have of predicate meanings and singular-term meanings. Therefore he cannot be thinking that those derive from concepts of satisfaction-condition and reference-condition.

Turning to the question of whether *intentional* psychological use-facts are supposed to be included amongst the meaning-constituting ones: our puzzlement about how a state of
belief or intention could have the content, say, *that I will scratch
my nose*, is no less than our puzzle ment about how the sentence "I will scratch my nose" could have that content. So it
would not be at all demystifying to explain the latter in terms
of the former. More helpfully, one might well go in the opposite explanatory direction and view contentful mental states as
relations to linguistic expressions whose meanings are independently explained in terms of their compositional structure
and the *uses* of their component words.[2]

So, given Wittgenstein's commitments and aspirations, it
would be incongruous for him to include within the "use" of a
word such properties as 'used to refer to so-and-so' or 'used to
express such-and-such beliefs'. Rather, the meaning-giving uses
of words must be restricted to *non*-semantic forms of use,
including physical, behavioural, and certain psychological
forms—for example, the internal acceptance of sentences.[3]

[2] Let me indicate why this is a plausible approach. Since meanings/contents
(including propositions) are immediately identified by the expressions used to
name them (e.g. the proposition *that dogs bark* = what is expressed by our sentence "dogs bark"), a relation to a given content is naturally analysed as a relation
to some expression that possesses the content (or that has the property responsible
for possessing it). So 'attitude' states—which are relations to contents—will be
explained in terms of relations to expressions with the appropriate contents (or
content-constituting properties). Thus one might say, following Fodor, that a
mental state qualifies as *believing that p* in virtue of its consisting in an internal
assent to (or 'holding true' of) some sentence whose meaning is *that p*. (See footnotes 4 and 5 for further discussion.) Or, accommodating those who cannot
stomach languages of thought, one might instead follow Sellars and say (to a first
approximation) that this belief is a matter of the state's tending, via compositional
laws, to provoke overt assent to such a sentence. In either case it will then remain
to explain how the sentence comes to mean what it does; and this is the point at
which Wittgenstein's use-conception can be invoked.
[3] Granted, we might well describe the use of a given word by relating it to
the uses of other words, *assuming that they have their normal meanings*. For

This interpretation is vindicated by Wittgenstein's *fairly* behaviouristic illustrations.[4] In the first paragraph of the *Investigations* he asks us to consider "the following use of language", and he tells us what is *done* with the word "five"—how it is *acted on*, how people *behave* with it (such as when counting out apples in a shop). And then he says "It is in this and similar ways that one operates with words", explaining that he has specified how the word "five" is used. Similarly, for all the primitive language games that he goes on to present—such as the one (described in paragraphs 2 and 8) in which a builder calls out "slab" (or "block", or "beam") then someone brings him a slab (or a block, or a beam). His examples of the meaning-constituting uses of words are never couched in semantic or intentional terms.[5]

example, we might say that "bachelor" means what it does by virtue of our being prepared to interchange it with the expression "unmarried man". And such accounts, as they stand, clearly violate the requirement that meaning-constituting usage be characterized in *non*-semantic terms. However, such violations are only temporary, since we can proceed to replace our references to the *meanings* of the terms in question by references to their *usage*. In particular, the use of some terms (such as "true" and "believes") will initially be given by relating them to "proposition" (as we understand it), which will in turn be related to "meaning" (as we understand it). But the definition of "meaning" as "use" will allow such temporary violations to be rectified. For further discussion see Chapter 5, footnote 16.

[4] Going perhaps beyond Wittgenstein, let me stress that (as suggested in footnote 2) his conception of word use—though it shouldn't be semantic or intentional—need not be *behaviouristic*. The linguistic activities that constitute meanings may take place within the mind, and not be outwardly expressed. In particular, these activities are likely to include 'internal assent' to *mental* sentences.

[5] It is sometimes maintained that the notion of *assent* is infected with intentionality—that the only way to distinguish assent (whether overt or internal) from other cases in which sentences are produced is to define it in terms of what those productions express: namely, *belief*. (I.e, "S assents to u" is defined as "S's production of u constitutes his believing the truth of the proposition expressed by u".) This view (amongst other considerations; see footnote 9 below) has led many commentators to suppose that Wittgenstein could not be aiming to explain meaning in entirely non-semantic terms. See, for example, Colin McGinn, *Wittgenstein on*

(C) Our way of using a word versus the point of so using it

When we speak, outside the context of language, about the *use* of a certain thing (such as a tool), we might be thinking of our *practice* with it—our *way*, or *method*, of using it. Or we could mean its *function*—the *point* or *utility* of it. So one might wonder, in the case of words, which of these two senses of "use" Wittgenstein intends.

Well, his text—for example, the above-mentioned paragraph 1—strongly suggests the former sense.[6] And that is not surprising. For it is hard to imagine a plausible account of meaning based on the latter interpretation. This is because there will generally be various alternative linguistic strategies for achieving one and the same goal; so the function of a word with a given meaning might have instead been performed by words with different meanings. For example, what is most useful about our truth predicate is that it enables us to formulate certain generalizations (e.g. "Everything of the form <pv-p> is true"). But this job might have been done by sentence-variables and quantifiers (allowing us to say "(p)(pv-p)").

Meaning, Oxford: Basil Blackwell, 1984; John McDowell, "Meaning and Intentionality in Wittgenstein's Later Philosophy", *Midwest Studies in Philosophy* XVII, 1992 40-52; Warren Goldfarb, "Wittgenstein on Understanding", *Midwest Studies in Philosophy* XVII, 1992 109-22; Barry Stroud, "Mind, Meaning and Practice", in his *Meaning, Understanding and Practice*, Oxford: Oxford University Press, 2000; and William Child, *Wittgenstein*, London: Routledge, 2011, pp. 101–4. But I find it hard to reconcile such a reading with Wittgenstein's many apparent efforts to characterize word-usage as non-semantically and non-intentionally as possible. Moreover, the philosophical plausibility of the approach that I am attributing to him can be defended against the above objection by explaining "internal assent" in terms of its *non-intentional* cognitive role: the sentences to which S internally assents are those deployed as premises in his reasoning (i.e. computations), and are the ground for his dispositions to *overtly* assert their vocal correlates. And with this account in place, 'attitude' phenomena (such as *believing that p*) are most naturally analysed in terms of meaning; so an explanation of meaning in terms of such phenomena would be unhelpful—indeed, perverse.

[6] And note PI 141, where what a person means by a word is identified with "the application which—**in the course of time**—he makes [of it]" (my emphasis).

Similarly, the function of "electron" is to help explain certain observable phenomena; but a different theory, whose terms would have had different meanings, might well have been proposed instead.

Wittgenstein certainly does emphasize the importance of being sensitive to the diverse functions of different words.[7] However, it is only supposed to be *how* a word is used, and not what it is *for*, that engenders its meaning.

(D) Triviality versus theory

Wittgenstein's definition of the meaning of a word as its use is not presented as a *theory*, properly so-called (as characterized in Chapter 2, Section 2.8). For it is supposed to do no more than record the evident fact that demonstrations of understanding reside in linguistic activity. We settle what someone means by a word by observing the way he uses it. We are convinced that a child has grasped what a word means when we see that her basic deployment of it is just like ours. We explain what a word means by describing how it is used—i.e., that such-and-such sentences containing it are accepted in such-and-such circumstances. These are obvious features of our practice (or of *one* of our practices) with the word "meaning", and Wittgenstein's definition is intended to do no more than register them.

This is not to deny that the equation of meaning with use may be found puzzling and questionable. But, for Wittgen-

---

[7] Awareness of a term's distinctive utility will make us less likely to exaggerate analogies between it and other terms, and thereby less prone to philosophical confusion. More specifically, although a word's meaning is not *constituted* by its utility, we might well, by attending to a word's utility, gain insight into which facts of use *do* constitute its meaning. For example, the above-mentioned idea that our truth-predicate serves as a device of generalization provokes the question of what particular method of deployment is neccessary and sufficient for it to perform that function—which leads, on reflection, to the conclusion that the basic (meaning-constituting) fact about our use of the word "true" is our underived acceptance of the schema, "<p> is true ↔ p".

stein, the controversial character of his claim does not betray it as the sort of philosophical *theory* that he opposes. Rather, such controversies are regarded as the result of confusions that lead us astray—lead us away from the definition of "meaning" that is plainly implicit in normal discourse, and towards various mistaken accounts of it. One such misbegotten account is the Augustinian–Tractarian view mentioned above. Other examples (as we will see in Section 4.3) derive from the tempting idea that what one means by a word is an introspected, guiding, mental state.[8]

Thus, although it may not *actually* be obvious to someone that 'meaning is use', it is *potentially* obvious; it is not hidden beneath the surface and credible only via a self-conscious inference to the best explanation; so its recognition does not qualify as a theory (explanation, conjecture, hypothesis) of the kind that we are supposed to be shunning.[9]

---

[8] Note that Wittgenstein's strategy is not simply to declare people confused just because they disagree with what *he* takes to be obvious. His criticism of proposals inconsistent with his definition must and can be supported by making their defects objectively plausible—for example, by showing that they have issued from the irrational methodology of T-philosophy (as discussed in Chapter 2 and in Section 4.3 below).

[9] McDowell (op. cit.) suggests that an analysis of "meaning" in terms of *non-semantic* facts of use is too theoretical a view to be reasonably attributed to Wittgenstein, since considerable evidence would be required to establish it. However, the sort of elucidation outlined here is all that is needed—and this involves nothing abductive or speculative. No doubt a fair amount of work must be done in order to defuse the various confusions that can prevent us from recognizing the correctness of Wittgenstein's definition. But that is not the same as providing evidence for a theory.

Granted his definition is a sort of *generalization*: it concerns *every* meaning. But definitions articulate psycho-linguistic propensities whose presence can be obvious. Moreover, Wittgenstein's objection is not to generalizations *per se*, but to an irrationally insistent attachment to them, a refusal to question them even in the face of counter-examples.

Granted also that if we wish to go beyond his superficial analysis of meaning as use, and seek to discover the particular meaning-constituting use-properties of particular words, then hard, empirical enquiry will be needed (as explained

(E) All words versus some

Let us now turn to the question of whether Wittgenstein intended his account to be completely general—applying to *all* words in *all* languages—or whether he thought that the meanings of only *certain* terms could be identified with their uses. The latter opinion might be read into the second part of paragraph 43:

> And the *meaning* of a name is sometimes explained by pointing to its *bearer*.

For he may seem to be suggesting that the meaning of a *name* is its *referent* rather than its use. But this would be a bad misunderstanding. What he is in fact saying here is merely that the meaning—that is, the use—of a name (in contrast with other words) is often best *conveyed* to someone by pointing to its bearer. That sort of ostention is often helpful in giving someone the ability to use a name. Moreover, the surrounding passages make it obvious that Wittgenstein takes his definition of meaning as use to apply to names, just as well as to other words. Remember his earlier remark (in PI 40) that if NN dies that does not make it meaningless to say "NN is dead".

But what about the explicit qualification with which paragraph 43 begins:

> For a large class of case—**though not for all**—in which we employ the word 'meaning' it can be defined thus: the meaning of a word is its use in the language. (My emphasis)

Is he not placing some restriction on the words to which the account is intended to apply? No, he is not. The intended

---

in sub-section (G) below, so the results will indeed be theoretical. But specific theses of that kind are not integral to Wittgenstein's conception. One could reasonably hold that their investigation belongs to linguistics rather than philosophy.

restriction is to a certain sense of "meaning", rather than to a certain subset of words. His point is that the term "meaning" is ambiguous. We sometimes use it to mean *referent*, sometimes *intended interpretation*, sometimes *implicature*—and in none of *these* senses does meaning amount to use.[10] But there is another very familiar sense of "meaning": namely, the literal semantic meaning of a word-type within a language—as when we say, for example, that the German "Wasser" has the same meaning as our "water", but not the same meaning as "H_2O". It is in this sense—which he takes to be the most fundamental of them—that the meaning of a word, *every* word, is its use.

(F) How a word ought to be used versus how it tends to be used

What is the normative or evaluative status of the features of use that, according to Wittgenstein, issue in the meanings of words? There would seem to be various choices. First, is he saying that a word's meaning is constituted by how it *should* be used—some fact of the form, 'We ought to use w in such-and-such a way'? Second, is he supposing, rather, that it is our *adoption* of some such norm—the fact that we *endorse* it—that provides the word with its meaning? And in either case, what would be the appropriate sense of "ought"? Would it be the one we deploy in maintaining "One ought not to believe what is false"; or the one involved in canons of justification, such as "One ought to believe simple theories that fit the evidence"; or is some further flavour of "ought" (*pragmatic*, perhaps) the relevant one? Third, maybe his idea is that meaning

---

[10] For example: "By 'Big Ben' the English mean the clock above their Parliament"; "By 'everyone' he meant 'everyone in the room'"; "In saying 'It is hot' he meant 'Open the window!'". These illustrate the ambiguity of the *English* word "meaning". However, in the case of Wittgenstein's own term, "Bedeutung", the main alternative to the sense in which it can be defined as "use" is the sense in which it means "referent".

a given thing by a word is a matter of *following imperatival rules* for its use ("Accept such-and-such sentences containing w!")? Or fourthly, could it be that the principles of use that Wittgenstein has in mind are mere regularities, or dispositions, or laws—wholly non-normative, non-regulative facts of linguistic activity?

It would be a mistake to suppose that we must pick just one from amongst this array of alternatives—for they are not mutually exclusive. Indeed, it seems probable that he has a number of them in mind. Most prominent, perhaps, is the third option. Analogies between languages and games are constantly cited by Wittgenstein, including the idea that words—like chess-pieces—are governed by rules. (Note his famous notion of 'language-game'.)

But what is it to follow such rules for the use of words? We do not, of course, proceed by first reading what the rules are (or by being told them, or by simply happening to have articulations of them explicitly in thought) and then deciding to do what they instruct us to do. For any such formulation would itself need to be understood; so there would need to be rules for understanding *its* words; and so on. Thus we would be confronted with an unsatisfiable regress. It must be, therefore, that the rules that provide our words with meaning are followed in some non-standard way that does not require any formulation of them to be engaged. In other words, there must be such a thing as following rules *implicitly*. But what is that?

This is a notoriously tough question. However, a good case can be made for the view, suggested by Wittgenstein, that rules are implicitly followed in virtue of a combination of (i) rough conformity with law-like regularities, and (ii) occasional self-correction:

> One learns a game by watching how others play. But we say that it is played according to such-and-such rules because an observer can read these rules off from the prac-

tice of the game—like a natural law governing the play.—
But how does the observer distinguish in this case between
players' mistakes and correct play? There are characteristic
signs of it in the players' behaviour. Think of the behaviour characteristic of correcting a slip of the tongue. It
would be possible to recognize that someone was doing so
even without knowing his language. (PI 54)[11]

And in paragraph 82 he allows that "the rule by which [a
speaker] proceeds" might be "The hypothesis that satisfactorily
describes the use of his words, which we observe". Thus, someone's meaning a certain thing by a word might consist in his
following a certain rule for its use, which might in turn be constituted (in large part) by his being disposed to operate with it
in a certain law-like way.

As for the *normative* import of all this, several distinct implications for 'what ought to be done' are fairly clear.

First, a person's following a rule incorporates his propensity to
correct himself, based (presumably) on his immediate reactions
of satisfaction or dissatisfaction to his initial inclination. Thus
we might well suppose that he manifests an "implicit *desire*" to
obey the rule—in which case it is natural for us to recognize a
self-interestedly pragmatic *reason* for him to do so. He *ought*
(other things being equal) to conform.[12]

---

[11] The prospect of *correction* is required to distinguish rule-following from
mere law-like regularity (as in the motion of the planets). We cannot, however,
simply identify the cases in which someone inadvertently deviates from the rule
he is implicitly following with cases in which he corrects himself (or has a disposition to do so)—because he may well tend not to notice certain cases of
non-compliance, and he may sometimes wrongly correct himself. Thus a person's rule cannot be straightforwardly read off his practice of self-correction.
Nonetheless, that practice is an important part of the empirical evidence that
can help us (in the way indicated in Chapter 5, Section 5.4) to reach plausible
conclusions as to which combination of ideal laws and occasional distorting
factors are influencing the person's activity.

[12] Like Wittgenstein (as I'm reading him), Hannah Ginsborg takes implicit
rule-following to derive in large part from a disposition to conform to the

Second, it is plausible that for the sake of smooth communication and its benefits, all the members of a community ought to follow the same basic rules of word use. So, if a word's communal meaning is constituted by the majority (or the 'experts') following a certain rule, then everyone else *ought* to follow that rule too.

And third, it is a *virtue* to pursue truth and avoid false belief. Therefore, the following of certain rules of use for a word will, in light of the meaning thereby constituted, imply the desirability of applying it to certain things and not others. For example, if following R(w)! constitutes w's meaning DOG, then anyone who follows R(w)! *ought* to desire to apply it only to dogs.

Thus the answer to the present question "Are Wittgenstein's meaning-constituting features of use supposed to be (i) normative facts, (ii) normative commitments, (iii) cases of imperatival (game-like) rule-following, or (iv) mere regularities?" is "More or less *all* of them".[13] We might reconstruct his picture as follows. At the bottom there are propensities to operate with words in one way or another;[14] these help constitute our implicitly follow-

corresponding regularity. But instead of supplementing this factor, as above, with 'occasional self-correction, based on feelings of satisfaction and dissatisfaction', her prosposed further requirement is (roughly) that a rule follower 'take each of his actions to be correct/appropriate". (See her "Primitive Normativity and Skepticism about Rules', *Journal of Philosophy*, 108 (5)(2011), 227–254). Possible misgivings about this suggestion are that it is introspectively unmotivated, over-intellectualized, and potentially regressive. However, Ginsborg might perhaps allow that her 'takings to be correct/appropriate' are merely occasional and merely implicit, and that the phenomena in which they are implicit could be feelings of satisfaction.—In which case her proposal would not be very different from ours.

[13] Only 'more or less', because the proper direction of explanation is not *from* the fact that one *ought* to do certain things with a word *to* its having a certain meaning, but the other way around.

[14] "...the meaning is the use we make of the word..." (PI 138).—That is, our *actual* use of the word, not the *correct* use or the use we *ought* to make of it!

ing the rules of our language game; and this activity of rule-following constitutes our words' meanings.[15] In light of the values of (i) desire satisfaction, (ii) smooth communication, and (iii) believing the truth, we can see that our meaning what we do has at least three kinds of normative import.[16] But according to this picture, meaning is not *intrinsically* normative—a word's meaning what it does is not *itself* an evaluative fact—but it does have a variety of evaluative implications.[17]

Pace Kripke (see Chapter 5), there is no suggestion that, in general, a word means F (such as DOG) in virtue of a propensity to apply it to fs (such as dogs).

[15] I myself am not convinced that it is always *via an intermediate level of rule-following* that regularities of word-use constitute meanings. For, as suggested above, I think we should leave room for the possibility that the contents of our propositional attitudes (our beliefs, desires, intentions, and so on) are carried by expressions within languages of thought, and that many of the computational, cognitive processes involving their component symbols are unconscious. But in that case, the sort of 'occasional self-correction' required to convert mere use-regularities into cases of rule-following would seem to be impossible. So one might well suspect that the meanings of such symbols are constituted by regularities alone, and that there would be no intermediate level of rule-following. For further discussion, see my "Regularities, Rules, Meanings, Truth Conditions, and Epistemic Norms", Chapter 7 of *Truth–Meaning–Reality*.

[16] Ginsborg ('Primitive Normativity') rightly calls attention to a further normative feature of rule-following. Not only, as just discussed, do we judge the actions of people as correct/appropriate or not *relative* to the rules we take them to be following; but, in addition we often make *absolute* judgements as to what is, or would be, correct/appropriate for them to do. In effect we are then assessing their rules themselves. Such judgements remain expressions of our own perspectives, of course. They issue from a sense of what we ourselves would have been inclined or disinclined to do in their circumstances. It seems to me that as long as Ginsborg's 'takings to be correct/appropriate' are merely *implicit* (as suggested in footnote 12 above) then her point is correct and provides a nice articulation of Wittgenstein's observation that some 'ways of going on' are natural for us (but not for all possible creatures) and others aren't.

[17] A common view of Wittgenstein is that he regarded meaning and rule-following as *constitutively* both normative and social, and that he could not therefore have accepted the sort of brutely causal/dispositional view that I am attributing to him. See, for example, John McDowell, "Wittgenstein on Following a Rule", *Synthese* 58, 1984, 325–63; Saul Kripke, *Wittgenstein on Rules and Private Language* (Oxford: Blackwell, 1982); and Meredith Williams, *Blind Obedience* (London: Routledge, 2010 (discussed in Chapter 2, footnote 30)). The allegedly social nature of meaning is examined in Chapter 5, Section 5.6.

(G) Core use versus overall use

Jerry Fodor and Ernie Lepore have objected to use-theories of meaning (including 'conceptual role semantics') on the grounds that they lead to an unacceptable form of 'holism'.[18] If the meaning of word, w, were identified with its use, they argue, then one's acceptance of even a single new sentence containing w—since that would amount to a slight change in the word's use—would have to be regarded as slightly altering its meaning; but what we mean is surely more stable (and more uniform across the community) than that!

In response, one might say that the 'use' of a word, in the intended sense, is not the same as its *overall* use; it is not made up of *every* particular deployment of the word; only certain special deployments (or *patterns* of deployment) are meaning-constituting.

But this response carries with it the obligation to specify how those special uses are to be demarcated. And many philosophers (under the influence of Quine's critique of the analytic/synthetic distinction) have come to think that this is an insoluble problem.

But Wittgenstein shows no sign of being troubled by it—and rightly so. For there is an intuitive and tolerably clear difference between the *basic* general rules of a practice and the host of specific applications of these rules. Roughly speaking, the difference is a matter of explanatory order: the applications *result* from following the rules. Thus one can tell which aspects of a word's use are meaning-constituting by identifying which aspects of its use suffice (given other factors) to explain the others.

For example, although we are inclined to accept both "A planet is a massive sphere that orbits a star" and "The Sun has eight planets", the meaning of the word "planet" seems to

---

[18] See J. Fodor and E. Lepore, *Holism: A Shopper's Guide*, Oxford: Blackwell, 1991.

involve the first of these inclinations but not the second. I am suggesting, on behalf of Wittgenstein, that this intuition can be accommodated by supposing that the meaning-constituting uses of a word are those that are explanatorily fundamental. In the present case, the first inclination is meaning-constituting because it helps explain everything else we do with the word "planet"—including our thinking "We have eight planets".

Of course, it is not uncommon for the meanings of words to evolve. We might find that a somewhat different meaning would be more useful. And exactly this happened to the word "planet" in 2006, when the XXVIth General Assembly of the International Astronomical Union voted to incorporate into the definition that a genuine planet be massive enough to have "cleared the neighbourhood of its orbit". The result—a rejection of what we used to accept (that "The Sun has *nine* planets")—was not an empirical discovery, but a mere by-product of our modifying the word's *basic* use.[19]

* * * * * * * *

Needless to say, these various suggestions about how best to develop a Wittgensteinian 'use conception' of meaning are mere indications of the directions in which one might well proceed. A great deal of further clarification is required.

Moreover, even in their present sketchy form the above ideas often go beyond what the *Investigations* says about meaning and use. However, it is reasonable for us to be guided not merely by the text, but by considerations of philosophical plausibility—by the attempt (in a spirit of charity) to articulate Wittgenstein's position in the most interesting and defensible way we can. And I have taken that liberty. Of course, if the

---

[19] For more detail see my *Meaning*, Oxford: Oxford University Press, 1998 (esp. Chapter 3), and *Reflections on Meaning*, Oxford: Oxford University Press, 2005 (esp. Chapter 2).

result is to be called "Wittgensteinian" it should not go *against* his explicit remarks. But as far as I can see, my proposals do no more than expand upon them.[20]

4.3 PARADOXES OF MEANING AND THEIR DISSOLUTION

Having fleshed out Wittgenstein's idea that the meaning of a word may be identified with its 'use', we are now ready to engage the main substance of his discussion of meaning and understanding, which occurs in paragraphs PI 138–242. For the problems he addresses in these sections consist in conflicts between that idea and a cluster of further things that we are easily seduced into thinking about meaning.

Wittgenstein's discussion here is a paradigm instance of the metaphilosophical framework described in Chapter 2 (Section 2.6): the schematic sequential analysis of problems in terms of (1) scientistic expectations, (2) linguistic analogies, (3) tempting generalizations, (4) linguistic idiosyncrasies, (5) conceptual tensions, (6) philosophical perplexity, (7) illegitimate theorizing, and (8) therapeutic dissolution. Therefore, by examining his remarks on meaning from the perspective of that framework, we can clarify both of these important aspects of his thought.

Case V: MEANING

Suggestive analogies and scientistic generalization

Our discourse with the words "meaning" and "understanding" is similar, in a variety of striking respects, to the way

---

[20] An early draft of this section appeared under the same title in Daniel Whiting (ed.), *The Later Wittgenstein on Language*, Basingstoke: Palgrave-Macmillan, 2009.

we speak of *mental* phenomena such as pains, colour sensations, and moods; and so we are inclined to suppose that someone's understanding a word in a certain way, his meaning a certain thing by it, is a matter of its occurrences (his hearing and saying it) being correlated with a characteristic conscious state of his mind—perhaps a certain mental image, or an interpretation, or a body of decisions about how the word is to be deployed. In which case, that associated mental state would be what is meant by the word, its meaning.

This assimilation of meanings to introspectable mental states is suggested by the following linguistic phenomena:

(a) Statements like "Those screams mean someone is badly hurt", "That glum look means he is sad", etc., purport to specify which states of mind are correlated with (and are indicated by) the screams, the *facial expression*, etc. Therefore, what is meant by the utterance of a word— a *verbal expression*—would also appear to be some inner feature of the person—perhaps an aspect of his conscious belief state—whose presence is indicated by that utterance.

(b) We are inclined to think that we become attentively *aware* of the meanings of utterances as and when they are produced: "...we understand the meaning of a word when we hear or say it: we grasp it in a flash" (PI 138). But what can strike us with such speed and immediacy other than an experiential event of which we are entirely conscious at a given time?

(c) What someone means by one of his words appears, like his sensations and conscious beliefs, to be something 'private'—that is, as directly known by him through introspection, but found out by other people only on the basis of his behaviour: "When I say that I understand...I am surely

not saying so because I have *found out* that up to now I
have applied the algebraic formula in such-and-such a way!
In my own case at all events I surely know that I mean
such-and-such..." (PI 147)

(d) We sometimes exclaim, "*Now* I understand!" (PI 151),
expressing a sudden dawning of what the speaker means—
a sudden 'sight' of the meaning that has been successfully
communicated from his mind to ours

(e) We think of ourselves as using a word *in light of* how we
understand it—as *guided* by our consciousness of its meaning—"The understanding itself is a state which is the source
of the correct use." (PI 146)

Thus there are various suggestive parallels between how we
think of instances of meaning and understanding, and how we
think of introspectable mental states.

Linguistic idiosyncrasy

But alongside these similarities there is a crucial difference. The
criterion we take to be ultimately decisive for settling what is
literally meant by a word-type within some community is its *use*
there—that is, how it is deployed. And the ultimate test for an
individual's way of understanding a word is his way of using it.
We do not in the end go by what speakers say (or think) they
mean by a term; rather, we go by what they *do* with it; we observe
how they *operate* with it. We do not care what sort of experience
(if any) is correlated with its being uttered or heard—whether,
for example, a certain word means CUBE has to do not at all with
whether it is accompanied by a certain mental image, but with
whether or not there is a certain practice of applying it and inferring with it:

> What is essential to see is that the same thing can come
> before our minds when we hear the word and the appli-

cation still be different. Has it the *same* meaning both
times? I think we shall say not. (PI 140)

Thus the meaning of a word is tied constitutively to its *use*.[21]

Conceptual tensions

The different conclusions induced by the analogies and the
disanalogy clash with one another. For the former suggest that
a meaning is a psychological entity (like a mental picture, or a
conscious conceptual analysis, or a set of private instructions);
but the latter requires that each meaning be linked to a certain
pattern of usage, of actual and potential applications. And
these demands seem impossible to reconcile. The tensions
highlighted by Wittgenstein take three interrelated forms.

In the first place there is a conflict (**I**) between the ideas

(i) that the meaning of a word is an introspectable mental
object

AND

(ii) that the use of a word is determined by its meaning

The problem is that the association of a word with some mental
presentation (such as the *image* of a cube) cannot guarantee its use
(for example, that it will be applied to what appear to be cubes):

> ... Can what we grasp *in a flash* accord with a use, fit or fail
> to fit it? And how can what is present to us in an instant,

---

[21] As Hans-Johann Glock puts it: "Words do not have linguistic meaning
intrinsically, as a matter of arcane factors accessible exclusively to scientists, but
only because speakers use and explain them in a certain way (see BB 27–8).
Therefore it is simply absurd to suggest that our term 'teddy-bear', for instance,
has a real meaning, and might, for all normal speakers know, refer to a type of
supernova." "Wittgenstein on Concepts", in A. Ahmed (ed.), *Wittgenstein's
Philosophical Investigations: A Critical Guide*, Cambridge: Cambridge University Press, 2010, p. 98.

> what comes before our mind in an instant, fit a *use?* ... The
> picture of the cube did indeed *suggest* a certain use to us,
> but it was possible for me to use it differently. (PI 139)

And it would not help to suppose that the meaning involves not
merely an image but also a method for its projection onto the
world. For such as system would be just another picture, itself
requiring a method of application. It would be tantamount to
an explicit rule-formulation, with which meanings would
already need to have been associated (yet there's no prospect of
an account of how that could have been done.)[22]

An important special case of this conceptual tension—
the clash between meanings as mental entities and meanings as determinants of use—arises when we consider what
is involved in following an explicitly formulated rule and
are tempted to suppose that our understanding of the formulation must consist in our giving it a certain *interpretation* (in the sense of an explicit articulation of what it
means). This is problematic; for such an interpretation is
nothing more than a reformulation 'written in the mind'—
a further string of symbols. Therefore, the usage that it
requires of us depends on how it in turn is interpreted, and
so on. In which case,

> ... how can a rule shew me what I have to do at *this* point?
> (PI 198)

---

[22] "Suppose, however, that not merely the picture of the cube, but also the
method of projection comes before our mind?—How am I to imagine this?—
Perhaps I see before me a schema shewing the method of projection: say a picture of two cubes connected by lines of projection.—But does this really get me
any further? Can't I now imagine different applications of this schema too?—
Well, yes, but then can't an *application come before my mind*?—It can: only we
need to get clearer about our application of *this* expression. Suppose I explain
various methods of projection to someone so that he may go on to apply them;
let us ask ourselves when we should say that *the* method that I intend comes
before his mind." (PI 141)

... our paradox: no course of action could be determined
by a rule ... (PI 201)

Thus we have a clash (**II**) between the following ideas:

(i) what a given rule has us do must depend on its interpretation, which must then depend on *its* interpretation, ... *ad
infinitum*—so no particular action can be determined;

AND

(ii) when we follow a rule, we feel we have no choice; it settles
what we do.

A third and somewhat different conceptual tension is articulated in the questions: How can the whole use of a word be
grasped in a flash? How can all the applications required by the
rules for its use be grasped in a flash?

> When someone says the word "cube" to me, for example,
> I know what it means. But can the whole use of the word
> come before my mind, when I understand it in this way?
> (PI 139)

How can one know, in a flash, what to do with a word—what
one would do—in a vast (perhaps infinite) range of circumstances. Surely one does not (indeed cannot) 'leap ahead' to
consider *all* of those circumstances and take a separate view, for
each one, about whether or not to apply the word in it! But
then understanding a term—which would surely have to incorporate all those decisions—would seem to be impossible. In
other words there is a conflict (**III**) between supposing

(i) that the state of knowing a word's meaning—the mental
act of grasping it—obtains wholly at a particular time;

AND

(ii) that this state incorporates decisions, regarding a huge
range of circumstances, about what is to be done with the
word in each of those circumstances.

Note that the tensions articulated in Paradoxes **I** and **II** derive from the fact that a mental concomitant cannot *determine* a use—however minimal that usage is imagined to be. But the present difficulty is that of seeing how a momentary state of understanding a word—even if it does *not* consist in its association with a mental *object* but is assumed to incorporate decisions about its use—could yield the vast body of usage that meanings do in fact determine. As Wittgenstein expresses the problem:

> ...when you gave the order +2 you meant that he was to write 1002 after 1000—and did you also mean that he should write 1868 after 1866, and 100036 after 100034, and so on—an infinite number of propositions? (PI 186)

Thus his third focus is on the tension between, on the one hand, the seductive idea that S's meaning F by w is a distinctive mental state, and on the other hand, our conviction that each such fact about S is conceptually tied to a vast number of characteristic potential utterances.

Notice that it is a *further* fact that, of these utterances, some would qualify as "correct" relative to the meaning at issue, and some incorrect. But the puzzle here is independent of such appraisals, and Wittgenstein shows no interest in them. Nor, as I see it, does he ever address the general question of how there could be an account of the distinct natures of different word-meanings that would explain their distinctive *correctness*-conditions, i.e. that would explain which predications would be *true*.

Here I am in stark disagreement with Kripke, who takes that general question to be Wittgenstein's predominant concern, and who interprets him as arguing, in light of it, that there can be no 'genuine' facts as to what words mean—not even dispositional facts. In Chapter 5 I will describe how I think Wittgenstein, given his deflationism about truth, would have responded to this further paradox, and explain why he wasn't bothered by it—why his attention was confined to the three interrelated conceptual tensions that I've just described.

Philosophical perplexity

These three paradoxes combine to produce in us the sense that meaning and understanding are extraordinary phenomena— unique, queer, and inexplicable:

> We are trying to get hold of the mental process of understanding which seems to be hidden behind those coarser and therefore more readily visible accompaniments. But we do not succeed; or, rather, it does not get as far as a real attempt. For even supposing that I had found something that happened in all those cases of understanding,— why should *it* be the understanding? And how can the process of understanding have been hidden, when I said "Now I understand" *because* I understood? And if I say it is hidden—then how do I know what I have to look for? I am in a muddle. (PI 153)

> Here I should first of all like to say: your idea was that that act of meaning the order had in its own way already traversed all those steps: that when you meant it your mind as it were flew ahead and took all the steps before you physically arrived at this or that one.

> Thus you were inclined to use such expressions as "The steps are *really* already taken, even before I take them in writing or orally or in thought. And it seemed as if this were in some *unique* way predetermined, anticipated—as only the act of meaning can anticipate reality." (PI 188)

> "It is as if we could grasp the whole use of the word in a flash." Like *what* e.g.?—Can't the use—in a certain sense—be grasped in a flash? And in *what* sense can it not?—The point is, that it is as if we could 'grasp it in a

flash' in yet another and much more direct sense than
that. (PI 191)

But I do not mean that what I do now (in grasping a
sense) determines the future *causally* and as a matter of
experience, but that in a queer way the use itself is in
some way present. (PI 195)

Thus meaning and understanding seem, on philosophical
reflection, to be intrinsically mysterious.[23]

Philosophical theories

These (and other[24]) assorted paradoxes, together with the puzzlement about meaning that they engender, have led philosophers
to a variety of *theoretical* reactions—including accounts of
meaning that are sceptical, revisionary, systematic, and
mysterianist.[25]

For example, the proper response, according to a sceptical
line of thought described by Kripke, is to conclude that there
are no facts as to what expressions mean. The idea in a nutshell
(see Chapter 5 Section 5.2 for details) is that, on the one hand,
a word's meaning would have to amount to mental instructions that guide our use of it; but on the other hand, such

---

[23] This retreat to the "occult", as McDowell puts it, is well described in
his "Are meaning, understanding, etc. definite states?", in A. Ahmed (ed.),
Wittgenstein's Philosophical Investigations: A Critical Guide, Cambridge: Cambridge University Press, 2010.

[24] There are many problems of meaning that are not discussed in detail by
Wittgenstein: for example, those relating to 'substitution into belief attribution'
(Frege, Mates, Kripke), compositionality (Davidson, Fodor), externalism
(Putnam, Burge), and pragmatics vs. semantics (Grice, Kaplan).

[25] See Chapter 2, Sections 2.3 and 2.5, for abstract characterizations and
criticisms of these forms of philosophical theory. Their various incarnations as
theories of *meaning* are much too numerous and complex to be dealt with here.
The following examples illustrate reactions merely to the limited set of problems raised by Wittgenstein. Other paradoxes of meaning will provoke quite
different theoretical responses within those four categories.

instructions could be understood only by means of further instructions, and so on—which would imply a vicious regress. So meanings cannot exist.

A less radical proposal—but still revisionary—is due to Quine. He responds to Wittgenstein's paradoxes by accepting that meanings cannot be mental entities and must somehow be matters of usage. But he holds that the relevant facts of use must be restricted to dispositions to assent and dissent, and draws the radical conclusion that only *observation* sentences have determinate meanings.

Turning from reformists to conservative theorists, there is no shortage of philosophers—such as Grice, Katz, Millikan, Brandom, and myself—who have (each in their own distinctive way) offered *a priori* systematizations of meaning-facts and their relations to both cognitive and linguistic activity.

And—of more interest to Wittgenstein, as we have just seen—there are reactions, such as Brentano's, that would transmute our puzzlement over how the mind can engage meanings into a mysterian theory whose central thesis is the queer uniqueness and inexplicability of this phenomenon.

Therapeutic dissolution

But in Wittgenstein's view, such theoretical responses to our puzzlement are irrational. What we should be doing, rather, is trying to expose and remove the various language-based confusions that engendered it:

> The criteria we accept for "fitting", "being able to", "understanding" are much more complicated than might appear at first sight. That is, the game with these words, their employment in the linguistic intercourse that is carried out by their means, is more involved—the role of these words in our language other—than we are tempted to think. (This role is what

we need to understand in order to resolve philosophical paradoxes...) (PI 182)

More specifically, we must come to see that the above-noted linguistic analogies—(a) through (e) on pp. 125–6—that were taken to show that meanings are objects of introspection, do not really justify that conclusion:

(a*) True, a person's behaviour can reveal his state of mind. In particular, his uttering a certain thing can indicate (i.e. in one sense, 'mean') that he has a certain belief. But it is not implausible that a belief-state is itself nothing more than a disposition to rely internally on a sentence expressing a given abstract proposition—'meaning' it, but in a *different* sense.[26] And we have no reason to think that what is meant, in this second sense, is a mental concomitant.

(b*) True, a person's understanding appears to be an inner activity of tracking the sequence of words-*meanings* spoken to him. But it might be that the aspect of this activity of which he is sometimes aware is merely his mentally representing/encoding the *words* he hears. Of course, those words (or their encodings) must also be understood. But we have no reason to conclude that this further requirement consists in an association with further mental objects.

(c*) True, we often take a person to be a special authority on what he means. But that is because he can decide, up to a point, how his thoughts are to be expressed—e.g. whether to express them fully or only elliptically, whether to express them literally or metaphorically, and so on. And, granted, we are typically much less reliable as to the

---

[26] Some support for this idea was offered in Section 4.2(B) of the present chapter.

speaker's intentions than he is. However, it may well be that the thoughts themselves consist in mental sentences. And the literal meanings of such sentences could not (on pain of regress) be a matter of the speaker's intentions. So they would not be something that he can judge any better than we can.

(d*) True, an awareness of what someone means can suddenly dawn. But—as in (c*)—that is typically a matter of recognizing the idiosyncratic *intentions* behind his utterance, rather than its literal meaning. When it is the literal meaning that dawns, this tends to be because the sentence is unusually complex and because one suddenly hits on a way of parsing it. Thus a palpable tension of incomprehension is suddenly relieved. But in normal communication there are no such difficulties, and no conscious experiences are associated with understanding.

(e*) True, it is not unnatural to think of our usage of words as being *guided* by our understanding of them. But (as we shall see in detail in Chapter 5) *feelings* of guidance are not often present; and, even when they are present, they should not be taken to imply the existence of a straightforwardly guiding mental entity—an inner instruction.

Thus the analogies between meaning-discourse and sensation-discourse do not run very deep. It is not in the end reasonable to expect there to be an introspectable object or state associated with a word and necessarily correlated with that word's being used in a certain way. Therefore, it should be unsurprising that no such object or state can normally be discerned by introspection. Evidently, we often deploy the word "cube" with no mental image (nor any other characteristic experience) to help us; evidently, uses of a word may be associated with an image of cube, and yet not mean CUBE.

Therefore Paradox **I**—the clash between (i) meanings as mental entities (such as images) and (ii) meanings as determinants of use—can be resolved by rejecting its first component:

> Try not to think of understanding as a mental process at all.—For that is the expression which confuses you. But ask yourself: in what sort of case, in what kind of circumstances, do we say, "Now I know how to go on", when, that is, the formula has occurred to me?—
>
> In the sense in which there are processes (including mental processes) which are characteristic of understanding, understanding is not a mental process.
>
> (A pain's growing more and less; the hearing of a tune or a sentence: these are mental processes.) (PI 154)

And note the final remark in Part I of the *Investigations*:

> And nothing is more wrong-headed than calling meaning a mental activity! Unless, that is, one is setting out to produce confusion. (It would also be possible to speak of an activity of butter when it rises in price, and if no problems are produced by this it is harmless.) (PI 693)

Turning to the intimately related Paradox **II**—the impression that no rule can specify what is to be done because that would depend on which interpretation it is given—this tension arises because if a meaning is to be a mental object capable of guiding our behaviour, we are tempted to suppose that it must amount to a set of mental instructions. Thus, on the one hand, we assume that in order to follow a rule we must first interpret it—that is, translate it into more basic, more immediately intelligible terms—but on the other hand, that assumption would lead to an infinite regress of reformulations—which would imply that no rule could ever determine our behaviour.

The solution is, first, to remind oneself (as above) of the limitations of the analogy between states of understanding and mental states; and second, to appreciate that some (indeed most) rules are followed without being interpreted. This is not, of course, to say that no meanings are given to them. It is to say that our understanding of them—our giving them meaning—consists in our simply responding to the words as we have been shown and taught:

> "But how can a rule shew me what I have to do at *this* point? Whatever I do is, on some interpretation, in accord with the rule."—This is not what we ought to say, but rather: any interpretations still hangs in the air along with what it interprets, and cannot give it any support. Interpretations by themselves do not determine meanings.
>
> "Then can whatever I do be brought into accord with the rule?"—Let me ask this: what has the expression of a rule—say a sign-post—got to do with my actions? What sort of connexion is there here?—Well, perhaps this one: I have been trained to react to this sign in a particular way, and now I do so react to it.
>
> But that is only to give a causal connexion; to tell how it has come about that we now go by the sign-post; not what going-by-the-sign really consists in.[27] On the contrary; I have further indicated that a person goes by a sign-post only in so far as there exists a regular use of sign-posts, a custom. (PI 198)
>
> What this [paradox] shews is that there is a way of grasping a rule which is *not an interpretation*, but which is exhibited in what we call "obeying the rule" and "going against it" in actual cases. (PI 201)

[27] As is confirmed by the immediately following response ("On the contrary..."), this objection pretty clearly comes from Wittgenstein's interlocutor, and really belongs in quotation marks.

In other words, the result of someone's genetic nature and education is that when he is given a certain instruction he simply acts in a certain way. He does not typically respond by first putting some interpretation on the instruction—that is, reformulating it to himself—and only then acting accordingly. Such an intermediate step is neither possible (in general) nor necessary:

> How can he *know* how he is to continue a pattern by himself—whatever instruction you give him?—Well, how do I know?—If that means "Have I reasons?" the answer is: my reasons will soon give out. And in the end I shall act, without reasons. (PI 211)

> When I obey a rule I do not choose.
> I obey the rule blindly. (PI 219)

Note that the rules that Wittgenstein is talking about here are followed on the basis of *explicit formulations* of them. And in maintaining that we obey them "blindly" he is surely implying not merely that we do not obey via *re*formulations of them in more basic terms, but also that we do not obey via *articulations* of the various rules of use that govern the various words involved in their formulation. Instead, we simply act. Our actions are, of course, mediated by our understanding of those words; they derive from our following the rules which govern them. But these rules are not *explicitly formulated*. Rather, our following them is *implicit* (as discussed in Section 4.2(F) above): constituted by the tendency for our linguistic activity to fit certain simple regularities.[28]

---

[28] Paul Boghossian (in "Epistemic Rules", *Journal of Philosophy*, 109 2008, 472–500) proposes that Wittgenstein's concern about "needing a rule to interpret a rule"—which I have interpreted as Paradox II—in fact concerns a quite different paradox, as follows. It would seem that any rule-governed action is the result of an *inference* whose premises are: (i) some general rule of the form, "In circumstances of type C, perform an action of type A!"; and (ii) the agent's belief that the rule's antecedent condition is satisfied—that is, that "The present circumstances *are* of type C". But it would also seem that inference is always a

As for Paradox **III**—"How can we, all at once, grasp the enormously many components of a word's entire use?"—its dissolution rests on the distinction between (as we now might put it) *explicit* and *implicit* cognitive states. Our knowledge of how far it is to the sun, of where Buckingham Palace is to be found, and of which President of the US preceded Bill Clinton, is explicit: we articulate these beliefs to ourselves; we formulate them in some language. But not everything one calls "knowledge" has this character. For instance, someone who knows how to ride a bicycle knows, when it tilts to one

---

matter of following rules. In particular, the inference from (i) to (ii) must be rule-governed. So it must itself be the product of inference. So we are faced with a vicious infinite regress!

However, although it may well be that this problem was at the back of Wittgenstein's mind, I think that the evidence for its being his main concern about rule-following is rather slim. For one thing, he never articulates it—whereas Paradox **II** and his response to it are quite explicit. And, for another thing, the passage from which Boghossian draws his interpretation need not be read in the way he suggests. He observes that, in PI 219, after an interlocutor says "'All the steps are already taken' means: I no longer have any choice. The rule, once stamped with a particular meaning, trace the lines along which it is to be followed through the whole of space", Wittgenstein replies "But if something of this sort really were the case, how would it help?" It would not help, according to Boghossian's Wittgenstein, because (if the regress is to be averted) one could not invariably use inference to get from a meaning-stamped rule to the dictated action. But we might suppose instead that what is said by Wittgenstein to be unhelpful is merely the image of the rule "trac[ing] the lines along which it is to be followed through the whole of space". This alternative would explain why Wittgenstein goes on to remark that that "only makes sense if it was to be understood symbolically. I should have said: *This is how it strikes me.*"

Finally, the solution (to his attributed paradox) that Boghossian attributes to Wittgenstein is that the state of accepting a rule cannot always be an explicit propositional attitude—such as an explicit (though perhaps merely internal) intention to always do A in C. This, supposedly, is the respect in which sometimes—as Wittgenstein puts it later in PI 219—"I obey the rule *blindly*". But again it seems to me that the evidence allows a perfectly plausible alternative interpretation.—As I noted in the text, Wittgenstein's discussion here appears to be focused on *formulated* rules—on cases in which there *is* an explicit propositional attitude—and he is saying that actions deriving from these states are typically "blind". So he must be prepared to acknowledge that *either* such a state engenders the dictated action *non-*inferentially *or*, if there is an inference, it is not the result of following a rule.

side by a certain angle, how to turn the handle-bars and shift weight in order to avoid falling. But this knowledge does not appear to be articulated; the rider does not appear to think it to himself in some language. The situation, rather, is that, as a result of training and practice he becomes disposed to react to a large variety of tilts of the bicycle with a variety of appropriate twists of the handle-bars and shifts of weight. And we regard this as a kind of knowledge. But in order to distinguish it from the more standard kind—which *is* articulated in a language—we might call it "implicit knowledge". This corresponds, of course, to the familiar distinction between 'knowing *that*' and 'knowing *how*'. So one might put the point by saying that certain special cases in which we ordinarily speak of 'knowing that p' really consist in knowing *how* to do something; and these cases might well be marked by calling them instances of '*implicitly* knowing that p'. An example is our so-called knowledge of the (syntactic) rules of grammar of our spoken language. We non-linguists cannot say what they are. Nor could psychoanalysis bring them to consciousness. Rather, our knowledge of them is implicit— implicit in the fact that certain psycho-linguistic laws are what determine the sentence structures with which we are able to engage.

According to Wittgenstein, our knowledge of what a word-type literally means—that is, our knowledge of how to use it—is similarly implicit. It consists in our disposition to do a certain variety of things with it in a certain variety of circumstances: for example, to respond to the order "Add 2" by writing 1004 after 1002, and so on. Therefore, there should be no puzzle about how the state of understanding a word—our grasping its meaning—can determine all these hypothetical actions. For that state is nothing more or less than the propensity to perform those actions. This becomes puzzling only if one forgets that the knowledge involved in understanding a word is merely implicit. For it would indeed be impossible to see how one might 'in a flash' *explicitly* think of all the things one is going to do.

> "But I already knew, at the time when I gave the order, that he ought to write 1002 after 1000."—Certainly; and you can also say that you *meant* it then; only you should not let yourself be misled by the grammar of the words "know" and "mean". For you do not want to say that you thought of the step from 1000 to 1002 at that time— and even if you did think of this step, still you did not think of other ones. When you said "I already knew at the time..." that meant something like: "If I had been asked what number should be written after 1000, I should have replied '1002'." And that I do not doubt. This assumption is rather of the same kind as: "If he had fallen into the water then, I should have jumped after him." (PI 187)

Thus Wittgenstein's view, quite clearly, is that the meaning consists in the disposition. And this idea, taken to be obvious, is immediately contrasted with the following seductive mis-impression of the extraordinary powers of meaning.—He ends the above paragraph by asking 'Now what was wrong with your idea?', and immediately answers that we were wrongly tempted to imagine meaning as something *extraordinary*—as a weird, mental 'leaping ahead':

> ...you were inclined to use such expressions as: "The steps are *really* already taken, even before I take them in writing or orally or in thought." And it seemed as if they were in some unique way predetermined, anticipated— as only the act of meaning can anticipate reality. (PI 188)

> "But I do not mean that what I do now (in grasping a sense) determines the future *causally* and as a matter of experience, but that in a *queer* way the use itself is in

some sense present."—But of course it is, 'in *some* sense'! Really the only thing wrong with what you say is the expression "in a queer way". The rest is all right; and the sentence only seems queer when one imagines a different language-game for it from the one in which we actually use it. (PI 195)

In our failure to understand our use of a word we take it as the expression of a queer *process*. (As we think of time as a queer medium, of the mind as a queer kind of being.) (PI 196)

"It is as if we could grasp the whole use of a word in a flash."—And that is just what we say we do. That is to say: we sometimes describe what we do in these words. But there is nothing astonishing, nothing queer about what happens. It becomes queer only when we are lead to think that the future development must in some way already be present in the act of grasping the use and yet is not present. (PI 197)

His point is that we have to be careful when we think of all the potential uses of a term as 'known' to us. This phenomenon will wrongly seem to be astonishing if we loose sight of the fact that the so-called knowledge here—unlike more familiar cases—is *not explicitly articulated* (either in public language or in thought), but is constituted, rather, by the laws governing that term's deployment.

The upshot, for Wittgenstein, of his treatment of such conceptual minefields is that meaning and understanding are not at all mysterious. Our confusions are exposed, the paradoxes they engendered dissolved, and our puzzlement removed. We are now able to see, as entirely obvious and unproblematic, that the meaning of each word consists in our basic propensities concerning its use.

> ... How does it come about that this arrow ⟫⟶ *points*? Doesn't it seem to carry in it something besides itself?—

"No, not the dead line on paper; only the psychical thing, the meaning, can do that."—That is both true and false. The arrow points only in the application that a living being makes of it.

This pointing is *not* a hocus-pocus which can be performed only by the soul. (PI 454)

5

Kripke's Wittgenstein

5.1 A SCEPTICAL ACCOUNT OF MEANING

Inspired by Wittgenstein's discussion of meaning in paragraphs 138–242 of the *Philosophical Investigations*, Saul Kripke has devised a sceptical line of argument that is very different from the purely therapeutic preoccupation I have just been reading into those passages, and in the present chapter I want to examine that alternative.[1] My focus will be on the *philosophical* plausibility of its central contentions. But this appraisal—since it comes from the Wittgensteinian perspective described in Chapter 4—will also reveal the substantial extent to which Kripke's Wittgenstein diverges from Wittgenstein himself.

Kripke's train of thought consists in a paradox, a solution to it, and an implication of that solution.[2] The paradox is an argument for a striking "sceptical thesis": namely, that there are no 'genuine' facts as to what people mean by their words. The proposed solution is to show not that the paradoxical argument is mistaken, but that its conclusion is not really counter-intuitive

---

[1] See S. Kripke, *Wittgenstein on Rules and Private Language*, Oxford: Blackwell, 1982. (Page references are to this book.) Some of his textual evidence is drawn from elsewhere in the *Investigations*, and some from Wittgenstein's *Remarks on the Foundations of Mathematics*.

[2] For convenience I will speak of this account of meaning as Kripke's, even though he credits Wittgenstein with its main elements and does not himself fully endorse it.

after all, for nothing in our ordinary practice of attributing meanings is threatened by accepting it. And a corollary of this solution is supposed to be that there can be no such thing as a 'private language'—i.e. that language is essentially *social*.

In order to establish that there are no 'genuine' meaning-facts, Kripke considers each ontological category to which, if there were such facts, they might with some plausibility belong—that is, the physical/behavioural, the mental, or the irreducibly semantic—and attempts to show, case by case, how none of these species of fact would do. (We shall return later to the question of what it takes for a fact to be 'genuine'; but for now it suffices to assume that any facts within these three categories would qualify.)

Against the idea that meanings are conscious mental entities—for example, that to mean CUBE by a word is to associate it with a mental image of a cube—Kripke mentions some of the Wittgensteinian considerations that I outlined in Chapter 4, Section 4.3: including that no fact of that sort could guarantee the pattern of deployment that we take to be indicative of a given word (such as "cube") meaning what it does. But his key objection (pp. 41–5) is that no such fact could explain which particular applications of the word would be *correct*. Similarly, against the idea that meaning-facts are irreducibly semantic Kripke says that the distinctive (infinitary) truth-theoretic and normative implications of different meanings would, on this account, be left mysteriously inexplicable (pp. 51–4). But the initially most promising view of the underlying nature of meaning-facts is the physical/behavioural option—more specifically, that they derive in some way from how we are disposed to use our words. This is the position that Kripke spends most of his time combating; and his objections to it, although at bottom the same as those he makes to the other two candidates, are developed in much greater detail. So this is the part of his discussion on which I will be concentrating.

It is worth emphasizing that although many interpreters (including myself in Chapter 4) would say that Wittgenstein's equation of meaning with 'use' (construed non-semantically) is the taken-to-be-obvious centrepiece of his view of the matter, according to Kripke's interpretation the centrepiece is his *criticism* of that equation!

5.2 THE RATIONAL-GUIDANCE ARGUMENT

Kripke marshals two principal arguments against the idea that to attach a given meaning to a word is to have a propensity to use it in a particular way (that is, to apply it in certain contexts and not in others). The first one may be formulated as follows:

1. Meaning a certain thing by a word is a matter of following certain rules for its use.
2. *Rational-Guidance Requirement*: If someone's following a certain rule were to be constituted by a certain underlying fact about him, then that fact would have to be capable of accounting for his being rationally guided by the rule: more specifically, it would have to somehow incorporate *instructions* which tell him what he ought to do and provide him with a *reason* for acting in that way.
3. But use-dispositions are knee-jerk reactions, and can neither involve, nor engender, any such instructions or rational guidance.
4. Therefore, following a certain rule for the use of a word (hence meaning something by it) cannot be constituted from dispositions with respect to its use.[3]

---

[3] This argument is a rendering of Kripke's remarks on pp. 11 and 22–4. One might instead read him as taking a shorter route to the conclusion—one that dispenses with premise (1) and that modifies the Rational-Guidance Require-

Even if it is conceded that the reasoning here is valid, and that premises 1 and 3 are correct, this argument would nonetheless fail; and that is because, given these concessions, premise 2 (the Rational-Guidance Requirement) could not be right.

One may grant that *explicit* rule-following involves guidance of the sort proposed. For in such cases the rules are *articulated*, we *understand* them, and they give us a statable, supporting *rationale* for acting as we do. But in so far as premiss 1 is correct—in so far as there is a kind of rule-following for the use of words that constitutes our *understanding* them—then *that* kind of rule-following cannot generally be explicit; it cannot always be a matter of understanding and respecting certain articulated instructions. For the need to account for our understanding of these instructions (and then of the further instructions behind that understanding, and so on) would lead to an unimplementable infinite regress.[4] Therefore the rule-following involved in our meaning what we do must be merely *implicit*. It cannot contain formulations and guidance of the kind familiar from explicit rule-following. Instead— and as Wittgenstein himself suggests—it may amount to

---

ment so that it begins, "If someone's *meaning some given thing by a word* were to be constituted by a certain underlying fact about him...etc.," and that later substitutes "meaning" for "rule". But the reading I have given has the virtue of integrating Kripke's evident view that rule-following and meaning are intimately related, and that the same sceptical paradox afflicts them both.

[4] I am allowing here that the instructions for how to use basic natural-language words might be formulated in a *language of thought*. But how could the instructions governing *its* basic terms be formulated? In a more fundamental language of thought? But what then?!

As for the version of Kripke's argument (mentioned in footnote 3) that skips rule-following and hinges on Rational Guidance by *meaning*, the parallel regress problem is that the meanings of the guiding instructions would need to be explained, and so on.

Note that, *pace* Crispin Wright's intention-based view of rule-following (in, for example, his *Rails to Infinity*, Cambridge, MA: 2001), intentions are in the same boat as instructions: in so far as they are explicitly formulated in thought, our understanding of such formulations will call for more basic intentions, and so on.

nothing more than (i) propensities to conform to regularities of word-use, conjoined with (ii) feelings of satisfaction or discontent that lead to occasional self-correction.[5] Therefore, as it stands, the Rational-Guidance Requirement must be rejected. So Kripke's first argument against dispositionalism is not successful.

But perhaps there is a better argument in the vicinity of that critique—one that does not rely on the implausibly strong requirement that rules must provide *explicit* guidance. Perhaps it suffices to insist that any decent analysis of 'following a rule' be able to explain why such activities provide *reasons* for conformity, and then to argue—still invoking premiss (3)—that no purely dispositional account could meet that weaker condition.

And this, perhaps, is how Kripke himself should be read. According to Alex Miller, Kripke has a nuanced double-barrelled position: first, that *from the perspective of the naïve assumption that there are individualistic 'genuine' facts as to which rules a person is following*, his reason to conform with them would indeed require *explicit* guidance, which (as we've seen) could not be constituted from dispositions; and second, that the *normative* import of rule-following can nonetheless be accommodated (as just suggested), but only by abandoning that naïve assumption and invoking a guiding and correcting *community* of speakers.[6]

However, it is not at all clear that any backing away from the naïve assumption is really needed in order to see how implicit rule-following engenders *reasons*. For the above-mentioned Wittgensteinian analysis of this phenomenon invokes *self*-correction-

---

[5] Wittgenstein's conception of 'implicit rule-following' was discussed in Chapter 4, Sections 4.2(F) and 4.3. See also various remarks below (esp. in footnotes 19 and 26 and in Section 5.7).

[6] See Miller, "Horwich, Meaning, and Kripke's Wittgenstein", *The Philosophical Quarterly*, 50:199, April 2000, 161–74.

behaviour, which can be regarded as manifesting the rule-follower's implicit *desire* to conform. Thus, despite being fully 'factualist' and 'individualistic', that analysis provides a perfectly natural explanation of why we regard it as (in some sense) "wrong" for someone to fail to obey the rules he is following. So it seems to me that Miller's reading of Kripke's first objection does no better than mine at leaving him with an effective argument.

5.3 THE TRUTH ARGUMENT

Kripke's second argument against the dispositional view of meaning attempts to demonstrate its inability to explain how words come to have the particular referents (or extensions) that they do. As I reconstruct it, his reasoning proceeds as follows:[7]

(1) *Explanation-of-Truth Requirement:* If a word has *meaning*-engendering properties they must account for its *correct* use. In particular, the underlying facts constituting a predicate's meaning F must explain why it is true of all and only the things that are f.[8]

(2) Therefore, S's meaning F by predicate w may be analysed *a priori* in terms of S's *use* of w only if it is possible to infer (read off) from that usage that $(x)(w$ is true of $x \leftrightarrow fx)$.

(3) This requires an analysis of (or at least a sufficient condition for satisfaction of) 'S's w is true of $x \leftrightarrow fx$' in terms of how S applies w. But there are possible circumstances in which S would mistakenly apply w to certain things that

---

[7] The steps below are not intended to offer a paraphrase of Kripke's exposition (pp. 22–32), but to bring out what I take to be its underlying argumentative structure.

[8] For example: the fact constituting S's meaning DOG by the word, w, must explain why S's w is true of all and only dogs. Note that, in line with the convention followed in earlier chapters, "DOG" is stipulated to name the meaning of the word "dog".

are *not* f, and circumstances in which he would fail to apply w (indeed deny its application) to certain things that *are* f. So the needed analysis will have to incorporate some way of filtering out such incorrect uses. It will have to speak of 'how S would apply w *in epistemiologically ideal conditions*'.[9]

(4) In sum: S's meaning F by word w could be *a priori* constituted by facts about his use of w only if they were to entail:

> For any object x: if S were in *epistemically* ideal conditions I with respect to x, then S would apply word w to x if and only if x were an f.

(5) But how might these 'epistemically ideal conditions' be articulated, given the work they are needed to do? Certainly not as 'conditions in which S's application of w to x could not be *mistaken*'; for this amounts to a *semantic* condition—one whose explication would presuppose the notion of meaning and thereby render the analysis circular.[10] And surely not as 'circumstances in which S is not tired, not drunk, has an infinitely large brain, lives forever, and so on, and so forth'. For who knows what would really happen in such an extraordinarily far-fetched scenario? It is merely an *a posteriori speculation* that each of our predicates "f" would, in those remote circumstances, be applied to fs and only fs.[11] Thus we may

---

[9] It is not being assumed that predicate application must take place *overtly*. Unvoiced *mental* application will do.

[10] "The circumstances of S's application of w to x are such that it could not be mistaken" comes to "The circumstances of S's application of w to x are such that, if w means F then x is an f, and if x is an f then w means something coextensive with F."

[11] Extremely hypothetical capacities and circumstances are needed because of the fact that, in the case of most predicates, certain objects are too remote, or too small, or too complex, or too something else, for an ordinary person to be able to tell whether they do, or do not, belong to the extension of that predicate.

conclude that the needed non-semantically-specifiable epistemologically ideal conditions, I, do not exist.

(6) Therefore, S's meaning F by w cannot be analysed *a priori* in terms of facts concerning S's use of w.[12]

5.4 APPRAISAL OF KRIPKE'S REASONING

I think that Kripke succeeds here in demonstrating that there can be no *a priori* use-theoretic analysis (in non-semantic terms) of the fact that a predicate has the particular extension that it does. But in order to reach the promised conclusion—namely, that such semantic facts are not 'genuine'—he needs

---

[12] A similar argument, but focused instead on *rule-following*, but focused instead on might begin with the assumption, paralleling (2), that:

> S's implicitly following rule R! could be analysed *a priori* in terms of how S acts (and would act) only if it were possible to read-off (that is, infer) from S's activities that R is the regularity to which he is (implicitly) attempting to conform.

Then, paralleling (3), it could be observed that

> S's activities will sometimes fail to conform to his rule; so the right analysis would have to incorporate a way of filtering out such mistakes.

From which we could infer, paralleling (4), that:

> S's implicitly following R! must be a matter of his conformity with it *in ideal conditions*.

However, for reasons similar to those provided in (5):

> These ideal conditions cannot be specified *a priori*.

Thus we might obtain the result, paralleling (6), that:

> S's implicitly following rule R! cannot be analysed *a priori* in terms of how he acts (and would act).

Notice that this argument, if combined with the assumption that meaning is a matter of rule-following, would provide an alternative route to the conclusion that S's meaning F by w cannot be analysed *a priori* in terms of his activity with the word.

to show, in addition, that there are also no *a posteriori* naturalistic reductions of them. And an argument to that effect is
in fact suggested in the context of his brief critique (on pp.
51–4) of the idea that the semantic facts might be 'primitive'
(that is, not explicitly definable *a priori*). He notes the
difficulty of seeing how a finite being's mental or neurological
or behavioural activities with word w could provide it with a
specific extension given the infinitary content of such a fact—
that is, its countless implications of forms, 'w is true of x' and/or
'w is not true of x'. And although this point calls for considerable elaboration, I believe it does in the end provide the basis
for thinking that there is indeed no *a posteriori* reduction of
"w is true of x"—hence no way of explaining (via such an
account) the truth condition of a predicate from non-semantic facts about its usage.[13]

But the irreducibility of "w is true of x" (either conceptually
or empirically) yields the conclusion that *meaning*-facts are
irreducible only if it is taken for granted that meanings are
based on reference/truth conditions. It must be assumed either
that a predicate's meaning what it does amounts to no more
than its having a certain extension, or that the meaning is constructed by starting with an extensional fact and then adding
some further ingredient or ingredients. This, of course, is the

---

[13] Some of the needed elaboration is given in Chapter 6 of *Truth–Meaning–
Reality* ("Kripke's Paradox of Meaning"). For those of us who are deflationists
about truth, Kripke's discussion provides welcome support for our view. From
our perspective, given the generalizing function of the concept of truth and
given the disquotation rule that is necessary and sufficient to account for it
(and therefore *implicitly* defines the concept), there can be no room for an
explicit definition, in *any* non-semantic terms, of "w is true of x". And there
can be no reason to expect an *a posteriori* reduction either.

The important observation that Kripke pays insufficient attention to the distinction between an *a priori* analysis of meaning attributions and an *a posteriori* reduction
of meaning-facts was made by Scott Soames in his "Skepticism about Meaning:
Indeterminacy, Normativity, and the Rule-Following Paradox", *Canadian Journal of
Philosophy*, Supp. Vol. 23, 1998, 211–50.

orthodox picture—reflected in mainstream truth-theoretic semantics. But it can perfectly well be resisted—and is resisted by Wittgenstein. As we saw in Chapter 4, Section 4.2(B), his alternative—an inversion of the orthodox direction of explanation—is to explain a predicate's extension in terms of its meaning, via the schema

> S's word w means F → S's word w is true of all and only the fs[14]

From this ("deflationary") point of view, our acceptance of that schema completely explains our overall usage of "true of" on the basis of our usage of the other expressions involved in its instances—that is, on the basis of our usage of meaning attributions (such as "w means DOG") and non-semantic terms (such as "dog"). It therefore implicitly defines "true of" in terms of a prior understanding of those other expressions.

And, in that case, an empirical investigation into whether a given property of w (such as a specific disposition for its use) constitutes w's meaning need not (indeed *should* not) be concerned with how that property could conceivably yield the word's extension. As long as we have found a property of w that explains the *non*-truth-theoretic import of w's meaning, we can infer that this property constitutes that meaning; and we can then infer—simply in virtue of the above schema—that it indirectly accounts for the word's truth-theoretic import as well. In this model the *only* inferential route from a word's use to its truth condition is *indirect*, going *via* the word's meaning. We must *first* establish that a word's meaning (say) DOG derives from a certain way of using it, (say) $U_{17}(w)$; *second*, cite the definitional entailment, that w means DOG → w is true of the

---

[14] Alternatively, there is Hartry Field's formulation: "f" (as I now mean it) is true of all and only the fs. For ease of exposition I follow Kripke in restricting the discussion to predicates whose extensions are not dependent on context of utterance.

dogs; and *third*, invoke transitivity to explain why $U_{17}(w) \rightarrow w$ is true of the dogs.[15]

In order to see what sort of evidence really *is* needed to settle the question of exactly how a given meaning is constituted, remember that, in general, a relatively basic property, B-ness, empirically constitutes a relatively superficial property, S-ness, when possession of B-ness explains the contingent symptoms of S-ness. (For example, 'being made of H_2O molecules' constitutes 'being a sample of water' in virtue of the fact that it explains why water is colourless, boils at 100° C, and so on.) Consequently, the feature of a word's (non-semantic) use that empirically constitutes its meaning is the one that explains what is contingently symptomatic of its having that meaning. And the main symptoms of a word's meaning what it does are all the thousands of cases in which sentences containing it are accepted—sentence-tokens that are caused in part by that semantic fact.

Now it is crucial to recognize that the *basic* use of a predicate "f"—that which accounts for our overall use of the word and hence constitutes its meaning—may well *never* turn out to be a disposition to apply it to all and only the fs. Clearly, the basic use of "bachelor" is not that we apply it (ideally) to all and only bachelors, but is roughly a matter of our accepting substitutions of "bachelor" for "unmarried men", and *vice versa*. Clearly, our fundamental way of using "true" is not a propensity to apply it to truths and only truths but, more plausibly, to accept

---

[15] By analogy, consider a term, "shmoo", that is introduced via the stipulation that anything made of plastic is shmoo of the dogs. Surely, it is no constraint on something—say XYZ—being a decent analysis of plastic that there be a *direct* explanation of why XYZ-things are shmoo of the dogs. Instead, we would look for entirely independent evidence to establish that XYZ is what empirically constitutes plastic. And we would then explain *indirectly* why all XYZ-things are shmoo of the dogs. This example is borrowed from "Kripke's Paradox of Meaning", Chapter 6 of my *Truth–Meaning–Reality*.

instances of the schema '<p> is true ↔ p'. And clearly the basic use of "red" is not to apply it to all and only red things but something more immediately and easily implementable, such as accepting "That is red" in the presence of *observed* red things (or perhaps, accepting "That is red" given a visual experience of the sort normally produced in humans by observed red things).[16]

But if, as these examples suggest, the use-fact that empirically constitutes S's meaning F by w is *anyway* not likely to be a disposition to apply w (ideally) to all fs and only to fs, then Kripke's observation that no legitimate conception of 'ideal epistemological conditions' could sustain *such* an account is somewhat beside the point—having no negative import for the existence of meanings.

However, this objection to Kripke's line of thought, though telling, is not quite enough to completely undermine it. For *whichever* the disposition (propensity, tendency, law-like regularity) of use may be in virtue of which S's word w means F, the question will arise as to what *exactly* this implies for S's actual and counterfactual use of w. After all, S's general disposition to con-

---

[16] The project of identifying the distinctive meaning-constituting properties of different words is bound to be dauntingly difficult—a massive job for empirical linguistics. For one thing, the explanations that will support any particular conjecture of that sort will also require conjectures about the meaning-constituting properties of the other words in the sentences whose acceptance is to be explained. Moreover (and as the above examples illustrate) a word's meaning-constituting property will typically dictate its usage in relation to other words *whose meanings are taken for granted*. For instance, the above suggestion about "bachelor" might be roughly right about its basic use, but only if "unmarried man" is given its usual English meaning. Therefore the aspiration to explain linguistic activity in *non-semantic* terms can be met only globally, as follows. There must be *some* terms—the most primitive ones—whose meanings are engendered by entirely non-semantic facts about their use in relation to one another. The meanings of certain less fundamental terms may then be explained via properties that presuppose the meanings of those primitive ones. And so on. Thus a hierarchy of meanings is gradually constructed. (For further discussion, see Chapter 2 of *Reflections on Meaning*.)

form to regularity, R, does not preclude there being circumstances in which he will not (or would not) conform. So the original Kripkean objection re-arises. For we will need to say that

> S has a disposition to conform to regularity R ≡
> S will (and would) conform to R, *as long as circum-*
> *stances are ideal.*

And paralleling Kripke's step (5), it will be argued that any attempt to articulate these 'ideal' (or 'non-ideal') conditions is bound to fail. Thus it would seem that we still do not have a viable strategy for reducing word-meanings to non-semantic properties.[17]

But there is an adequate response to this last-ditch version of Kripke's sceptical objection. The idea on the table is, in effect, that a word's meaning-constituting use is a matter of its *being governed by the ideal law, R*. And we can respond to his imagined critique of it by defending the legitimacy of *this* particular notion of 'ideal' (unlike the original one)—observing that its deployment is a common and legitimate feature of scientific theorizing, even within physics. There is nothing normative, non-naturalistic, unempirical, or spooky about it. Kepler's proposal for ideal laws of planetary motion and Chomsky's for ideal laws of linguistic competence are subject to the same methodological constraints as are any other scientific postulate. That is to say, we find that the standardly desired blend of empirical adequacy,

---

[17] "Dispositional analysis" is sometimes used for analyses of the unqualified form, "S is disposed to do A"—where this is intended to be consistent with "S does not (or would not) *always* do A" and is taken to mean roughly the same thing as "S tends to do A" and "S has a propensity to do A". But the term is also used—by Kripke, for instance—for analyses of the explicitly *counterfactual* forms, "S would do A in condition C" or "S would do A in ideal conditions". Clearly, he does not think that an analysis of the first kind (i.e unqualified) suffices to show that the analysed phenomenon is 'genuinely' factual. What would be needed, in his view, is a yet deeper *counterfactual* analysis—but one that it does not involve what he regards as unacceptable notions: for example, that of 'ideal conditions'.

simplicity, and explanatory power is sometimes best achieved by means of a theory whose two-pronged form is to postulate certain *ideal laws* (or *ceteris paribus* laws) and certain *distorting factors*—where the laws describe how the systems in question would behave in the absence of these factors, and the factors are characterized together with specifications of how their presence would alter that behaviour.[18]

It should be emphasized that this strategy of response would not have worked against Kripke's *original* step (5)—that is, against his argument that there are no non-circularly specifiable 'ideal *epistemic* conditions' (in which one is bound to conform to the regularity, 'Apply w to fs and only fs'). For, as we have seen, it is not plausible to suppose that an unprejudiced empirical investigation into the causes of "f"'s overall deployment (whatever "f" may be) will reveal that our *basic* ideal law for its use takes that truth-oriented form. Remember, for example, the above-mentioned cases of "bachelor", "true", and "red". It is only to be expected that our nature as human beings will permit the inculcation of certain basic propensities but not others. Thus one may perfectly well countenance the existence of ideal laws in general, and the existence of ideal laws of word-use in particular, without

---

[18] In some cases, talk of an "ideal law" is tied to specific simplifying stipulations (for example, that the planets are point masses and that they exert no gravitational forces on one another)—stipulations relative to which the law can be deduced from (hence explained by) a more fundamental theory. But in other cases—including the phenomenon of word-use—some combination of an ideal law with a collection of potentially distorting factors is postulated on empirical, explanatory grounds, with the usual understanding that revisions of both the alleged law and the list of distorting conditions may well be needed.

No doubt it can happen (and occasionally will happen) that alternative combinations of 'law of word-use and set of potential distorting factors' will seem equally simple and plausible, and so we shall be uncertain which such combination is correct. But this will not lead to any uncertainty as to what the word means. However unsure we are about what provides the word "dog" with its meaning, we are in no doubt that it means DOG and is true of the dogs.

Thanks to Paul Boghossian and Allan Gibbard for pressing me on these issues.

embracing the much more controversial assumption that, for any not-explicitly-definable predicates "f", there is a basic ideal law of the form, 'Apply it to all and only the fs'—or in other words, that there are such things as 'non-circularly specifiable, *epistemically* ideal conditions'.[19]

Therefore, *pace* Kripke, one might after all suppose that a person's meaning what she does by a word consists in her activity with it being governed by a *ceteris paribus* law whose existence is manifested in the standard way—that is, by its being part of the best explanation of what she does. Thus we can see that his anti-dispositionalist conclusion, (6), is far from having been established. On the contrary, it is plausible that one *can*

---

[19] Although the scientific respectability of the notion of 'ideal conditions' cannot salvage the attempted analysis of 'S means F by w' to facts entailing 'S would ideally apply w to x ↔ fx', it *does* salvage the above-mentioned Wittgensteinian *a priori* analysis (subjected to a Kripkean critique in footnote 12) of 'S implicitly follows rule R!' to facts entailing 'S conforms to regularity R in ideal conditions'. The naturalistic credentials of the latter use of "ideal" reside in the fact that empirical research *will* often identify specific instances of R, and specific favorable conditions, C1, C2,..., in which S would conform to that regularity. Thus we will often be able to move towards a detailed *a posteriori* account of what it is for S to implicitly follow the rule, "Conform to R".

The above proposal has a certain limited affinity with David Lewis' idea (in "Putnam's Paradox", *Australasian Journal of Philosophy* 62, 1984, 221–36) that *natural* properties (which "cut the world at its joints") are more susceptible to being referred to than others—that they are "reference magnets" (to use Harold Hodes' term). For we might think (picturesquely) of the import of our proposal as being that those few regularities that are *ideal natural laws* of human psychology (and are correction-susceptible) are the ones that 'magnetically attract' our rule-following and semantic endeavours. But it is another matter to suppose, as Lewis does (and see also Ted Sider's *Writing the Book of the World*, Oxford: Oxford University Press, 2011—esp. chapter 3, section 2), that *S's word w means F* in virtue of the ideal natural law that S applies w to fs and only to fs—or, as they would put it, in virtue of S being fairly disposed to apply w to all and only fs, where f-ness is a *natural* property (and hence a reference magnet). For, as we have seen, very few words (if any) acquire their meanings in that way. Dispositionalism is rescued from Kripke's critique *not* by restricting which dispositions of the form 'to apply w to fs and only to fs' can qualify as meaning-constituting, but by appreciating that meaning-constituting dispositions of use do not take that form. So there is simply no room for the metaphor of *reference* magnets.

specify underlying use-theoretic conditions—broadly dispositional in character—for our meaning what we do.[20]

In sum: the response to Kripke's paradox advocated above takes the form of a '*straight* solution'—a way of seeing that the reasoning-to-an-implausible-conclusion is defective. However, the faults that have been identified in that reasoning are quite

---

[20] A nice objection to dispositionalism is ventured by Paul Boghossian in his "Epistemic Rules", *Journal of Philosophy* 109, 2008, 472–500. His argument is based on the intuition that a person's following a certain rule helps explain both what she actually does *and what she is disposed to do*, and her meaning a certain thing by word, w, helps explain both how she actually uses w *and how she is disposed to use it*. But surely nothing can help explain itself! And nor can anything be constituted by what it explains. So how could rule-followings or meanings be constituted by dispositions?

Wittgenstein puts some such intuition into the mouth of his interlocutor: "The understanding itself is a state which is the *source* of the correct use" (PI 146, my emphasis). And his response to it (as to other objections to his equation of meaning with use) is (i) to attribute it to an overstretching of analogies between meanings and conscious presentations, such as images or mental instructions; (ii) to reiterate that only a person's *usage* provides *definitive* evidence of what she means; and (iii) to note that no state of the mind/brain that might *cause* that telltale usage could be inferred *a priori* from it. Thus:

> What is one really thinking of here? Isn't one thinking of the derivation of a series from its algebraic formula? Or at least of something analogous?—But this is where we were before. The point is, we can think of more than *one* application of an algebraic formula; and every type of application can in turn be formulated algebraically; but naturally this does not get us any further—The application is still a criterion of understanding. (PI 146)

Further tempting overgeneralizations that conspire to foster the mistaken intuition are: (a) irrational extrapolation from familiar *explicit* rule-following (which clearly *does* explain the propensity to conform) to the relatively technical/theoretical phenomenon of *implicit* rule-following; (b) irrational extrapolation from *public* words (sounds), whose dispositions of use *are* plausibly *explained* by what they mean—in so far as those meanings are identified with dispositions for the deployment of correlated terms in *thought*—to these language of thought terms themselves; and (c) irrational extrapolation, in the case of *implicit* rules and *LOT-term* meanings, from the fact that they explain a certain batch of *particular* dispositional facts to the conclusion that they must also explain the corresponding *general* propensities.

distinct from those alleged in other straight solutions proposed in the literature. The great majority of these *either* resist his argument that no non-semantic analysis of a word's meaning (in terms of use-dispositions, for example) could directly explain how it comes to have the particular extension it does (e.g. Blackburn[21]), or they suppose that, although Kripke is right about that, the moral is simply that meaning-attributions, though factual, are irreducible (e.g. Boghossian[22]).

The present Wittgensteinian response, in contrast, accepts (indeed applauds) Kripke's arguments against definitions or reductions of 'w is true of x'. But it denies that the postulation of empirically irreducible states of meaning such-and-such and meaning so-and-so could be satisfactory (for it would make a mystery of why each meaning has the distinctive *use*-theoretic import that it does). Our 'third way' has been to argue—from the deflationary assumption that a predicate's extension (e.g. the set of dogs) is a definitional consequence of its meaning (e.g. DOG)[23]—that our basic use practice with the word *indirectly* explains its extension by first explaining its meaning. And—as one would expect from property-constitution claims elsewhere in science—a specific core practice *will* first do that by explaining the predicate's *overall use* (since that is the main *symptom* of its meaning). Given this adequacy condition, there is no reason at all to expect a meaning-constituting use-fact to take the form, 'S would apply w (when queried in ideal conditions) to x iff fx'. Therefore, there is no need for the sort of '*epistemologically* ideal conditions' that Kripke

[21] "The Individual Strikes Back", *Synthese* 58, 1984, 281–302.

[22] "The Rule-Following Considerations", *Mind*, 98, 1989, 507–49.

[23] Support for this deflationary assumption comes not merely from examination of the function and meaning of our truth predicate (see my *Truth*, Oxford: Oxford University Press, 1998), but also from the fact that, as just argued, it alone yields a non-sceptical and explanatorily adequate view of meaning.

shows to be non-existent—the sort that would ensure the *truth* of predications, and thereby yield a reduction of 'w is true of x'. The concept of idealization that we *do* need (namely, the one deployed in 'ideal laws' or '*ceteris paribus* laws') is another thing entirely—a perfectly familiar and respectable element of scientific methodology.

5.5 THE PARADOXICAL CONCLUSION

Kripke's overall thesis—that there are no 'genuine' facts as to what words mean—is somewhat obscure. But it is supposed to derive from his critique of dispositionalism, together with his additional arguments (mentioned initially) that meanings cannot be engendered by mental facts and cannot be irreducibly semantic. Therefore, in so far as there turn out to be substantial flaws in his case against *a posteriori* dispositionalism, then we can safely take it that his sceptical conclusion—whatever it means exactly—will also be unproven.

Still, one might wonder about the precise content of that thesis. Which facts are the 'genuine' ones? Since Kripke does not say, we are forced to guess what he has in mind on the basis of what he takes the import of the thesis to be and on the basis of the considerations he takes to establish it. Now—as will be confirmed in the next section—he himself does not think he has discredited our *ordinary* attributions of meaning (such as "Jones means PLUS by '+'"). Moreover, as he concedes (p. 86), there is a perfectly legitimate *deflationary* conception of fact in which those claims trivially entail that there *are* such things as meaning-facts (such as "It is a fact that Jones means PLUS by '+'"). Therefore, it is clear that his denial of meaning-*facts* involves a special, more restrictive, 'robust' conception.

Specifically, the kinds of fact he entertains and rejects as the possible underlying bases of meanings are all *causal/explanatory/ naturalistic* in character—that is, facts of the sort that enter into causal and explanatory relations and are therefore dealt with in the empirical sciences.[24] *These* are the facts that, according to Kripke's arguments, cannot explain the truth-theoretic and normative import of words meaning what they do. Thus it seems fair to conclude that his overall sceptical conclusion is, roughly speaking, the thesis that there are no causal/explanatory/naturalistic facts as to what words mean.[25]

An implication of Kripke's conclusion, as he emphasizes (p. 97n), is that any *explanatory* deployment of implicit rules of language (e.g. *à la* Chomsky) is put into question. However, one might well prefer to apply *modus tollens* to that relation of implication, and reason that in so far as we *do* deploy attributions of meaning (and implicit rule-following) in satisfactory explanations of what people do and say (e.g. which string of words they take to be grammatical) then there must be something wrong with Kripke's sceptical conclusion, hence mistakes in his reasoning. Our appraisal (in Sections 5.2 and 5.4) of his two main lines of argument purports to pinpoint these mistakes.

---

[24] A more familiar alleged example of a 'non-genuine' fact (in what appears to be Kripke's sense) is *the fact that killing is wrong*. From the emotivist/expressivist point of view, in so far as we accept "killing is wrong" we should also accept that there is such a fact (in a deflationary sense); but this fact will not be part of the causal nexus; in particular, its existence will not be what explains our belief in it.

[25] Note that this interpretation of "genuine facts" as "causal/explanatory/naturalistic facts" is a *charitable* one, in that it rationalizes Kripke's inferring (from his anti-dispositionalism, and so on) that there are no 'genuine' meaning-facts.

A less charitable alternative would be to suppose that the notion of 'genuine', 'robust' fact that he is deploying is the notoriously elusive concept on which realist-antirealist debates are typically focused (see Kit Fine, "The Question of Realism", *Philosophers' Imprint*, 1:1, 2001). This alleged notion is highly contentious: controversies surround not merely its intension and extension, but its very existence. Arguably, it *cannot* be made legitimate, because it is an expression of the confused idea that physical facts have a peculiar ontological weight which makes them 'more real' than the merely deflationary facts of ethics, arithmetic, and so on.—See my *Truth–Meaning–Reality*, Chapter 13 ("The Quest for REALITY").

5.6 KRIPKE'S "SCEPTICAL SOLUTION"

Let us spend a little time on Kripke's "sceptical solution" to the paradox—his attempt to defang the sceptical argument by showing, not that it contains a fallacy (which would be giving a "straight solution"), but that its conclusion is, on reflection, perfectly tolerable.

To that end, he emphasizes that our practice of meaning-attribution—of asserting things like "Jones means PLUS by '+'"—does not depend for its coherence on its being concerned with 'genuine' (causal/explanatory) facts. What is required is merely that there be rules for the deployment of such meaning-attributions (i.e. 'assertibility conditions' for them), and that the practice, as governed by those rules, serve some purpose. Thus the substance of Kripke's sceptical solution consists in his roughly articulating the rules for meaning-attribution and indicating their utility.

Specifically, he notes (pp. 90–1) that if we have observed that S has in the past used word w (subject to communal correction) more or less as *we* do, then we are allowed to assert, tentatively, that S is following the same rules for it as we do

---

Granted, this 'quietist' dismissal of the notion may be incorrect. Still, we would need some compelling story about 'robustness'—something well beyond what Kripke provides—in order to be in a position to see how his arguments against dispositionalism (and against other accounts of meaning-facts) could yield the conclusion that they are not 'robust'.

An even less charitable interpretation, it seems to me, would be to suppose that Kripke is not invoking a notion of 'robustness', and is concluding that there are *no* facts at all (not even in the weak deflationary sense) as to what words mean. Not only (as already mentioned in the text) is this hard to square with his explicitly allowing that meaning attributions may be perfectly justified, but it is hard to square with his claim to be giving a reading of Wittgenstein, whose metaphilosophy is famously anti-revisionist. On this final point see Gordon Baker and Peter Hacker's *Scepticism, Rules and Language*, Oxford: Blackwell, 1984.

(and therefore meaning the same by it). And he suggests that the purpose of such an assertion is to express our confidence in S—to label him as someone whose sincere w-statements ought to be relied on.

Now, as we have seen, there is no need for any such sceptical solution, for we already have a straight one. We have found mistaken premises in Kripke's arguments against the possibility of reducing meaning-facts to use-facts.

But it is worth appreciating, in addition, that his particular way of giving substance to a sceptical solution—his particular specification of the assertibility conditions for meaning-attributions—points in exactly the same direction: namely, towards our straight solution. For the best explanation of our endorsement of these assertibility conditions is our acknowledgement that there *are* causal/explanatory facts of meaning and that they are use-regularities.

To see this, notice that the observation that S has *until now* used w pretty much as we do is canonical inductive evidence for the genuinely factual conclusion that S has had, and still has, *a general tendency* (propensity, disposition) to use w in that way. So if, as Kripke says, such an observation is recognized as the condition for a certain meaning-attribution to be assertible—that is, justifiably maintained—the obvious explanation lies in our taking this meaning-attribution to be made true by S having that general tendency.[26] Thus an ironic feature of Kripke's sceptical solution to his paradox is the way that it leads directly to the correctness of a straight response.

---

[26] Similarly for rule-following attributions. Kripke does not specify the assertibility conditions for "S is implicitly following the rule 'Conform with R'" (where R may have nothing to do with language). However, extrapolating from what he says about *meaning*-attributions, one might take his view to be that we are allowed to provisionally accept such a thing if we have observed (i) that R is the simplest of the simple regularities to which S's behaviour to date roughly conforms, and (ii) that this behaviour is subject to correction. But the first of these observations is standard inductive evidence that R is an ideal law govern-

5.7 INDIVIDUALISTIC LANGUAGE

A quick word on the alleged corollary of Kripke's solution—its alleged implication that languages are essentially *communal*; that someone can understand a given language only if other people do too; so there can be no 'private' (=individualistic) languages. The argument here is simple. What has been learned (supposedly) from the paradox is that we can legitimately assert of someone that he means a given thing by one of his words only if there is a tendency (or potential) for departures from its ordinary use to be *corrected*. Consequently, in attributing meanings we presuppose the existence of other people who mean the same thing. Thus we arrive at the conclusion that so-called 'private' languages are impossible.[27]

But one might well resist this reasoning. Although it is somewhat plausible that attributions of meaning to verbal activity are in place only when there is the prospect of *some* form of correction—that is, only when the relevant use-propensity is displayed within contexts of positive and negative reinforcement—it is unclear that an individual's practice of *correcting himself* would not suffice. As we first saw in Chapter 4, Section 4.2(F), Wittgenstein (the alleged arch-communitarian!) makes just this suggestion in connection with rule-following. Consider (again) a game of which

ing S's behaviour—past, present, future, and counterfactual. So why not regard that conclusion as the first component of the fact constituting S's following the rule, 'Conform with R'?—our straight solution!

[27] Other commentators who have interpreted Wittgenstein as urging a view of language as necessarily communal include John McDowell in his "Wittgenstein on Following a Rule" (*Synthese* 58, 1984, 325–63), Norman Malcolm in his *Nothing is Hidden* (Oxford: Blackwell, 1986) and 'Wittgenstein on Language and Rules' (*Philosophy* 67, 1989, 5–28), and Meredith Williams in her *Blind Obedience* (London: Routledge, 2010). For a more nuanced view see John V. Canfield, "The Community View" (*Philosophical Review* 105:4, 1996, 469–88).

we say that it is played according to such-and-such rules because an observer can read these rules off from the practice of the game—like a natural law governing the play— But how does the observer distinguish in this case between players' mistakes and correct play?—There are characteristic signs of it in the players' behaviour. Think of the behaviour characteristic of correcting a slip of the tongue. It would be possible to recognize that someone was doing so even without knowing his language. (PI 54)

In opposition to our reading of Wittgenstein, which prioritized this passage, textual support for a 'communal' interpretation is often taken to come from his denying that rule-following can be a "private" matter:

And hence also 'obeying a rule' is a practice. And to *think* one is obeying a rule is not to obey a rule. Hence it is not possible to obey a rule 'privately': otherwise thinking one was obeying a rule would be the same thing as obeying it. (PI 202)

But "private", as it appears here, does not mean "independent of others". It means, rather, "the sort of state, like an experience, that its subject is peculiarly well-positioned to pronounce upon, since someone tends to be in it when and only when he *thinks* he's in it." So the alternative to '*private* rule-following' that Wittgenstein is insisting upon is 'rule-following as an objective *practice*'—and that can perfectly well be grounded in the regular activity of a single isolated person, independently of anyone else.[28]

---

[28] In PI 243, when Wittgenstein explicitly turns his attention to the philosophy of mind, he raises the question of whether a person could devise and deploy a special language to describe her own "private sensations"—construed (for example, in PI 272) to be the peculiar ways that sensations feel to her (that is, *what they are like for her*): so the language cannot be understood by anyone else. And the temptation to think that there exist such 'raw-feels' (qualia) is one that he subjects to extended therapeutic criticism (as we shall see in Chapter 6). Thus, in a *further* sense of "private", he does indeed deny that there could be

5.8 THE DIFFERENCES BETWEEN KRIPKENSTEIN AND WITTGENSTEIN

Despite superficial similarities between the Wittgensteinian and Kripkean lines of thought, we have seen that they diverge in fundamental respects. Here again are the main points of disagreement.

First: although they both maintain that the meaning of a word is provided by its 'use', their operative conceptions of 'use' are crucially different.—For Wittengstein meanings are a matter of *actual* use-dispositions, whereas for Kripke they are *correct* use-dispositions (i.e. the applications that would be *true*).

Second: having argued that there is no naturalistic analysis of 'w is true of x', Kripke concludes that there can be no naturalistic reductions of *meaning*-properties either (that is, properties such as 'w means DOG'). For he assumes that these are constructed *from* truth conditions, so that any such reduction would determine a predicate's truth condition by incorporating *its* naturalistic basis (which has been shown not to exist!). But from Wittgenstein's deflationary perspective—whereby predicative truth is introduced and defined

---

private languages, i.e. languages in which these qualia are mentioned. But he is not thereby denying that someone's *ordinary* language may be 'individualistic'—not dependent upon non-semantic relations to anyone else, and not necessarily understood by anyone else. On the contrary, PI 243 explicitly contrasts a private sensation language with "human beings who spoke only in monologue; who accompanied their activities by talking to themselves. An explorer who watched them and listened to their talk might succeed in translating their language into ours."

Others who have interpreted Wittgenstein as open to 'individualism' about meaning include Gordon Baker and Peter Hacker in *Scepticism, Rules and Language* (Oxford: Blackwell, 1984) and in *Wittgenstein: Rules, Grammar, and Necessity*, 2009, Oxford: Blackwell, 149–68), Colin McGinn in *Wittgenstein on Meaning* (Oxford: Blackwell, 1984, 77–93), and Malcolm Budd in "Wittgenstein on Meaning, Interpretation and Rules" (*Synthese* 58, 1984, 303–23).

in terms of meaning by the schema, "w means F → (x)(w is true of x ↔ fx)"—an empirical investigation into the naturalistic basis of 'w's meaning DOG' is not in the slightest constrained by the fact that words with that meaning are true of the dogs.

Third: both philosophers' paradoxes derive in part from the premise that *meanings are actual use-dispositions*. But for Kripke, the puzzle, as we have just seen, is how to reconcile this idea with meaning's truth-theoretic implications, and his solution is to abandon it.—Whereas for Wittgenstein the puzzle is to reconcile it with a tempting view of meanings as *mental*, and *that* is what must be abandoned.

Fourth: the difference between Wittgenstein and Kripke on rule-following is analogous. They would agree that someone's implicitly following a given rule is a matter both of his conforming with it in ideal circumstances and his being subject to correction. For Kripke the confusion to avoid is that of regarding this story as naturalistic ('genuinely' factual). He baulks at both "ideal" and "correction". But Wittgenstein displays no such concerns. He is content to invoke the behavioural signs of *self*-correction; and seems to appreciate that the circumstances that tend to engender (or inhibit) divergences from a rule's dictates are perfectly susceptible to empirical identification. For him, the dangerous confusion is that of regarding rule-following as a kind of subjective mental stance, and *failing* to see it as an objective regularity.

Fifth: Kripke also supposes (unlike Wittgenstein) that *meaning* something by a word requires correction *by others*, so that language is essentially social.

And sixth: they agree that although there are certainly *facts* of meaning (in the ordinary, deflationary sense), there are no 'facts' of meaning (in one or another special, metaphysical sense). But the metaphysical facts they renounce are very different. For Kripke the illusion is that of 'genuine' (=naturalistic) meaning–facts. But Wittgenstein, the disposionalist, has of course no qualms about these. What he dismisses are the occult "superlative facts" that we feel drawn to invoke when we confusedly imagine meanings as introspectable, guiding states of explicit knowledge—states that are entirely present at an instant, yet somehow incorporate a vast body of decisions about future use:

> "It is as if we could grasp the whole use of the word in a flash." Like *what* e.g.?—Can't the use—in a certain sense—be grasped in a flash? And in *what* sense can it not?—The point is, that it is as if we could 'grasp it in a flash' in yet another and much more direct sense than that.—But have you a model for this? No. It is just that this expression suggests itself to us. As the result of the crossing of different pictures. (PI 191)

> You have no model of this superlative fact, but you are seduced into using a super-expression. (It might be called a philosophical superlative.) (PI 192)

These fantasized *facts* are the essentially paradoxical projections of our initial confusion.

6

The "mystery" of consciousness

6.1 PSEUDO-PROBLEMS

A *genuine* question is provoked by ignorance: we have good reason to believe that there is some fact meeting a certain specification—e.g. the identity of the murderer, the mass of the sun, or the cause of the dinosaurs' disappearance—and we want to know what that fact is. In each such case the statement of the question, together with generally accepted background assumptions, direct us towards the unknown information, and our task is to find it. A *pseudo*-question, on the other hand, is prompted by confusion rather than ignorance. In such cases, had we been thinking properly, we would have been able to tell that, initial appearances to the contrary, no fact is implicitly indicated, no fact is at issue. What time is it on the sun? Where is the number three? Why is there something rather than nothing? These apparent questions are defective because the impression that each of them gives of pointing towards an answer presupposes assumptions that are products of muddled thinking. Thus a pseudo-question, or pseudo-problem, is one that we should not attempt to answer—not because it is too difficult, but because there is every reason to expect that no objectively correct answer exists.

Nice illustrations of such problems are to be found in the philosophy of time. For example, it is tempting to suppose that, in some sense, *time flows*. But in trying to imagine such a phenomenon we can find ourselves entangled in perplexities. In what does the flow or passage of time consist? How fast does it go? Is some sort of 'meta-time' required? Would this lead to an infinite regress? Could time flow backwards? If not, why not? No one who has taken these questions at face value—as calling for a profound metaphysical theory—has ever been able to provide satisfactory answers to them. And, arguably, this is because the presumption that time flow is a basic feature of the universe is misconceived. Let me elaborate a little.

If, at successive times t_1, t_2, and t_3, someone says, "Now it is t_1", "Now it is t_2", and "Now it is t_3", then—given the meaning of the word "now"—each of these statements will be true. But suppose "now" is regarded as the name of a single, localized, temporal entity or quality. Then we may conclude that this 'Now-ness' was once located at t_1, then at t_2, and then at t_3—which implies that 'it moved' in the direction from past to future. Hence the flow of time!

So far so good. There is nothing puzzling in this idea *as so explained*. It becomes puzzling only if we exaggerate the analogy between *this* 'motion of Now' and ordinary physical motion—that is, only if we allow ourselves to overlook certain crucial differences between them. When something moves through space, it occupies a series of different places at different times: say, p_1 at t_1, p_2 at t_2, ..., and p_9 at t_9. The average speed of the motion is defined as the distance along that path divided by the length of time between t_1 and t_9. And we can easily make sense of the possibility of a motion along that very path but at a different speed, or in exactly the opposite direction. But, although it is perfectly coherent to speak of Nowness moving through time—meaning, as we have just seen, merely that it is entirely located first at t_1, then at t_2, ..., and so on—the existence of *this* phenomenon (in contrast with the movement of a given physical thing) is not a substantive contingent matter; it is an empty conceptual necessity. Given the meaning of "now", and given our definition of "movement with respect to time", it is trivially provable that Now-ness moves into the future at a rate of 1 second per second. So there can be no deep issue as to *why* time passes at the speed it does, or whether it could go in the opposite direction. Such questions are tempting only given an irrational overstretching of the superficial analogy between 'time flow' and normal motion.

Thus the picture *in itself* of Now-ness as an 'entity' with variable location is non-committal and harmless. The trouble comes from interpreting that picture in the wrong way, from thinking of this 'entity' as more like a spatially-located moving *physical object* than it really is—hence, as capable of something very like genuine motion. This interpretation is a perverse inflation of the linguistic similarities on which the initial picture is based. And once that error is identified our perplexities about 'time flow' disappear.[1]

This example helps us to appreciate the question with which we are concerned in the present chapter. Is the aura of mystery surrounding *consciousness* derived from a set of genuine problems prompted by our ignorance of various deep and subtle facts about a truly extraordinary phenomenon—the mind? Or is it provoked rather by a cluster of pseudo-questions, which, like 'the mystery of time-flow', are based on a confused response to our ways of speaking and thinking of experience?

I will be trying to explain sympathetically Wittgenstein's view that the traditional and still widely debated perplexities of con-

---

[1] It might be thought that the confusion operating here is deeper than I have just suggested—that it really consists in overlooking the fact that "now" is merely an *indexical* (picking out different times on different occasions of use) and so cannot be regarded as standing for any sort of *constant* entity. But although I would grant that the picture of 'Now-ness' as a constant feature is not particularly useful or appealing, and that it brings us to the *brink* of misunderstanding, I do not believe that it is *inevitably* confused and paradoxical.

sciousness are indeed the result of recognizably defective assumptions rather than the incompleteness of scientific knowledge and of our conceptual repertoire. The rough idea is that—just as in the case of "now"—our ways of using the words for feelings and sensations suggest a certain picture of what is happening; and although that picture is innocent in itself, we are tempted to misapply it, to exaggerate the linguistic analogies on which it is based. This misapplication is what creates the various puzzles that make conscious experience seem incomprehensible; and so our perplexities will evaporate once it is acknowledged and corrected.

6.2 THE CASE OF CONSCIOUSNESS

Let us begin by reviewing some of the notorious puzzles, beginning with those relating to our *knowledge* of mental phenomena.

In ordinary life we take ourselves to have a fair ability to say what is being experienced by another person. We observe certain behaviour and the circumstances in which it occurs, and often find ourselves in a position to judge (sometimes with complete certainty) whether someone is in pain, whether she is feeling hot or cold, whether something looks green to her, whether she is sad, and so on.

However, on philosophical reflection it can seem that we in fact have no right to pronounce upon such matters. For is it not obvious that mental life is *private*, so that only the individual undergoing an experience really knows which one she is undergoing? Could not it be that the visual sensations others have when they look at things we all call "green" are like the sensations I have when I look at things we all call "red"? And similarly for other types of experience. How can any of us tell how someone else feels when he screams and exhibits other so-called "pain behaviour"?

Worse still, the privacy of experience would seem to imply that we cannot be at all sure that there even *exist* any experiences besides our own. Perhaps everyone else is a zombie, the behaviour of which is not associated with any conscious experience at all. How can this be ruled out?

Surely the legitimacy of our ruling it out is not based merely on *analogy*—on reasoning inductively that other bodies are likely to exhibit roughly the same correlations between circumstantial/behavioural characteristics and mental activity that we notice in ourselves. For no such extrapolation from a *single* case—suggestive as it might be—could rationalize the unshakeable confidence with which we often judge what someone else is feeling or sensing. It could not justify our absolute certainty that we are 'not alone'.[2] "Just try—in a real case—to doubt someone else's fear or pain" (PI 303).

Further problems concern how to tell which experiences, if any, can be had by non-humans. Do worms have emotions? How about robots or space aliens? What is it like to be a bat? We feel that there are definite facts of the matter here. But they appear to be accessible only to those 'creatures' themselves![3]

---

[2] Suppose I know (somehow!) that another person is in exactly the same internal *physical* state I am in. Could I not then be certain that he is also in the same *mental* state? Not really—for it is not *a priori* obvious that mental facts supervene on physical ones. Perhaps the best direct evidence for that supervenience hypothesis would be the discovery of strong correlations between facts of these two kinds—correlations ranging across a variety of individuals. But how could such correlations ever be discovered unless the epistemic problem at issue had *already* been solved? We would have to already have a justified way of telling what mental states other individuals are in. Moreover, even if knowledge of another's brain-states were a *potential* route to knowledge of his mental states, there would remain the question, given our *present* ignorance of neural–mental correlations, of what could justify our *present* convictions about the mental states of others.

[3] See Thomas Nagel, "What is it like to be a bat?", *Philosophical Review* 83, 1974, 435–50.

Besides all these *epistemological* worries there are *metaphysical* puzzles that deepen the sense of mystery. How could experiences—sensations like *THIS* (pinching myself)—be nothing but certain physical events within the body, such as instances of a characteristic form of neurological activity! For experiences appear to have features that physical events cannot have. They strike us as peculiarly 'flimsy' and 'weightless'; as occupying an ethereal world shared only by other experiences belonging to the same person; as somehow both palpably real yet frustratingly incommunicable—whereas brain-events are essentially concrete, public, objective, and equally accessible to a variety of investigators. Thus we find it impossible to understand how experiences could simply *be* bodily events. We cannot even understand how such events could *engender* experiences.[4] So we are pushed towards the conclusion that mental phenomena are made out of a quasi-magical non-material stuff whose mode of interaction with the physical world defies comprehension—a conclusion totally at odds with our contemporary scientific world view.

Each of these perplexities of consciousness calls for further elaboration. But it is pretty clear that they are what constitute the fundamental mystery. And the central question of this chapter is whether—like the mystery of time-flow—it can be exposed as a collection of pseudo-problems. Can we find, lying behind these perplexities, some appealing picture of mental phenomena—something innocuous in itself perhaps, but liable, through linguo-conceptual overgeneralization, to puzzle-engendering misinterpretation?

According to Wittgenstein there is indeed such a picture, and its central element is that experiences are *private*. We imagine

---

[4] Such an "explanatory gap" (to use Joe Levine's term) has been described by David Chalmers as constituting "the *hard* problem of consciousness". He thinks that its intractability leaves us "entirely in the dark about how consciousness fits into the natural order" (*The Conscious Mind*, Oxford: Oxford University Press, 1996, pp. xi–xii).

each conscious mind as an arena in which events take place that can be witnessed only by the person whose mind it is. The sole form of access others have to this private arena is indirect—via inference from the person's behaviour and circumstances. It is rather like the difference between watching a movie from inside the cinema, and trying from the outside to figure out what is happening on screen from hearing the audience's reactions.[5]

As it stands, the image of 'private arenas of experience' is a *mere* picture, which leaves open how it is to be applied: that is, which of its features are to be taken seriously. But one tempting and common interpretation of it involves the following more specific commitments:

(i) Each sensation-term (such as "pain") is defined ostensively—understood by each individual in virtue of its association with a certain introspected phenomenal quality ('quale') of his own.

(ii) Consequently, the epistemologically basic and unquestionably justified uses of such terms occur in the context of first-person reports (such as "*I* am in pain").

(iii) Such judgements will have to be the basis for our ability to accurately describe the experiences of *other* people. That is to say, our practices of third-person attribution (such as "*S/he* is in pain") will be justified only to the extent that their reliability can be inferred (given collateral information) from the assumed reliability of first-person reports.

Call this the *inflated*-private-arena model.

We'll come eventually to the question of why that inflation is tempting. But first let us look at how it leads to various perplexities—including the epistemological and metaphysical problems just mentioned.

---

[5] Daniel Dennett calls this model "the Cartesian theatre". He discusses its dangers in his *Consciousness Explained*, Boston: Little Brown, 1991.

An immediate puzzle is to see how the requirement on justification that is specified in (iii) might be satisfied. How, on the basis of my understanding of the word "pain" as provided by its association with the introspected distinctive quality of my own pain sensations (that is, by my rule for the use of "I am in pain"), can I derive a compelling reason to suppose that someone screaming and writhing in front of me has an experience with *that* quality: that is, that she is feeling *pain* (in *my* sense of the word)? The answer appears to be that I cannot! For the only available argument—the 'argument from analogy with my own case'—rests on the implausible conjecture that I (as a child!) took careful note of the causes and effects of my pains. And even if I had collected a mass of such data, an inductive extrapolation from it would, at best, provide me with only *some* justification for attributing pain to others, falling short of the confidence that would often be appropriate.

It may be objected that "pain" is a word of *English*—a *communal* language—and that its meaning includes the legitimacy, without any need for argumentative support, of attributing pain to others on the basis of the usual circumstantial and behavioural evidence. However, a common puzzle-preserving response is to concede this point about the *public* word "pain", but to suppose that each individual might deploy an extra term of her own to refer to the private quality of her own pain-states—a term that *is* defined solely by means of introspective ostension.[6] And she may then raise the epistemological question using that term: "Do others get into *such* a state—which *I* am calling 'Q_{17}'? Is *this* what it is like for others who are in pain?" Thus the inflated-private-arena

---

[6] As Wittgenstein asks (rhetorically!): "[I]s it like this: the word 'red' means something known to everyone; and in addition, for each person, it means something known only to him?...[As] if when I uttered the word I cast a sidelong glance at the private sensation, as it were in order to say to myself: I know all right what I mean by it." (PI 273–4).

model implies that everyone has ways of representing the 'what-it-is-like-for-me' of her own experiences—ways of forming thoughts like "I am having an experience of type Q_{17} again", and "My experience when I stub my toe is almost always of type Q_{17}". And she can then reasonably wonder—but cannot easily decide—whether others have Q_{17}-type experiences when they are in pain.

Thus epistemological problems of consciousness arise regardless of whether one identifies the introspectively-defined sensation-concepts with ordinary communal concepts, such as PAIN, or with private qualia-concepts, such as Q_{17}. The puzzles derive, on either view, merely from supposing that each of us possesses experiential concepts whose application to ourselves is based on introspection, and whose possession conditions are captured by that usage, but whose conditions of application to others must be inferred.[7]

The metaphysical mystery of consciousness is also provoked by the inflated-private-arena model. For, on the one hand, any phenomenon that has characteristic physical causes and effects can be expected to itself boil down to something physical. So, in particular, a person's pains, since they tend to be brought about by injuries to his body and tend to induce flinching, crying, withdrawal, and so on, ought to be identifiable with phys-

---

[7] One might think that these epistemological problems do not necessarily presuppose a commitment to private phenomenal qualities (hence, to *every* feature of the inflated private-arena model). For it will suffice (one might think) that first-person judgements are simply assumed to be fundamentally and unquestionably justified—in contrast with third-person judgements, whose conditions of justification are to be rationalized on the basis of the legitimacy of this first-person practice. However, it is hard to see what could *motivate* that assumed asymmetry other than the feeling that a first-person judgement of experience is based on introspection *properly so-called*—the feeling, in other words, that such a judgement is fundamentally akin to a perceptual judgement of an external quality, in that *both* are taken to rest on some distinct mental state that points us towards the judged fact.

ical (presumably, neurological) events.[8] But on the other hand, a feature of the inflated picture of experience is that we are aware (or *can*, by paying special attention, *become* aware) of its qualitative characteristics. And these characteristics appear to have peculiarities so extreme (to the point of *indescribability*) that no physical reduction of them is imaginable.

This pro-dualist sentiment—somewhat arm-waving as it stands—may be bolstered by the following more precise argument. It is plausible that facts of 'immediate constitution' are *never* susceptible to explanation. There is, for example, no explanation of why H_2O makes water, or why the temperature of a gas is constituted by the mean kinetic energy of its molecules. Nevertheless, what we *can* sometimes do—indeed *must* do in order to *establish* any such property-constitution claim—is to explain the characteristic *symptoms* of the superficial property in terms of its association with the alleged underlying property. We must be able to show why bodies of H_2O are colourless and boil at 100° C. We must show how the mean kinetic energy of a collection of gas molecules will issue in those phenomena that *manifest* its temperature. So it is only to be expected that even if my pains really are reducible to brain events of type B, it will be impossible to explain why this is so. But what *does* count against any such reducibility claim—at least, from the perspective of the inflated-private-arena model—is that it will also be impos-

---

[8] The reasoning is that if pain were not so constituted, then its behavioural effects *either* would lack sufficient causes that are entirely physical, *or* they would not and would therefore have two independent but individually sufficient causes: namely, the pain and the brain-state. But the first possibility would contravene the well-supported idea that the realm of the physical is causally complete. And the second possibility would involve an enormously improbable, limitless series of coincidences (since the correlated instances of pain and brain-state would not be causally connected). See Donald Davidson, "Mental Events" (1970), reprinted in his *Essays on Actions and Events*, Oxford: Oxford University Press, 1980; and David Papineau, *Thinking About Consciousness*, Oxford: Clarendon Press, 2002.

sible to show how these brain events engender all the character-istic *symptoms* of pain. For, from that perspective, each person recognizes his own experiences via their private phenomenal qualities—a pain is identified as such by some telltale 'what-it-is-like'. But these qualia cannot be expressed in *public language*. A person's terms for them cannot be understood by anyone else. So there can be no explanatory deduction from the presence of brain-state, B (which *is* described in public language) to the exemplification of such a quality. Thus there can be no adequate basis for reducing pain to something physical. And the same goes for any other experience-type.[9] Hence, mind–body dualism.

Summarizing, we have seen that from the intrinsically innocent image of each mind as a private arena one can slip into the more precise and demanding idea that everyone is vividly and fully acquainted with a panoply of personal and private mental qualities; and this commitment will issue in our epistemological and metaphysical puzzles. So it is fairly clear that we have identified both the initial imagery, and the substantive elaboration of it, that are responsible for the mys-tery of consciousness.[10] Not so clear, however, and remaining

---

[9] The philosophical literature contains a variety of further arguments, also designed to show how qualia preclude mind–body identity. Amongst the best known of these are Saul Kripke's modal argument in *Naming and Necessity* (Cambridge, MA: Harvard University Press, 1980), Frank Jackson's epistemo-logical argument in "What Mary Didn't Know" (*Journal of Philosophy* 83, 1986, 291–5), and David Chalmers' explanatory-gap argument in *The Conscious Mind*. This is not the place for an assessment of these various lines of thought. But it seems to me that the first two of them are undermined in Brian Loar's "Phenomenal States", *Philosophical Perspectives*, vol. 4, J. Tomberlin (ed.), Atascadero: Ridgeview Publishing Co., 1990, pp. 81–108; and the third is put in question by Ned Block and Bob Stalnaker, "Conceptual Analysis, Dualism and the Explanatory Gap", *Philosophical Review*, January 1999, 1–46.

[10] Let me repeat that the private-arena model is not itself a *theory* but merely a *picture*—a way of *imagining* the phenomena of conscious experience. Still, such a thing can make certain theoretical commitments seem plausible. In particular, it can foster the idea that each person possesses clear and complete conceptions of

to be shown, is that the inflated model is a misleading and dispensable linguo-genetic illusion—i.e. that the notorious problems of consciousness are pseudo-problems. What solid reasons are there for rejecting that model? In addition, it will remain to identify which facts about our ways of expressing and describing experience it derives from, and to explain just how they lead us into trouble.

Here is one substantial objection to the idea that each person is vividly acquainted with the qualities of his own experiences. Our ordinary understanding of the expression "vivid acquaintance with a quality" derives from our knowledge of *external-world* properties such as the redness and the roundness of physical objects. In such cases our awareness of the quality depends on our having some experience of it. We are acquainted with worldly redness in virtue of our sensations of red. But there is surely no experienced awareness of an experience of pain. No such *meta*-experiences (let alone *meta*-meta-experiences!) are ever revealed by introspection, but surely would be if they occurred. So we cannot coherently take ourselves to be vividly acquainted with the qualities of our experiences.[11]

experience features that are derived entirely from his introspection. And this is an assumption that leads inexorably to the above-mentioned perplexities. No doubt it is conceivable for a philosopher to make that problematic assumption on the basis of some *other* reason (or for no reason). But the private-arena model is an especially natural and common breeding ground for it.

[11] In response, a qualia theorist might protest that the 'vivid acquaintance' we have of our qualia need not and should not be assumed to have exactly the same character as our cognitive relation to observed *external* qualities. For a decent account of the former phenomenon must be responsible to its idiosyncratic features. So, perhaps, our understanding of "vivid acquaintance with qualia" comes directly from our being *in* such states of acquaintance?

But such a qualia theorist would be admitting that what is indescribable in public language goes beyond the qualia themselves, and also includes crucial elements of their philosophical justification. He would be admitting that when we have experiences we are *somehow* convinced—via some inarticulate method—that they possess distinctive personal qualities. And the view thereby becomes increasingly contrived, obscure, and unappealing.

And here is another objection. Acquaintance with a property requires the possession of a corresponding *concept*. And any concept is individuated by its distinctive psychological role. For example (and very roughly speaking), a person possesses the everyday concept, RED, in virtue of being disposed, by visual experiences of the kind typically provoked in normal conditions by red things, to have a tentative belief whose content is, THAT IS RED. But what could be the defining role of my alleged qualia-concept, $\text{RED}^*_{\text{HOR}}$ — the one corresponding to the alleged phenomenal quality of what it is like for something to look red to me? Presumably, at least a part of that role would be that I am disposed to believe the proposition, I HAVE $\text{RED}^*_{\text{HOR}}$, when and only when I actually have a token of the quale, $\text{red}^*_{\text{HOR}}$. But now we face a problem. For this quale is not supposed, as a matter of conceptual necessity, to be my own personal property. The associated concept is supposed to allow for a determinate fact as to whether or not some other person on a given occasion is having a quale of the same type as mine. And that requires the concept's psychological role to include or imply rules for the (tentative) acceptance of *S/HE HAS* $\text{RED}^*_{\text{HOR}}$.[12] But the

---

[12] Christopher Peacocke disagrees with this conclusion. He maintains, for example, that our objective concept, IS IN PAIN, is grasped by our recognition *that a subject falls under it when s/he is in the same conscious state that we are in when we perceive ourselves to be in pain*. But the problem (as Wittgenstein makes clear) is that our recognition of this fact is trivial—too weak for there to be any prospect of its inducing any grounds for applying the concept to others, hence too weak to sustain an understanding of what it is for that concept to apply:

> "But if I suppose that someone has a pain, then I am simply supposing that he has just the same as I have so often had."—That gets us no further. It is as if I were to say: "You surely know what 'It is 5 o'clock here' means; so you know what 'It is 5 o'clock on the sun' means. It means simply that it is just the same time there as it is here when it is 5 o'clock."—The explanation by means of *identity* does not work here. For I know well enough that one can call 5 o'clock—here and 5 o'clock there "the same time", but what I do not know is in what cases one is to speak of its being the same time here and there.
> In exactly the same way it is no explanation to say: the supposition that he has a pain is simply the supposition that he has the same as I.

addition of such rules would leave us with the wrong concept!—
no longer one that is graspable and definable *purely* in virtue of
introspective awareness. Instead we would be left with the
uncontroversial '*non*-phenomenal' *public* concept, LOOKS RED![13]

Thus there are at least two things seriously wrong with the
'introspective acquaintance' assumption—the assumption into
which we can be led by the private-arena model, and from
which flow the notorious epistemological and metaphysical
problems of consciousness. So let us now turn to the question
of exactly why the initial model might be appealing, and why
we are tempted to misapply it.

Wittgenstein's answer to the first part of this question
emphasizes a couple of features of sensation talk. One of them
is that the syntactic form and the usage of a first-person expression of experience—like "I am in pain"—resembles the form
and use of an empirical, descriptive occasion-sentence, "Object

> For *that* part of the grammar is quite clear to me: that is, that one will
> say that the stove has the same experience as I, if one says: it is in pain
> and I am in pain. (PI 350)

What is needed for concepts—of type F, say—to be successfully explained in
roughly Peacocke's way is an account of how we grasp the identity, x HAS THE
SAME F-PROPERTY AS Y, in terms of some more fundamental equivalence-relation
concept. (For example: "x and y have the same length-property iff they are con-
gruent", "Straight lines x and y have the same direction-property iff they are
parallel", and Frege's "sets x and y have the same numerocity iff there's a 1–1
correspondence between their members".) But no such more-fundamental
equivalence relation appears to be available to explain our understanding of "x
is in the same conscious state as y". See Peacocke, "Conceiving of Conscious
States", in his *Truly Understood*, Oxford: Oxford University Press, 2008.

[13] One rather desperate move that has been made to distinguish the phenomenal concept of a red-quale from the ordinary 'LOOKS RED' concept is to
suppose that any deployment of the former includes instances of the quale
itself! Thus, my beliefs about the occurrence of red*$_{HOR}$ would involve my having that very 'raw feel'. Similarly, someone's belief about his pain-quale would
incorporate that quale! (See David Papineau, *Thinking About Consciousness*). So
the cost of propping up the theory of 'phenomenal qualities' now extends to a
bizarre *ad hoc* account of concepts. Not to mention that my "I do *not* now have
red*$_{HOR}$" threatens to be self-falsifying!

x has property f".[14] The other pertinent fact is that a person saying "I am in pain" is not normally to be challenged (except with respect to linguistic competence and sincerity); each person is normally treated as the ultimate authority on his own experiences. Thus, "He thinks he is in pain but perhaps he is mistaken" and "I am not sure if I am in pain" are considered deviant, anomalous—a sort of violation of linguistic rules.[15]

Now, for most empirical occasion-sentences (such as "x is red"), one can be in a better or worse situation for judging whether they are true. So it is natural to think of reports of experience in that way too, and to take first-person reporters as relatively well placed and third-person reporters as not. Thus the picture of the mind as a private arena emerges when we assimilate first-person sensation reports to certain paradigm empirical descriptions of states of affairs, and then go on to imagine their quasi-incorrigibility as attributable to the fact that each such state of affairs is immanently detectable by just that person.

So far so good. We are not yet in trouble. This picture is still nothing but a picture, vague and non-committal: an expression of certain real similarities. But from there we can easily descend into confusion. The tempting and problematic further move is to regard 'immanent detection' as more like ordinary observation than it really is—specifically, to assume that our awareness of our own pains (for example) is based upon introspective apprehension of a telltale phenomenal quality, and that inferential support is needed for our practice of attribut-

---

[14] As Wittgenstein puts it:

> Perhaps the word "describe" tricks us here. I say "I describe my state of mind" and "I describe my room". You need to call to mind the differences between language games. (PI 290)

> What we call "*descriptions*" are instruments for particular uses. (PI 291)

[15] "... it makes sense to say about other people that they doubt whether I am in pain; but not to say it about myself." (PI 246)

ing pain to other people (since their states are beyond the scope of our faculties of introspection).

This inflation of the initial picture encourages (and is itself encouraged by) a couple of further confusions. More specifically, the central feature of that inflation—which is our thinking that when we focus our attention on an experience we are able to apprehend its private phenomena quality—involves, first, a failure to distinguish between *apprehending* an experience and '*immersing oneself in it*'; and second, a failure to distinguish between awareness of the quality *of* an experience and awareness of the quality it *presents*.

In fact, when we do what we call "focusing our attention on an experience" we are not thereby making ourselves especially aware of the original experience. Rather we are replacing it with a somewhat different one. We are *modifying* the collection of our simultaneous experiences, making that one more intense and sharp and informative, and others less so. Therefore, what we become especially aware of is not some quality of the experience, but simply whatever quality the experience represents as being 'out there'. For example, attending to an experience of 'looking red' is really just a matter of *amplifying* it. And the result is not an apprehension of what the original experience is like. Rather, it is a more intense 'looking red' experience—one in which one is more acutely aware of the real-world quality of being red.[16] Similarly, if you focus on the throbbing pain in your knee, you do not thereby encounter the incommunicable, intrinsic, phenomenal quality of that experience. Rather, you focus on your knee, and the quality of which you are vividly

---

[16] "But how is it even possible for us to be tempted to think that we use a word to *mean* at one time the colour known to everyone—and at another the 'visual impression' which I am getting *now*? How can there be so much as a temptation here?—I don't turn the same kind of attention to the colour in the two cases. When I mean the colour impression that (as I should like to say) belongs to me alone I immerse myself in the colour—rather like when I 'cannot

aware is simply the throbbing-pain quality that is purportedly located there.[17]

I have been suggesting, on behalf of Wittgenstein, that lying behind the 'mystery' of consciousness is an inflated-private-arena model of experience, and that lying behind this inflation is an exaggeration of the similarities between sensation reports and observation reports. However, if that suggestion is correct, then we should be able to see how the overstretched analogies would *directly* engender our various problems. We would then be able to understand how someone might become ensnared by these problems despite never having consciously entertained the private-arena model.

To that end, note first that the basic use of an observation predicate "D" (such as "red") is captured by a rule specifying the circumstances in which a person, S, should, with maximal confidence, apply it. Very roughly, S is to apply "D" to an observed object when and only when it provokes sensations in him of the sort that are normally provoked by objects that are D. Such applications of the term are not taken to require evidential support. But any further applications—to things that are *not* present—are regarded as justified only to the extent that they can be inferred, partly on the basis of observation reports. Thus one might infer that a certain unobserved object is likely *now* to be D from the fact that when it *was* observed it certainly *was* D.

So if we think of "pain" as an observation term[18] we will be led to demand (as we do with other observation terms) that the

get my fill of a colour'. Hence it is easier to produce this experience when one is looking at a bright colour, or at an impressive colour scheme." (PI 277)

[17] The qualia-promoting role of a failure to distinguish between awareness of some (alleged) quality *of* an experience and awareness of the quality it *presents* is emphasized in Gilbert Harman's "The Intrinsic Quality of Experience", *Philosophical Perspectives* 4, 1990, 31–52.

[18] Let me stress that the ur-mistake, according to Wittgenstein's diagnosis, is *not* a self-conscious endorsement of the false theory that expressions of sensation are simply a kind of observation report (i.e. that we literally observe our experi-

rule governing the privileged first-person applications provides a rationale for the other, less confident, non-definitive applications: namely, the third-person attributions of pain. But the only available argument will be to reason inductively ("by analogy") from our own case. And that seems much too weak— incapable of explaining the high degree of confidence we often place in judgements about what others are experiencing. This is how our overstretching of the analogy between sensation terms and observation terms gives rise to the familiar sceptical puzzles.[19]

In addition, we fall into problematic assumptions about the *determinacy* of facts of experience. For however difficult it may be to put ourselves in a position to observe whether or not a certain *extremely distant* object is (say) red, we do not, merely on that account, deny that there is a definite, objective fact of the matter. Therefore the impression that sensation terms tend to function like observation terms inclines us to suppose that there is generally

---

ences). It is less committal and less explicit than that—merely a tendency to exaggerate the analogies between these two linguistic practices—a tendency to regard (say) "I have a toothache" as more like a description of something observed than it actually is. To put it another way, the source of our perplexity is *not* supposed to be the belief that the observation model of introspection (= the inflated-private-arena model) is entirely accurate; but rather, a fuzzier state of mind in which we overestimate the extent to which it is. Similarly, one may claim that puzzles in the philosophy of mathematics stem from a tendency to overstretch the analogies between numerals and names of things like planets—a tendency to misread the heuristic picture of numbers as physical objects (see Chapter 1, Section 1.5). But that is not to impute a commitment to the theory that numbers really *are* physical objects! Thus it may well be that some philosophers who believe in qualia explicitly reject the 'inner observation' model of self-knowledge. But it is nonetheless possible that their belief stems from exaggerating the similarities between introspection and perception.

[19] Alternatively (as we have seen), someone might acknowledge that it is not the *English* word "pain" that functions like an observation term, but rather the private terms introduced by people as names for the introspected qualities of their pains. So the sceptical upshot will be that we each have insufficient reason to think that other peoples' pains resemble our own in possessing the same private quality as ours.

a *determinate* answer—whether knowable or not—to questions of the form, "Do creatures of type X have experiences of type Y?" And this does not sit comfortably with our sense that for many such questions—for example, "Do worms have feelings?"—we cannot conceive of any reasonable way of settling the matter.

Regarding ontology, the exaggerated analogy causes trouble because the implied 'phenomenal qualities of experience' are indescribable in public language. So their presence cannot be deduced from, hence explained by, any neurological states of affairs. But if pains have features that cannot be explained in terms of underlying brain-states, then they cannot be identical to, nor realized by, such states. Thus pains are ontologically bizarre—as are all mental phenomena.

These puzzles will disappear if we can learn not to apply the private-arena model so indiscriminately. And that will happen once we are able to recognize (and keep clearly in focus) certain crucial respects in which sensation reports and observation reports are *not* analogous.

For example, the meaning-constituting use of "pain" is crucially different from that of "red". As already noted, the basic use of "red" is (roughly) our tendency to apply it when we have the sort of visual sensation typically produced in human beings by red things. But the basic use of "pain" is (roughly) to apply it to ourselves when we are in the state that tends to make us cry, flinch, and so on, *and* to tentatively apply it to others when we see them exhibit such symptoms.[20]

Thus we teach someone how to use "red" by encouraging or correcting him in such a way as to bring it about that his application of it to what *he* sees is to things that *we* can see are red. He then proceeds to apply the term to things he cannot see,

---

[20] The present conjectures about the meaning-constituting properties of "red" and "pain" seem plausible. But, as argued in Chapter 5, Section 5.4, such matters call for painstaking empirical enquiry.

extending his basic use of it by means of inductive and abductive inference.

In the case of "pain", however, people are so trained that the state that causes their moaning, grimacing, recoiling, and so on, also causes their utterance of "I am in pain"; they come to make that utterance *instead* of moaning.

> ... words are connected with the primitive, the natural, expressions of the sensation are used in their place. A child has hurt himself and he cries; and then adults talk to him and teach him exclamations and later sentences. They teach him new pain behaviour. (PI 244)

In addition, the child comes to assert "S/he is in pain" of people who are observed to exhibit those patterns of behaviour. Thus the conditions for third-person attributions are *not* inferred from the first-person practice (plus collateral information). We do not first notice that our utterances of "I am in pain" correlate with our shrieking, writhing, and so on; second, jump to the generalization that, in *anyone*, shrieking and writhing will be a likely indicator of pain; and third, on that basis, arrive at our belief, concerning the shrieking and writhing child before us, that he is probably in pain. Rather, there appears to be an innate, unreasoned tendency[21] for the observation of someone shrieking and writhing to induce the conviction that he is in pain.[22] Thus the first-person and

---

[21] Note that (as also illustrated by the case of enumerative induction) "unreasoned" (in the sense of "without argumentative support") does not imply "irrational". As Wittgenstein puts it: "To use a word without a justification does not mean to use it without right." (PI 289)

[22] Arguably, the causal process involves *mirror neurons*: my observation of someone's pain behaviour causes discomfiting brain activity in me that is analogous to activity in that person's brain—which in turn engenders my conviction that he is in pain. See Alvin Goldman, "Imitation, Mindreading, and Simulation", in S. Hurley and N. Chater (eds.), *Perspectives on Imitation: From Cognitive Neuroscience to Social Science*, Cambridge, MA: MIT Press, 2004;

third-person practices are consistent with one another—they interlock. However, each of them is epistemologically basic; neither is inferred from the other, and neither is taken to stand in need of justification.

Our neglect of these phenomena—our neglect of the *actual* relations between first-person and third-person sensation reports—is what allows us to think of introspection as closely akin to observation, which in turn gives rise to the idea that there are 'accessible' realms to be perceived and 'inaccessible' realms to be conjectured about. But absent an overly observational picture of introspection, absent the taken-too-seriously private-arena model, and absent the underlying doxastic substance of these inflated images—namely, the assumption that our introspections alone provide each of us with our experience-concepts—the familiar epistemological problems disappear. My belief that the child before me is in agony is an immediate causal consequence of what I see and hear. The step from those observations to that belief is not based on reasoning, and is legitimate independently of my ability to articulate any grounds for it. No doubt we do eventually come to *self-consciously* associate such convictions with particular observed patterns of circumstance and behaviour. And *these* explicit general beliefs must and can be justified empirically and inductively. But they play a merely occasional and relatively superficial role in our practices of attributing experiences to others.

Turning to our inclination to think that there must exist a *determinate* fact as to whether a given type of thing (a worm, a fish, a computer...) can occupy a given type of mental state: again it is the false analogy between the (non-introspectible)

A. Goldman C. and Sripada, "Simulationist Models of Face-based Emotion Recognition", *Cognition* 94/3, 2005, 193–213; and P. Jacob and F. de Vignemont, "What is it like to feel another's pain", *Philosophy of Science*, 79:2 2012, 295–316.

sensations of others and the (unobservable) qualities of faraway objects that lies behind it. So, in correcting this error, we remove the puzzlement about not being able to settle such questions. We get rid of the sense that there must always be a definite answer, even though we cannot see how to find it. We can easily accept that (just as in the case of applying vague terms to borderline cases) there will often be no *objective* facts as to which types of creature can have which types of experience.[23]

Finally, on the metaphysical front, the result is that since we do not recognize our pains via their private, incommunicable, qualitative character, the case in favour of a mysterious dualism collapses. It can no longer be argued that since my pains are identified via their inexplicable phenomenal qualities, then no constitution thesis of the form "pain = brain state B" could be true. For—without qualia in the picture—the only facts whose explanations are required in order to justify a neural reduction of pain are the facts about which forms of bodily change tend to cause pain and which forms of behaviour tend to ensue. And why should not a correlation between pain-states and brain-states be able (in principle) to account for those relations?

I have been suggesting that our neglect of the special use and function of experience-talk is what inclines us to over-interpret the private-arena model and to suppose that sensation-terms express ineffable phenomenal qualities. But once this misunderstanding has taken hold of our imagination it can survive the

[23] In Ned Block's opinion, questions about how to figure out the mental lives of non-humans constitute the "harder" problem of consciousness; for he finds them to be even tougher than what Chalmers (see footnote 4) termed the "hard" problem—that is, the metaphysical mind–body problem. In view of his commitment to qualia, Block's epistemological difficulty is unsurprising. (But one would have expected him to be no less puzzled about the metaphysical situation.) See his "The Harder Problem of Consciousness", *Journal of Philosophy* XCIX(8), 2002, 1–35.

concession that ordinary language words, such as "pain", are not designed for that job and do not do it. For, as we have seen, there is a tempting strategy of retrenchment whereby each of us deploys his own (ostensively defined) *private language terms* for that purpose. But this is surely a strained and irrational manoeuvre. For if the over-literal private-arena model really is—as argued here—a product of confusion about our ordinary sensation-terms, then an appreciation of their true conceptual and linguistic role ought to remove any inclination to embrace that model, and should undermine the temptation to think that there exists anything for the alleged *private* languages to describe.

To summarize, let us cast Wittgenstein's treatment of the 'mystery of consciousness' into the eight-stage schema for the rise and fall of philosophical problems that was elaborated in Chapter 2, Section 2.6.

Case V: Sensation

(1) *Background scientism.* The aspirations and methodology of traditional philosophical theorizing encourage our attribution of simple, common structures to different conceptual practices—especially when they *somewhat* resemble one another.

(2) *Analogy.* Our usage of "pain" is similar in striking respects to our usage of empirical descriptive predicates such as "red". In particular, each tends to be most confidently asserted of 'local' phenomena—either in the speaker's own immediate environment, or in his own mind.

(3) *Generalization.* Everyone knows of his own pain through its peculiar phenomenal quality; but such a private feeling may legitimately be attributed to other people only on the basis of our evidence that the behaviour they are exhibiting (such as screaming) tends to correlate with that quality.

(4) *Idiosyncrasy.* In fact, our use of "S/he is in pain" in the presence of screaming, etc. is *not* a reasoned extension of the first-person practice; the third- person use is taken to be equally basic. Moreover we do not accept "I am in pain" in response to our *awareness* of pain, or in response to some 'raw feel' that is provoked by pain; rather, pain itself is the unmediated cause of such beliefs.

(5) *Paradoxical tensions.* We are led by the 'linguistic analogy' to suppose that experiences occur in a private realm—that we are directly aware of our own pains, but are epistemically obliged to rationalize the conditions in which other peoples' pains are attributed. However those attribution-conditions cannot be adequately justified; so it would appear that we actually have no right to pronounce on the experiences of others. Moreover, although it is a central feature of our (highly successful) scientific world view that all causally-potent properties supervene on physical phenomena, the qualitative characteristics of a person's pains are so thoroughly detached from the objectively-describable non-phenomenal world that no grounding of experience in brain processes is conceivable.

(6) *Bewilderment.* Pain (and experience in general) is metaphysically bizarre and (in large part) epistemologically inaccessible.

(7) *Philosophical theories*

    (a) *Sceptical eliminativism*: there is really no such thing as pain over and above behaviour; its existence is an illusion (e.g. Gilbert Ryle, Georges Rey, Daniel Dennett).

    (b) *Revisionary solipsism*: there are no pains other than mine (e.g. Wittgenstein's *Tractatus*).

    (c) *Mysterianistic dualism*: pains are composed from an immaterial form of stuff that bears unknown relations to physical reality (e.g. René Descartes, Frank Jackson,

Galen Strawson, David Chalmers). We might well be
incapable of acquiring the conceptual resources or the
scientific knowledge needed for an understanding of
these phenomena (e.g. Thomas Nagel, Colin McGinn).

(d) *Conservative systematization*: the nature of pain is fixed
by the collection of basic *a priori* platitudes about it
(e.g. David Lewis).[24]

(8) *Therapeutic dissolution.* We must come to appreciate the
distinctive usage of pain attributions, thereby demolishing
the inflated-private-arena picture, removing the worry that
other peoples' pains might be different from our own, and
undercutting arguments for dualism.[25]

The preceding account gives, I believe, the main thrust of Wittgenstein's discussion of sensation in the *Philosophical Investigations*—his attempt to dissolve the sense of mystery surrounding

[24] Gibert Ryle, *The Concept of Mind,* Chicago: University of Chicago Press, 1949; Georges Rey, "A Reason for Doubting the Existence of Consciousness", in R. Davidson, G. Schwartz, and D. Shapiro (eds), *Consciousness and Self-Regulation*, vol. 3, New York: Plenum, 1983, pp. 1–39; Daniel Dennett, "On the Absence of Phenomenology", in D. Gustafson and B. Tapscott (eds.), *Body, Mind and Method: Essays in Honor of Virgil C. Aldrich*, Dordrecht: D. Reidel, 1979, pp. 93–114; René Descartes, *Meditations on First Philosophy* (1641), in *The Philosophical Writings of René Descartes*, trans. by J. Cottingham, R. Stoothoff, and D. Murdoch, Cambridge: Cambridge University Press, 1984, vol. 2, pp. 1–62; Frank Jackson, "What Mary Didn't Know", *Journal of Philosophy* 83, 1986, 291–5; Galen Strawson, "Realistic Monism: Why Physicalism Entails Panpsychism", in A. Freeman (ed.), *Consciousness and Its Place in Nature*, Imprint Academic, 2006, pp. 3–31; David Chalmers, *The Conscious Mind*; Thomas Nagel, "What is it like to be a bat?"; Colin McGinn, "Can We Solve the Mind–Body Problem?", *Mind* 98, Issue 391, 1989, 349–66; David Lewis, "Mad Pain and Martian Pain", in *Readings in the Philosophy of Psychology*, vol. I, N. Block (ed.), Cambridge, MA: Harvard University Press, 1980, pp. 216–22.
[25] Deflationary accounts of experience, along more or less Wittgensteinian lines, have been offered in a variety of works, including G. E. M. Anscombe's "The Intentionality of Sensation: A Grammatical Feature", in R. J. Butler (ed.), *Analytic Philosophy*, Oxford: Blackwell, 1965, 55–75; Daniel Dennett's *Consciousness Explained*; Gilbert Harman, "The Intrinsic Quality of Experience"; and Meredith Williams, *Wittgenstein, Mind and Meaning*, London: Routledge, 1999.

conscious experience. Let me now flesh out this approach a little by trying to answer some questions that are often raised about it. What exactly is his much-debated 'private language argument'? Is Wittgenstein nothing but a behaviourist? If not, what is he? What on earth could he mean by saying of a sensation of pain that "It is not a *something*, but not a *nothing* either" (PI 304)? And how does he respond to the notorious inverted-spectrum problem?

6.3 THE "PRIVATE LANGUAGE ARGUMENT"

Wittgenstein begins his discussion of experience by raising the question of whether someone might devise a special language to keep track of his sensations

> ...for his private use... The individual words of this language are to refer to what can only be known to the person speaking: to his immediate private sensations. So another person cannot understand the language. (PI 243)

He proceeds to devote a sequence of passages to this question and related puzzles. And that material has been generally interpreted to constitute a deep and sophisticated argument—the so-called "private language argument"—whose conclusion is that no such language is possible. The issues around which critical commentary has revolved are what exactly the argument is, and whether or not it is valid (in particular, whether it is vitiated by verificationist presuppositions).

However, this common framing of Wittgenstein's remarks strikes me as potentially misleading. For it fails to take into account: (i) that he considers and addresses *various* ways of understanding his initial question; (ii) that the imposition of *essential* conditions for 'being a language' runs contrary to his post-Tractarian views; and (iii) that his aspiration is therapeutic—merely the unmasking of confusions and not the establishment of profound results, and so the term "private language *argument*" (which Wittgenstein does not himself use) conveys the wrong impression.

According to what I take to be the most philosophically important construal of his question, it concerns a language whose terms cannot be understood by another person because they are introduced by someone to refer to the peculiar introspected qualities of his own experience—that is, to refer to his own 'qualia'. As we have seen, Wittgenstein's fundamental critical point concerning that issue—namely, that our standard sensation terms do not function (in relevant respects) like observation terms—was based, not on argument, but on simply reminding us of what we say, of how we use these different kinds of expression. And the following further ideas were pretty obvious consequences of this point: that third-person rules of ascription do not need to be justified on the basis of the first-person rule; that narrowly circumscribed sensation-types have no subjective character, capable of varying from one individual to another; and therefore that a person cannot develop a language in which these (non-existent) introspected subjective characters are named. We find no deep and sophisticated arguments here—and certainly no reliance on verificationism.[26]

But there is a further sense—not tied to qualia—in which Wittgenstein deploys the term "private language". He uses it in

---

[26] One of Wittgenstein's techniques to help loosen the grip of the ostensive-definition (inflated-)private-arena model is to note various anomalies that it would engender. It would imply, for example, that we would each constantly be having to assume, without evidence, that we had not forgotten what our paradigm quality of pain (—the one used in our ostensive definitiion—), was like (see PI 258, 265). But the concern we are supposed to have about this assumption is not (*à la* verificationism) that it would be *incoherent*, but that our right to make it would be questionable.

PI 258 to refer to what a person comes out with after she has gone through the ceremony of introducing a term (say "S") to name what she *takes* to be some peculiar, new experience of hers—peculiar in that it has *no* characteristic environmental cause, and that it has no behavioural manifestation except that from time to time she says "Now I have S again" (despite recognizing that no one can understand her). Call her use of words a "putative private language".

Now one might wonder whether such 'languages' are possible—that is, whether this sort of speechifying could qualify as *language* properly so-called, whether its terms would be truly *meaningful*. And one might take a negative answer to *this* question, rather than the previous one, to be the intended upshot of Wittgenstein's 'private language argument'.

But that would be a mistake. No such conclusion could be squared with his rejection of Tractarian essentialism about language—his rejection of the view that genuine languages, strictly speaking, have certain necessary characteristics (see PI 65, quoted in Chapter 3). Moreover, Wittgenstein never goes so far as to say that a *putative private language* is impossible. What he says, rather, is that such a practice—such a way of introducing and using words—would differ in important respects from familiar linguistic activity. In particular, there would be no *point* to it—no practical purpose would be achieved with it. Moreover, there would be no possibility of correcting someone's application of the terms of such a language—there would be no distinction between an application's *being* right and its *seeming* right. Of course, in certain ways a *putative private language* is quite analogous to English: its words are combined into sentences, which are asserted when the speaker feels it is appropriate to do so. But in other ways, just mentioned, it is very dissimilar to what we ordinarily call "language".

So is it a language or not? Do the words have meanings or don't they? For Wittgenstein these are poor and pointless questions. LANGUAGE is a family resemblance concept: there are no necessary and sufficient conditions for its application. In particular, there is no objective fact of the matter as to whether *putative private languages* are sufficiently like paradigm languages, such as English, to qualify. For there is no objective fact as to whether the uses of its terms are sufficiently like the uses of paradigmatically meaningful terms to count as meaningful. Moreover, it is of no importance how this issue is decided. What is important is to be aware of the similarities and differences between *putative private language* and ordinary language. Provided all this is out in the open then Wittgenstein allows that we can decide to say whatever we like, and

> ...sounds which no one else understands but which I *'appear to understand'* might be called a "private language". (PI 269)

6.4 BEHAVIOURISM

Wittgenstein wants to make it absolutely clear that he is *not* a behaviourist; that he is certainly not denying that pains (and other experiences) exist over and above behaviour. For he is aware that several of his remarks may give a contrary impression:

> ...only of a living human being and what resembles (behaves like) a living human being can one say: it has sensations; it sees; is blind; hears; is deaf; is conscious or unconscious. (PI 281)

> Only of what behaves like a human being can one say that it has pains. (PI 283)

> An inner state stands in need of outward criteria. (PI 580)

> [A sensation] is not a something... (PI 304)

However, as he insists, none of these statements amounts to behaviourism—either in its *eliminativist* form whereby the existence of experience is simply denied, or in its *reductionist* form according to which attributions of mental states may be translated without loss of meaning into attributions of behaviour and behavioural dispositions.[27]

His point, rather, is that the basic regularities of use underlying sensation language—those regularities in word use whose mastery our understanding of that language consists in—include the tendency to make simple third-person attributions of experience in the appropriate behavioural and environmental circumstances. But it is not that we have (or *should* have) *inferred* those beliefs from assumed correlations between sensation types and forms of behaviour. We may well have no explicit knowledge of such correlations. The situation, rather, is that our observation of the behaviour has a natural tendency to bring about the beliefs. Thus we *implicitly* master something like a function, "The probability that he is in pain, given that he exhibits behaviour of type B in conditions C, is x", which specifies how much confidence, x, to have in a third-person pain attribution, as a function of behaviour and other circumstances, B&C. But this rule is

---

[27] Conceptual reductive behaviourism comes in a variety of forms. At its crudest it might include theses along the lines of:

x is in pain ≡ x is crying, etc.

But Wittgenstein is no less opposed to more sophisticated forms of behavioural analysis, e.g. (again, vastly oversimplifying):

x is in pain ≡ x is *disposed* to cry, etc.
x is in pain ≡ x is *in an internal state* that tends to cause crying, etc.
x is in pain ≡
    x is in an internal state that (a) tends to cause crying, etc. that (b) is itself caused by bodily damage, and that (c) bears blah-blah causal relations to other internal states that themselves have so-and-so environmental or internal causes and such-and-such internal and/or behavioural effects. (Analytical functionalism.)

not *explicitly* known or followed; so it does not permit any translation of pain-talk into behaviour-talk. Moreover, the *first*-person attributions are not covered by this rule. So, for both of these reasons, we are a long way from reductive behaviourism.

Turning to the *eliminativist* brand, what Wittgenstein clearly *does* deny is the existence of pain *qualia*, of private 'raw feels'. But he is not denying the existence of *pain*. He is rejecting the idea that we understand the word for it, "each from our own case", by acquaintance with its referent and mediated by its 'raw feel'.

This is an instance of a general change in outlook, from the *Tractatus* to the *Investigations*, on the relationship between meaning and reference. The *Tractatus* view was that the meaning of a word—the important thing about it, the thing that anyone who understands it must know—is what it refers to. But (as we saw in Section 4.1 of Chapter 4) this view is attacked at the very beginning of the *Investigations*, where it is argued that the most fundamental aspect of the meaning of a word is its *use*, and that only in certain cases (such as names of people, of mountains, of colours, of certain shapes) is that use explained by indicating a reference. The terms deployed in humdrum empirical descriptions (of houses, for instance) are like this. In other cases, although we can always, once we understand a term, trivially specify its reference (by adverting to the schema, "N" refers to N), we do not arrive at that understanding by focusing on the reference (note Wittgenstein's remarks about the numerals in PI 10). And this is the situation with the word "pain". What it refers to is, trivially, pain. But its meaning-constituting use is not a matter of our applying it to events that appear to be pains. Indeed there are no such 'appearances', distinct from the pains themselves and capable of varying from one person to another.

These ideas are illustrated in the following vivid passage:

> Now someone tells me that he knows what pain is only
> from his own case!—Suppose everyone had a box with
> something in it: we call it a "beetle". No one can look
> into anyone else's box, and everyone says he knows
> what a beetle is only by looking at his beetle.—**Here**
> [unlike in the case of pain] it **would** be quite possible
> for everyone to have something different in his box.
> One might even imagine such a thing constantly
> changing.–But suppose the word "beetle" had a use in
> these people's language?–If so it would not be used as
> the name of a thing. The thing in the box has no place
> in the language game at all; not even as a something:
> for the box might even be empty.–No one can 'divide
> through' by the thing in the box; it cancels out, what-
> ever it is. (PI 293)
>
> *[My emphasis and parenthetical insertion]*

His central point is that a sensation in mind is *not* like a
beetle in a box—which is something that retains a distinctive
appearance even if that appearance plays no role in public
beetle-talk. It is a fiction, induced by false analogies, to
imagine sensations as entities to which we can refer
ostensively (as we can to private beetles). Thus Wittgenstein
asks himself:

> Are you not really a behaviourist in disguise? Aren't you
> at bottom really saying that everything except human
> behaviour is a fiction?

and answers:

> —If I do speak of a fiction, then it is a *grammatical* fic-
> tion. (PI 307)
>
> The paradox disappears only if we make a radical break
> with the idea that language always functions in one way,
> always serving the same purpose: to convey thoughts—

which may be about houses, pains, good and evil, or anything else you please. (PI 304)[28]

6.5 INVERTED SPECTRA

One of the classic philosophical puzzles about sensation is the
so-called inverted-spectrum problem. Is it possible that what it
is like for me to see red things is what it is like for other people
when they see green things, and *vice versa*? It's often supposed
that a positive answer to this question is a vote for the inflated-
private-arena model, for the possibility of a private language
whose terms might determinately be applied to the sensations
of others, and for the existence of peculiar experiential features
(qualia) to which the terms of such a language refer—whereas
a negative answer is taken to mark a more behaviouristic (Wittgensteinian?) rejection of all these ideas.

But as it stands, this way of putting the issue is oversimpli-
fied, for it fails to distinguish two quite separate forms of the
inverted-spectrum question—one which presupposes that the
nature of experience may be captured entirely in ordinary lan-

---

[28] Immediately preceding this quoted passage Wittgenstein responds to the
charge of behaviourism as follows:

> "And yet you again and again reach the conclusion that that the sensa-
> tion itself is a *nothing*." Not at all. It is not a *something*, but not a *noth-
> ing* either! The conclusion was only that nothing would serve just as
> well as a something about which nothing could be said. We have only
> rejected the grammar which tries to force itself on us here. (PI 304)

What he means is that the picture of a person introspecting the intrinsic character of his pains, and of noticing either one private quality, or another, or perhaps *nothing*, is entirely wrong. The supposition that someone finds an absence
of qualia is just as confused as the supposition that he finds a particular one.

Thus I am disagreeing with Dennett, who interprets Wittgenstein as saying
here that a quale is "a something about which nothing can be said." See his
"Quining Qualia", in N. Block, O. Flanagan, and G. Guzeldere (eds.), *The
Nature of Consciousness*, Cambridge, MA: MIT Press, 1997, pp. 48–9.

guage, by means of expressions such as "like smelling a rose", "painful", and "looks red", and which asks whether, relative to such characterizations, an inverted-spectrum hypothesis might be true or plausible; and the other which presupposes that there exists a deeper, intrinsic, private way of describing one's experience, and which raises the inverted-spectrum possibility with respect to that terminology.

In its ordinary use, "What is it like to be in circumstances C?" is a request for an English characterization of someone's experience in C; and it can be answered either directly, by naming the sort of sensation we have in C (such as itchy, amusing, exhilarating, and so on), or indirectly, by reference to the type of experience as that which we tend to have in certain different circumstances C* ("It's like swallowing an oyster", "It is like looking at a ripe tomato"). In answering such questions—in making assertions of the form "What it's like to be in C is so-and-so"—we apply the familiar terminology of experience ("painful", "looks red", and so on) in the way we have been taught, according to the regularities of use we have absorbed. Sometimes a given expression will be confidently applied, at other times confidently withheld, at other times there will be uncertainty, and sometimes, when the situation in question is particularly bizarre—involving peculiar drugs, brain operations, weird organisms, and so on—we might well feel, not merely that we do not know what is being experienced, but that there is no determinate fact of the matter.

According to the rules of use for such ordinary expressions, another person's visual experience when he looks at red things will, under normal circumstances, be just like mine—and there is no answer to the question of what that is like. Consider, by analogy, the following exchange: "How long is the table?", "It is as long as this rug", "But how long is that?", "Five feet long". At this point it would not normally make sense to persevere with "And how long is five feet long?" Similarly, our familiar "What is it like?" questions tend to 'bottom out' at terms such as "painful" and "looks red".[29] Thus if the inverted-spectrum question is raised relative to normal conditions, and with respect to ordinary language characterizations of experience, the answer is, trivially, that there is no such possibility: if everything is normal, red things look red, and they look that way to everybody.

Of course, what those who worry about inverted spectra *typically* have in mind is a quite different hypothesis—one whose coherence presupposes a deeper, more intimate level of description. This worry involves the inflated-private-arena model, the possibility of a generally applicable private language, and the existence of qualia. And, as Wittgenstein has shown, the question in this form is a pseudo-question: there are no such private qualities and private terms, and the whole issue arises from a confused assimilation of first-person sensation reports to observations.[30]

---

[29] But note PI 278:

> "I know how the colour green looks to me"—surely that makes sense!
> Certainly: what use of the proposition are you thinking of?

Wittgenstein seems to have in mind playful answers like, "The way grass looks". Hence his very next remark:

> "Imagine someone saying: 'But I know how tall I am'" and laying his hand on top of his head to prove it." (PI 279)

[30] In notes from 1934–36 Wittgenstein himself considers two kinds of inverted-spectrum scenario. The first, which he takes to be entirely conceivable, involves a friend who one day announces that all of a sudden red things have begun to look blue to him, and blue things look red. The second is the supposition that roughly half the population sees colours (and has always seen them) in that deviant way; and this latter hypothesis he takes to be incoherent, since there could be no fact of the matter as to which half sees things correctly and which half sees red things as blue.

Neither of those inverted-spectrum hypotheses corresponds to either of the pair of hypotheses that I have just distinguished. However, Wittgenstein does mention the qualia-presupposing one in his *Philosophical Investigations*:

> The essential thing about private experience is really not that each person possesses his own exemplar, but that nobody knows whether

It is important to see, however, that our ability to make *ordinary* sense of questions about what it is like to be in various circumstances—hence our ability to make sense of the 'ordinary language' inverted-spectrum hypothesis—does not imply the inflated-private-arena model or the prospect of a private language. Therefore it is not necessary for someone who dismisses the 'mystery of consciousness' as a pseudo-issue, to claim that an inverted-spectrum hypothesis is nonsensical. It isn't even necessary to maintain that it is, in *all* circumstances, clearly false. Certainly, if raised with respect to *normal* circumstances it is indeed clearly false, as we have seen. But consider a person who (i) grows up normally, (ii) has an operation on his visual system such that red things start to look green to him, and *vice versa*, (iii) eventually learns nonetheless to apply colour terms just as we do, and (iv) then suffers amnesia so that he no longer remembers his early experiences. If it is asked whether this unfortunate individual has the same sensations as we do, the answer is not so obvious. It may be 'yes' or 'no', or it may well have no determinate answer; but it does not presuppose the private-arena model, the possibility of a private language, or the reality of qualia.[31]

other people also have *this* or something else. The assumption would be possible—though unverifiable—that one section of mankind had one sensation of red and another section another. (PI 271)

Needless to say, Wittgenstein is not himself endorsing the possibility of this hidden inversion. He is merely saying that it would follow from the existence of private experience—that is, qualia.)

I am grateful to Ned Block for alerting me to Wittgenstein's notes, first edited and published by Rush Rhees under the title "Wittgenstein's Notes for Lectures on 'Private Experience' and 'Sense Data'" (*Philosophical Review* 77(3), 1968, 271–5). They are discussed by Sidney Shoemaker in his "The Inverted Spectrum" (*Journal of Philosophy* 79, 1982, 357–81) and by Block in his "Wittgenstein and Qualia" (*Philosophical Perspectives*, 21 (Philosophy of Mind) 2007 73–115). Both of them argue, against Wittgenstein, that the inverted-spectrum possibility he accepts entails the possibility of the one he dismisses. For a response to that criticism see the following section.

[31] This four-stage scenario comes from Block's "Wittgenstein and Qualia" (op. cit.), pp. 91–5. A similar thought experiment had appeared in Shoemaker's

6.6 PSEUDO-QUALIA

Given that qualia are typically regarded by their advocates as *introspectively obvious*, there is something immediately puzzling about the suggestion that *theoretical arguments* are needed, and are available, to demonstrate their existence. One might well suspect that the argued-for entities are not really what they are advertised as being—i.e. that they are not *qualia* properly so-called. A case in point, it seems to me, is a line of thought of Ned Block's—an argument that invokes the four-stage scenario to which we have just alluded.

He reasons, in effect, that:

> (A) Although red things look green to the subject at stage iii (because of the operation on his visual system), they must be said "to look red to him" at stage iv. (That's because his speech behaviour has by then become entirely normal, and we should assume a 'normalcy principle' to the effect that '*in normal circumstances things look the same to all normal obeservers*'). Thus there is a change in the way red things look to the subject.

> (B) Yet there is surely *something* is his experience that remains the same from iii to iv.

> Hence, there are qualia. QED[32]

But neither of these premises is compelling. In particular, it is quite natural to say, in opposition to (A), that if red things look green to the subject at stage iii they must also look green at stage iv (since his intervening amnesia surely could not make a difference to how things look). Granted, we would then be

---

"The Inverted Spectrum". Shoemaker and Block (unlike myself) take it to provide an argument in favour of qualia. But see the immediately following discussion.

[32] "Wittgenstein and Qualia", pp. 91–6.

forced *either* to reject Block's 'principle of normalcy' (namely, that F-coloured surfaces look F to normal observers in normal circumstances), *or* to suppose, in virtue of the subject's extraordinary history, that, at stage iv, either he himself, or his situation, does not qualify as *normal*. But neither of these alternatives to (A) would be unreasonable.

Nor (and more to the present point) would it be at all unreasonable to reject Block's qualia-introducing thesis (B): that, granting the "looks green"–"looks red" inversion from iii to iv, something *experiential* 'surely' remains the same. Where does the "surely" come from? Is it the conviction that nothing relevant to experience has changed in the subject's brain? But in that case, how could we acknowledge the "looks red"–"looks green" inversion? And if those familiar categories of experience do not have to supervene on brain-states, why suppose that there is a further type of experience—a phenomenal quality— that does have to? It would seem that Block is simply *stipulating* that this is so! In which case one might well doubt whether the so-called "qualia" whose existence has been 'established' here are really the sort of thing whose existence has been in dispute within philosophy.

We can shed further light on this issue by looking at another of Block's "arguments for qualia"—one that he bases on the subtle physiological and behavioural differences amongst people undergoing the same experiences.[33]

It is not controversial that ordinary experience types (such as toothaches, itchy noses, sensations of red, and so on) are identified fairly crudely in terms of certain characteristic causes, behavioural effects, and relations to other mental states. And, again uncontroversially, such experiences might be *realized* by specific bodily states (presumably, neurological states): it may

[33] See his "Wittgenstein and Qualia"', pp. 86–9. Shoemaker had developed an analogous position in "The Inverted Spectrum", pp. 372–8.

be that there is a correlation between experience types and human brain-states such that the latter relate causally to sensory inputs, behavioural outputs, and to each other in just the ways that the associated experiences do. Moreover, it is not implausible—and this is reinforced by the scientific evidence cited by Block—that different peoples' experiences are physiologically realized in slightly different ways. Perhaps there are even some *radical* differences in the ways that different peoples' experiences are realized. Certainly, there may well be merely *hypothetical* realizations of certain experience types that differ radically from their *actual* realizations.

Now we might conceivably say—as Block suggests we do—that these different physical realizations of ordinary experiences engender differences in "what the experiences are like", in their "qualitative characters", in the "qualia" that are possessed. This would be a coherent way of speaking—perhaps even worthwhile for certain purposes. But would it involve a commitment to *genuine qualia*—that is, to *immediate phenomenal qualities*, to the contentious mental entities that have been at issue under these labels in the philosophical literature and in this chapter? I think not—and for the following reasons:

> First, although we might decide to *say* that differences in realizing brain-state constitute differences in "experienced quality", this would be a matter of linguo-conceptual *legislation*. For no reason has been given for supposing that what we *already* understand by "experienced quality" makes that the *right* thing to suppose.

> Second—and related to the first point—genuine qualia have been traditionally taken by their advocates (including Block himself in earlier work[34]) to be *obviously*

---

[34] See, for example, his "Troubles with Functionalism" (in C. W. Savage, (ed.), *Minnesota Studies in the philosophy of Science,* Minneapolis: University of Minnesota Press, 1978, pp. 261–326), where he describes qualia as "immediate

there—not to be merely conjectured *theoretical* entities whose rational acceptance hinges on the results of sophisticated empirical research.

And third, it is in the nature of genuine qualia to engender the epistemological and metaphysical controversies discussed in section 6.2. However, Block's new-fangled pseudo-qualia do not. So let them exist, by all means. But why, as philosophers, should we care?

Finally—but along similar lines—it is worth mentioning one more potential "argument for qualia", also mentioned by Block.[35] Suppose that we discover that in half the population, observed red things fire up one part of the visual cortex and green things a different part. But for the rest of us it turns out to be the other way round. Would not this give us *some* reason to suspect there is some "experiential" difference—a qualia difference—between people in the two groups when they look at red things? Certainly we can introduce that way of speaking. But, as before, such talk of so-called "qualia" would not engender the perplexities that give genuine qualia their philosophical importance.

6.7 CONCLUSION

It can seem patently obvious to someone reflecting on his own conscious life that together with (or included within) his sensations of things looking red there is the entirely private matter

---

phenomenal qualities" and suggests that if someone asks what they are, he should be answered in the way that Louis Armstrong answered the question "What is jazz?"—namely, "If you gotto ask, you ain't never gonna get to know."

[35] "Wittgenstein and Qualia", p. 80. For further critical reactions to that paper, see John Canfield, "Ned Block, Wittgenstein, and the Inverted Spectrum", *Philosophia* 37(4), 2009, 691–712.

of *what it is like for him* to have that sort of sensation; that alongside the persistent itchiness of his nose there is *how it subjectively feels* for him to have an itchy nose; that he can recognize the *incommunicable phenomenal character* of his own intense desires; and so on.

And if such intimations are taken seriously the phenomenon of consciousness becomes highly perplexing. For it will follow that we don't have the knowledge we ordinarily take ourselves to have of what others are experiencing. And it will also follow that these events cannot be located within the causal-explanatory nexus: experience emerges as a supernatural phenomenon; science is thrown into crisis; radically new concepts and theories are urgently required!

But, says Wittgenstein, this flap is quite unnecessary. We can all calm down. For a compelling case can be made that the troublesome 'impressions of obviousness' should *not* be taken seriously—that they are misleading products of confusion. As we've seen, not only are such supposed obvieties—the alleged 'private qualia'—impossible to make sense of, but one can give a plausible *undermining* explanation of our grounds for believing in them.—We are so moved by the evident similarities between observation reports and first-person sensation claims— by both of them being peculiarly basic and peculiarly authoritative—that we go too far in our analogizing and come to think that the latter, like the former, reflect a vivid awareness of intrinsic qualities—qualities whose 'local' presence is immediately knowable and whose conditions of 'non-local' possession (by faraway things, or by the experiences of others) will have to be inferred.

By paying closer attention to the *actual* use and function of sensation terms we can learn to appreciate the incorrectness of this stretched analogy and can thereby unravel the perplexities of consciousness. There turns out to be absolutely no need for a scientific revolution; indeed, no need—at least as far as these pseudo-problems are concerned—for any sort of *theory* of mind.

What sort of progress is this? The fascinating mystery has been removed—yet no depths have been plumbed in consolation; nothing has been explained or discovered or reconceived. How tame and uninspiring, one might think. But perhaps, as Wittgenstein suggests, the virtues of clarity, demystification, and truth should be found satisfying enough.[36]

---

[36] I would like to thank Ned Block for guiding me through the literature on consciousness, and for his invaluable criticism of earlier drafts of this chapter.

Bibliography

Ahmed, A. (ed.). *Wittgenstein's Philosophical Investigations: A Critical Guide*. Cambridge: Cambridge University Press, 2010.

Anscombe, G. E. M. *An Introduction to Wittgenstein's 'Tractatus'*. London: Hutchinson, 1959.

—— "The Intentionality of Sensation: A Grammatical Feature", in R. J. Butler (ed.), *Analytic Philosophy*. Oxford: Blackwell, 1965, 158–80.

—— "A Theory of Language?", in I. Block (ed.), *Perspectives on the Philosophy of Wittgenstein*. Cambridge, MA: MIT Press, 1981, 148–58.

Augustine. *Confessions*, translated by H. Chadwick. Oxford: Oxford University Press, 2008.

Ayer, A. J. "Can There Be a Private Language?", in G. Pitcher (ed.), *Wittgenstein: The Philosophical Investigations*. New York: Doubleday, 1966, 251–66.

Baker, G. and Hacker, P. *Scepticism, Rules and Language*. Oxford: Blackwell, 1984.

—— *Wittgenstein: Meaning and Understanding: Volume 1 of an Analytical Commentary on the 'Philosophical Investigations'*. Oxford: Blackwell, 2005.

—— *Wittgenstein: Rules, Grammar, and Necessity*, 2nd edition. Oxford: Blackwell, 2009.

Black, M. *A Companion to Wittgenstein's Tractatus*. Cambridge: Cambridge University Press, 1964.

Blackburn, S. "The Individual Strikes Back", *Synthese* 58, 1984, 281–302.

—— *Truth: A Guide*. Oxford: Oxford University Press, 2005.

Block, N. "Troubles with Functionalism", in C. W. Savage, (ed.), *Minnesota Studies in the Philosophy of Science*, vol. IX, Minneapolis: University of Minnesota Press, 1978, 261–326.

—— "Inverted Earth", *Philosophical Perspectives* 4, (Action Theory and Philosophy of Mind). Atascedero: Ridgeview Publishing Company, 1990, 53–79.

—— "The Harder Problem of Consciousness", *Journal of Philosophy* XCIX(8), 2002, 1–35.

—— "Wittgenstein and Qualia", *Philosophical Perspectives*, 21 (Philosophy of Mind), 2007, 73–115.

—— and Stalnaker, R. "Conceptual Analysis, Dualism and the Explanatory Gap", *Philosophical Review* 108: 1, January 1999, 1–46.

Boghossian, P. "The Rule-Following Considerations", *Mind* 98, 1989, 507–49.

—— "Epistemic Rules", *Journal of Philosophy*, 105, 2008, 472–500.

Budd, M. "Wittgenstein on Meaning, Interpretation and Rules", *Synthese* 58, 1984, 303–23.

—— *Wittgenstein's Philosophy of Psychology*. London: Routledge, 1989.

Canfield, J. V. "The Community View", *Philosophical Review* 105:4, 1996, 469–88.

—— "Ned Block, Wittgenstein, and the Inverted Spectrum", *Philosophia* 37(4), 2009, 691–712.

Cavell, S. *The Claim of Reason: Wittgenstein, Skepticism, Morality and Tragedy*. Oxford: Oxford University Press, 1979.

Chalmers, D. *The Consciousness Mind: In Search of a Fundamental Theory*. Oxford: Oxford University Press, 1996.

Chihara, C. and Fodor, J. "Operationalism and Ordinary Language: A Critique of Wittgenstein", in G. Pitcher (ed.), *Wittgenstein: The Philosophical Investigations*. New York: Doubleday, 1966, 384–419.

Child, William. *Wittgenstein*. London: Routledge, 2011.

Cioffi, F. "Wittgenstein and the Fire-festivals", in I. Block (ed.), *Perspectives on the Philosophy of Wittgenstein*. Cambridge, MA: MIT Press, 1981, 212–38.

Clark, R. W. *The Life of Bertrand Russell*. New York: Knopf, 1975.

Conant, J. "Must We Show What We Cannot Say", in R. Fleming and M. Paine (eds.), *The Senses of Stanley Cavell*. Lewisburg, PA: Bucknell University Press, 1989, 242–83.

Davidson, D. "Mental Events" (1970), reprinted in his *Essays on Actions and Events*. Oxford: Oxford University Press, 1980, 207–27.

Dennett, D. "On the Absence of Phenomenology", in D. Gustafson and B. Tapscott (eds.), *Body, Mind and Method: Essays in Honor of Virgil C. Aldrich*. Dordrecht: Reidel, 1979, 93–114.

—— *Consciousness Explained*. Boston: Little Brown, 1991.

—— "Quining Qualia", in N. Block, O. Flanagan, and G. Guzeldere (eds.). *The Nature of Consciousness*. Cambridge, MA: MIT Press, 1997, 619–42.

Descartes, R. *Meditations on First Philosophy* (1641), in *The Philosophical Writings of René Descartes*, translated by J. Cottingham, R. Stoothoff, and D. Murdoch. Cambridge: Cambridge University Press, 1984, vol. 2, 1–62.

Diamond, C. *The Realistic Spirit*. Cambridge, MA: MIT Press, 1991.

Drury, M. O'C. "Conversations with Wittgenstein", in R. Rhees (ed.), *Recollections of Wittgenstein*. Oxford: Oxford University Press, 1984, 97–171.

Dummett, M. "Wittgenstein's Philosophy of Mathematics", in G. Pitcher (ed.), *Wittgenstein: The Philosophical Investigations*. New York: Doubleday, 1966, 420–47.

—— *The Interpretation of Frege's Philosophy*. Cambridge, MA: Harvard University Press, 1981.

—— *The Seas of Language*. Oxford: Oxford University Press, 1993.

Fine, K. "The Question of Realism", *Philosophers' Imprint*, 1:1, June 2001.

Flanagan, O. *The Science of the Mind*. Cambridge, MA: MIT Press, 1991.

Fodor, J. and Lepore, E. *Holism: A Shopper's Guide*. Oxford: Blackwell, 1991.

Fogelin, R. *Wittgenstein*, 2nd edition. London: Routledge, 1995.

—— *Taking Wittgenstein at his Word*. Princeton, NJ: Princeton University Press, 2009.

Forster, M. "Wittgenstein on Family Resemblance Concepts", in A. Ahmed (ed.), *Wittgenstein's Philosophical Investigations: A Critical Guide*. Cambridge: Cambridge University Press, 2010, 66–87.

Frege, G. "Concept and Object", in P. Geach and M. Black (eds.), *Translations from the Philosophical Writings of Gottlob Frege*. Oxford: Blackwell, 1952, 42–55.

—— *Begriffsschrift*, translated by T. Bynum as *Conceptual Notation*. Oxford: Oxford University Press, 1972.

Geach, P. "Saying and Showing in Frege and Wittgenstein", *Acta Philosophica Fennica* 28, Nos. 1–3 (*Essays in Honour of G.H. von Wright*, ed. J. Hintikka), 1976, 54–70.

Ginsborg, H. "Primitive Normativity and Skepticism about Rules", *Journal of Philosophy*, 108:5, 2011, 227–54.

Glock, H. "Wittgenstein on Concepts", in A. Ahmed (ed.), *Wittgenstein's Philosophical Investigations: A Critical Guide*. Cambridge: Cambridge University Press, 2010, 88–108.

Goldfarb, W. "Wittgenstein on Understanding", *Midwest Studies in Philosophy* XVII, 1992, 109–22.

—— "Metaphysics and Nonsense: On Cora Diamond's *The Realistic Spirit*", *Journal of Philosophical Research* 22, 1997, 57–74.

Goldman, A. "Imitation, Mindreading, and Simulation", in S. Hurley and N. Chater (eds.), *Perspectives on Imitation: From Cognitive Neuroscience to Social Science*. Cambridge, MA: MIT Press, 2004, 79–94.

—— and Sripada, C. "Simulationist Models of Face-based Emotion Recognition", *Cognition* 94/3, 2005, 193–213.

Goodman, N. *Fact, Fiction and Forecast* (1955), 4th edition. Cambridge, MA: Harvard University Press, 1983.

Hacker, P. *Wittgenstein's Place in 20th Century Analytic Philosophy*. Oxford: Blackwell, 1996.

—— "Was He Trying to Whistle It?", in A. Crary and R. Read (eds.), *The New Wittgenstein*. London: Routledge, 2000, 353–88.

Harman, G. "The Intrinsic Quality of Experience", *Philosophical Perspectives* 4, 1990, 31–52.

Horwich, P. *Asymmetries in Time*. Cambridge, MA: MIT Press, 1987.

—— *Truth*. Oxford: Oxford University Press, 1998 (1st edition, Oxford: Blackwell, 1990).

—— "Meaning and Metaphilosophy", *Philosophical Issues* 4, 1993, 153–8.

—— *Meaning*. Oxford: Oxford University Press, 1998.

—— *From a Deflationary Point of View*. Oxford: Oxford University Press, 2004.

—— *Reflections on Meaning*. Oxford: Oxford University Press, 2005.

—— "Rorty's Wittgenstein", in A. Ahmed (ed.), *Wittgenstein's Philosophical Investigations: A Critical Guide*. Cambridge: Cambridge University Press, 2010, 145–61.

—— *Truth–Meaning–Reality*. Oxford: Oxford University Press, 2010.

—— "Williamson's Philosophy of Philosophy", *Philosophy and Phenomenological Research* 82, 2010, 524–33.

—— "Naturalism, Deflationism, and the Relative Priority of Language and Metaphysics", in H. Price (ed.), *Expressivism, Pragmatism and Representationalism*. Cambridge: Cambridge University Press, 2013.

Hutto, D. *Wittgenstein and the End of Philosophy: Neither Theory nor Therapy*. Second edition. Basingstoke: Palgrave, 2006.

Ishiguro, H. "Use and Reference of Names", in Peter Winch (ed.), *Studies in the Philosophy of Wittgenstein*. London: Routledge and Kegan Paul, 1969, 20–50.

Jackson, F. "What Mary Didn't Know", *Journal of Philosophy* 83, 1986, 291–5.

Jacob, P. and de Vignemont, F. "What is it like to feel another's pain", *Philosophy of Science*, 79:2, 2012, 295–316.

Kant, I. *Critique of Pure Reason*, edited and translated by P. Guyer and A. Wood, Cambridge: Cambridge University Press, 1998.

Katz, J. *The Metaphysics of Meaning*. Cambridge MA: MIT Press, 1991.

Kenny, A. "From the Big Typescript to the Philosophical Grammar", *Acta Philosophica Fennica* 28, Nos. 1–3, 1976, 41–53.

Kremer, M. "The Purpose of Tractarian Nonsense", *Nous* 35, 2001, 39–73.

Kripke, S. *Naming and Necessity*. Cambridge MA: Harvard University Press, 1980.

—— *Wittgenstein on Rules and Private Language*. Cambridge, MA: Harvard University Press, 1982.

Lewis, D. "Mad Pain and Martian Pain", in N. Block (ed.), *Readings in the Philosophy of Psychology*, vol. I. Cambridge, MA: Harvard University Press, 1980, 216–22.

—— "Putnam's Paradox", *Australasian Journal of Philosophy* 62, 1984, 221–36.

Loar, B. "Phenomenal States", in J. Tomberlin (ed.), *Philosophical Perspectives: Action Theory and Philosophy of Mind*. Atascadero, CA: Ridgeview, 1990, 81–108.

Malcolm, N. *Ludwig Wittgenstein: A Memoir*, 2nd edition. Oxford: Oxford University Press, 1974.

——*Nothing is Hidden*. Oxford: Blackwell, 1986.

——"Wittgenstein on Language and Rules", *Philosophy* 67, 1989, 5–28.

McDowell, J. "Wittgenstein on Following a Rule", *Synthese* 58, 1984, 325–63.

——"Meaning and Intentionality in Wittgenstein's Later Philosophy", *Midwest Studies in Philosophy* XVII, 1992, 40–52.

——"Are meaning, understanding, etc. definite states?", in A. Ahmed (ed.), *Wittgenstein's Philosophical Investigations: A Critical Guide*. Cambridge: Cambridge University Press, 2010, 162–71.

McGinn, C. *Wittgenstein on Meaning*. Oxford: Blackwell, 1984.

——"Can We Solve the Mind–Body Problem?", *Mind* 98, 1989, 349–66.

McGinn, M. "Between Metaphysics and Nonsense: Elucidation in Wittgenstein's *Tractatus*", *Philosophical Quarterly* 49, 1999, 491–513.

McGuinness, B. "Language and Reality in the *Tractatus*", *Theoria* 5, 1985, 135–44.

——(ed.) *Wittgenstein in Cambridge*. Oxford: Blackwell, 2008.

Miller, A. "Horwich, Meaning, and Kripke's Wittgenstein", *The Philosophical Quarterly* 50:199, April 2000, 161–74.

Moore, G. E. "Wittgenstein's Lectures in 1930–33", in J. Klagge and A. Nordmann (eds.), *Philosophical Occasions*. Indianapolis, IN, and Cambridge, MA: Hackett Publishing Company, 1993, 46–114.

Moyal-Sharrock, D. *Understanding Wittgenstein's On Certainty*. Basingstoke: Palgrave Macmillan, 2004.

——(ed.). *The Third Wittgenstein: The Post-Investigations Works*. Aldershot: Ashgate, 2004.

Nagel, T. "What is it like to be a bat?", *Philosophical Review* 83, 1974, 435–50.

Papineau, D. *Thinking About Consciousness*. Oxford: Clarendon Press, 2002.

Peacocke, C. *Truly Understood*. Oxford: Oxford University Press, 2008.

Pears, D. *The False Prison*, vols. 1 and 2. Oxford: Oxford University Press, 1987.

——*Paradox and Platitude in Wittgenstein's Philosophy*. Oxford: Oxford University Press, 2006.

Popper, K. "The Nature of Philosophical Problems and Their Roots in Science", *British Journal for the Philosophy of Science* 3(10), August 1952, 124–56.

Price, H. "Naturalism Without Representationalism", in D. Macarthur and M. de Caro (eds.), *Naturalism in Question*. Cambridge, MA: Harvard University Press, 2004, 71–88.

Proops, I., "The New Wittgenstein: A Critique", *European Journal of Philosophy* 9 (3), 2001, 375–404.

Ramsey, F. P. "Critical Notice of L. Wittgenstein's *Tractatus Logico-Philosophicus*", *Mind* NS 32, No. 128, October 1923, 465–78.

Rey, G. "A Reason for Doubting the Existence of Consciousness", in R. Davidson, G. Schwartz, and D. Shapiro (eds.), *Consciousness and Self-Regulation*, vol, 3. New York: Plenum, 1983, 1–39.

Rhees, R. "Wittgenstein on Language and Ritual", *Acta Philosophica Fennica* 28, Nos. 1–3, (*Essays in Honour of G.H. von Wright*, ed. J. Hintikka), 1976, 450–84.

Ricketts, T. "Pictures, logic, and the limits of sense in Wittgenstein's *Tractatus*", in H. Sluga and D. Dunn (eds.), *The Cambridge Companion to Wittgenstein*. Cambridge: Cambridge University Press, 1996, 57–73.

Rorty, R. "Wittgenstein and the linguistic Turn", in A. Ahmed (ed.), *Wittgenstein's Philosophical Investigations: A Critical Guide*. Cambridge: Cambridge University Press, 2010, 145–61.

Russell, B. *My Philosophical Development*. London: George Allen and Unwin; New York: Simon and Schuster, 1959.

——"Report to the Council of Trinity College", in Brian McGuinness (ed.), *Wittgenstein in Cambridge*. Oxford: Blackwell, 2008, 183.

Ryle, G. *The Concept of Mind*. Chicago: University of Chicago Press, 1949.

Schiffer, S. *The Things We Mean*. Oxford: Oxford University Press, 2003.

Schulte, J. *Wittgenstein: An Introduction*. Albany, NY: SUNY Press, 1992.

——*Experience and Expression*. Oxford: Oxford University Press, 1993.

Shoemaker, S. "The Inverted Spectrum", *Journal of Philosophy* 79, 1982, 357–81.

Sider, E. *Writing the Book of the World*. Oxford: Oxford University Press, 2011.

Soames, S. "Generality, Truth Functions, and Expressive Capacity in the *Tractatus*", *The Philosophical Review* XCII, No. 4, 1983, 573–89.

——"Skepticism about Meaning: Indeterminacy, Normativity, and the Rule-Following Paradox", *Canadian Journal of Philosophy*, Supp. Vol. 23, 1998, 211–50.

——*Philosophical Analysis in the 20th Century, vol. 2: The Age of Meaning*. Princeton, NJ: Princeton University Press, 2003.

Stenius, E. *Wittgenstein's Tractatus: A Critical Exposition*. Oxford: Blackwell, and Ithaca: Cornell University Press, 1960; 2nd edition, 1964.

Strawson, G. "Realistic Monism: Why Physicalism Entails Panpsychism", in A. Freeman (ed.), *Consciousness and Its Place in Nature*. Exeter: Imprint Academic, 2006, 3–31.

Strawson, P. "Review of Wittgenstein's Philosophical Investigations", in G. Pitcher (ed.), *Wittgenstein: The Philosophical Investigations*. New York: Doubleday, 1966, 22–64.

Stroud, B. "Wittgenstein and Logical Necessity", in G. Pitcher (ed.). *Wittgenstein: The Philosophical Investigations*. New York: Doubleday, 1966, 477–96.

——"Mind, Meaning and Practice," in his *Meaning Understanding and Practice*. Oxford: Oxford University Press, 2000.

Sullivan, P. "What is the *Tractatus* About?", in B. Weiss and M. Kölbel (eds.), *Wittgenstein's Lasting Significance*. London: Routledge, 2004, 32–45.

Tuomela, R. "Psychological Concepts and Functionalism", *Acta Philosophica Fennica* 28, Nos. 1–3, 1976, 364–93.

Whiting, D. (ed.). *The Later Wittgenstein on Language*. Basingstoke: Palgrave Macmillan, 2009.

Williams, M. *Wittgenstein, Mind and Meaning: Towards a Social Conception of Mind*. London: Routledge, 2002.

—— *Blind Obedience*. London: Routledge, 2010.

Williams, M. J. "Wittgenstein's Refutation of Idealism", in Denis McManus (ed.), *Wittgenstein and Scepticism*. London: Routledge, 2003, 76–96.

—— "Wittgenstein on Truth and Certainty", in B. Weiss and M. Kölbel (eds.), *Wittgenstein's Lasting Significance*. London: Routledge, 2004, 249–84.

Williamson, T. *The Philosophy of Philosophy*. Oxford: Blackwell, 2007.

—— "Reply to Paul Horwich", *Philosophy and Phenomenological Research* 82, 2010, 534–42.

Wittgenstein, L. *Tractatus Logico-Philosophicus*. London: Kegan Paul, 1922.

—— *Philosophical Investigations*. Oxford: Blackwell, 1953.

—— *Notebooks* 1914–1916. G. E. M. Anscombe and G. H. von Wright (eds.). Oxford: Blackwell, 1961.

—— *The Blue and Brown Books*. Oxford: Blackwell, 1958.

—— *On Certainty*, G. E. M. Anscombe and G. H. von Wright (eds.). Oxford: Blackwell, 1969.

—— *Last Writings on the Philosophy of Psychology*, Vol. II, H. Nyman and G. H. von Wright (eds.). Oxford: Blackwell, 1992.

Wright, C. *Wittgenstein on the Foundations of Mathematics*. London: Duckworth, 1980.

—— "Wittgenstein's Rule-following Considerations and the Central Project of Theoretical Linguistics" (1989), reprinted in his *Rails to Infinity* 170–2.

—— *Rails to Infinity*. Cambridge MA: Harvard University Press, 2001.

Index